Lecture notes...

Cavendish
Publishing
Limited

REVENUE LAW

TITLES IN THE SERIES

Cavendish
Publishing
Limited

REVENUE LAW

Philip Ridgway, BA, LLM, Barrister, ATII
Senior Manager, Coopers and Lybrand, London

First published in Great Britain 1996 by Cavendish Publishing
Limited, The Glass House, Wharton Street, London WC1X 9PX
Telephone: 0171-278 8000 Facsimile: 0171-278 8080

British Library Cataloguing in Publication Data.

Ridgway, Philip
Revenue Law – (Lecture Notes Series)
I Title II Series
344.2034

ISBN 1 874241 89 9

Cover photograph by Jerome Yeats
Printed and bound in Great Britain

Preface

Tax law is becoming increasingly complex. The latest legislation 'simplifying' the system is over 50 pages long. Consequently, this does not pretend to be a comprehensive textbook of taxation. It covers the three main areas of undergraduate and professional exams; namely, income tax, corporation tax and capital gains tax.

In producing this book I owe an immense debt of gratitude to Sarah Bush and Meena Patel, who together typed (and retyped and retyped) the manuscript; to all at Cavendish Publishing who put up with my excuses; to my parents without whom this would not have been possible and finally; to Debra, my long suffering wife who put up with so much whilst complaining so little.

Philip Ridgway
April 1996

CONTENTS

Table of Cases

Table of Statutes

Chapter 1

Definitions, Economics and Policy

This chapter examines certain fundamental questions: for example, what is a tax; why do we need taxes; and what makes a tax either good or bad? It is, of course, possible to practise and study revenue law without addressing any of these questions. However, if we wish to study revenue law in depth, to critically appraise it and offer improvements, we must grasp the basic issues which underpin the subject.

This chapter looks at tax policy and the reasons for taxation. It also examines the tax base and the question of who bears the burden of tax.

The question 'what is a tax?' is often paid very little attention in the study of revenue law, notwithstanding that this is clearly central to the whole subject. There are probably two reasons for this. First, it is not strictly necessary to know what a tax is; the tax statutes state what is to be taxed. Second, a definition is hard to give. It has been said that, unlike elephants which are easy to recognise but difficult to define, taxes are difficult both to define and to identify.

The Organisation for Economic Co-operation and Development (OECD) classifies taxes under six broad headings:

- taxes on income, profits and capital gains;

- social security contributions;

- taxes on payroll and workforce;

- taxes on property;

- taxes on goods and services; and

- other taxes.

However, it is first necessary to identify a payment as a tax in order to classify it. To do this, it is necessary to examine those characteristics which are common to all taxes and then to consider a particular payment to see whether it exhibits those attributes.

1.1   Introduction

1.2   What is a tax?

1.2.1	Some elements of a tax	Taxes have certain common characteristics:

- taxes are compulsory;

- taxes are paid to the State/government/public authority; and

- taxes are unrequited.

These characteristics are examined in the paragraphs below.

1.2.2	Taxes are compulsory	The idea of compulsion is a complex one. Although the payment is compulsory, it will only be effective if there is some element of consent to its imposition on the part of those paying. It is not sufficient to force compliance by imposing heavy penalties or imprisonment. A certain consensus derives from electing a government which then has a mandate to impose taxation that will raise the revenue necessary to implement its policies. One of the watchwords of the American War of Independence was 'no taxation without representation'.

The introduction of the community charge, or 'poll tax' was fraught with difficulties even though sanctioned by Parliament. The tax eventually had to be abandoned because, amongst other things, a substantial minority of the public objected to it and refused to pay. The system of general rates which the community charge replaced was generally perceived to be unfair, but it was paid because people had always paid it. This is one of the reasons why it is often said that 'a good tax is an old tax'.

1.2.3	Taxes are paid to the State	The payment must be made to the State. This includes local government and may include certain organs of central government, eg the BBC. In this respect, the television licence fee may be regarded as a tax. A payment made to the private sector (for example, to travel along a private road) is not, on this definition, a tax.

1.2.4	Taxes are unrequited	When it is said that a payment is unrequited, this does not mean that the person paying receives nothing in return; undoubtedly, one of the purposes of taxation is to finance public spending. It is the proportionality of the payment that is in question. The benefit received by any particular person will rarely be proportional to the amount paid by that person. The road fund licence costs the same regardless of whether a car is used once a week for a trip to the supermarket or every day to travel around the country on business. However, the road fund licence may be seen as requited in that it provides a benefit as a result of payment: namely, the right to use the

roads. If it is the right that is paid for, the receipt is in proportion to the payment; no one has a greater right to use the roads as a result of paying the fee than anyone else.

The road fund tax is an example of an hypothecated tax, that is, a tax which contributes to a specific fund. The hypothecated tax has its origins in the benefit approach to taxation. Historically, this was seen as the correct approach and proceeded on the basis that the taxpayer gets something in return for the payment. The principal service provided by the State was law and order; those with more to protect were required to pay more. Hypothecated taxes are now rare and few of those taxes which have their origins in an hypothecated tax have retained this attribute/feature. The road fund simply forms part of the general government coffers and expenditure on roads bears no relation to the amounts contributed by motorists.

Very little turns on the identity of the payer. There has been much publicity recently regarding the Queen's electing to pay income tax on personal income in her capacity as an individual. Obviously, there would be no point in her paying tax on money received from the civil list; the State would be giving with one hand and taking with the other. Accordingly, the payer must be someone other than the State or someone representing the State.

1.2.5   The payer

Taxes are generally considered to have four purposes:

- raising revenue for the provision of public goods;

- correcting external costs;

- redistribution of income/wealth; and

- managing the level of demand.

1.3   What are taxes for? Why are taxes levied?

The primary purpose of taxation is to raise money for public spending. Public spending finances two different types of goods: public goods and merit goods.

1.3.1   Raising revenue

- A public good exhibits two characteristics. First, a person who has not paid cannot be excluded from the benefit provided, eg law and order or national defence. Second, consumption by one person of a public good does not exclude consumption by another, eg street lighting. It would be inefficient to exclude those not wishing to pay because part of the benefit would be unused.

- Merit goods differ from public goods in that it is possible to withhold their benefit from those who do not wish to pay. Further, provision of the benefit becomes more expensive as the number of users increases. However, the State provides merit goods because it is considered that the whole State benefits from them as well as the individual. An example of such a 'good' is education.

The imposition of taxes not only pays for merit goods but can also discourage the consumption of 'demerit' goods, eg tobacco and alcohol.

1.3.2	External costs	The correction of external costs is also affected by taxation. An example is the tax on cigarettes. Smoking creates a cost to the State in the provision of health care. By imposing a tobacco duty, part of this cost is imposed on the consumer. The increase in cost of cigarettes resulting from the imposition of the duty reduces demand which, in turn, helps to reduce the cost of health care. This argument cannot be taken too far. Those who might otherwise have died will impose an extra cost on the State by contracting other illnesses at a later date and possibly by calling on state resources to provide care in old age.
1.3.3	Redistribution of income	It is generally agreed that one use for taxation is to provide for those who are unable to provide for themselves. Without the redistribution of income those with little or no resources would not survive. However, the means by which this is to be achieved differs as one moves through the political spectrum. Generally, the political right wing believe only in the relief of absolute poverty. The centre-left advocate the relief of relative poverty, which means reducing the disparity in wealth distribution.
1.3.4	Control of demand	While it is generally agreed by all political parties that the raising of revenue, correction of external costs and redistribution of income are desirable, the fourth, control of demand, is an instrument of the political left. The right argue that the free market, left to itself, will become stable and supply will approximate to demand. The left argue that there are inefficiencies in the system and that it is the role of the State to stimulate demand wherever there is a shortfall when compared to the supply. The converse of increasing demand by the increase in public spending is the reduction of demand by the private sector.
1.4	**Tax policy**	Income tax was first introduced in 1799 in Britain to finance the war against Napoleon. It was repealed in 1802 but reintroduced in 1803. With the final defeat of Napoleon it was again repealed in 1816. The present income tax has its origins

in the tax imposed in 1842 by Robert Peel as a first step to the repeal of the corn laws. The tax in its current form has evolved gradually since 1842. The adage 'a good tax is an old tax' militates against reform. Wholesale reform of the tax system is very difficult because, in any reform, some may benefit while others may be penalised. Recent years have seen the introduction of new taxes without any significant reduction in the number of old taxes. Taxes are not always introduced with a view to raising revenue. Capital gains tax was introduced in 1965 'to provide a background of equity and fair play'.

CGT is often described as a punitive tax. However, it should be remembered that the rate is the same as that for income tax, that CGT is levied only when the asset is realised, that there are reliefs for gains made on retirement, and that there is no CGT on disposals on death. The view one takes of CGT may depend upon whether one thinks there should be a tax on capital gains or not.

Adam Smith in his seminal work of 1776, *An Inquiry into the Nature and Causes of the Wealth of Nations*, identified four principles, or canons, of taxation. Today, these are often referred to by economists who wish to assess the merits of taxes, although a fifth is usually added. They are: equity; certainty; convenience; economy; and neutrality.

1.4.1   The canons of taxation

Equity means 'fairness'. It comprises two aspects: vertical equity and horizontal equity.

1.4.2   Equity

- **Vertical equity** looks at how people in different circumstances should be taxed. It necessarily concerns distinguishing between the rich and the poor, and addresses the redistributive element of taxation. Historically, vertical equity manifests itself in the benefit approach to taxation. Prior to the development of the welfare state, the principal object of taxation was to provide law and order; those with more property assets had more to protect, and it was incumbent upon them to pay more. The community charge has its origins in the benefit approach. Its creator, Douglas Mason of the Adam Smith Institute, argued that, as all inhabitants of a certain area received the same local government services (eg street lighting and refuse collection) they should each contribute an equal amount. However, certain households in an area may receive more services than others. In this regard, the community charge was an unrequited payment and more akin to a tax. The net result was that the public perceived it as an inequitable tax because the rich paid the same as the poor.

Vertical equity states that those with more should pay more, although there is still debate as to how this should be achieved. Should the tax be proportional (see para 1.6.1), or should it be progressive (see para 1.6.2)? Arguably 10% of the income of someone earning £4,000 is worth more to that person than 10% of the income of a person earning £40,000. Therefore, a taxation rate of 10%, although taking more from the wealthy, probably takes more from the poor.

- **Horizontal equity** states that those in similar circumstances should be taxed equally. This is not as simple as it sounds. At first sight it would imply that a person earning £10,000 should pay the same tax as another person earning £10,000. However, two questions need to be addressed. First, on what unit should taxes be levied? Should it be the individual, the family or some other measure? Second, when are circumstances similar? Is it to be measured in purely monetary terms or should personal circumstances be taken into account? For example, in the UK a married couple is considered to be in different circumstances from an unmarried couple. A married couple will receive the married couple's allowance which allows a husband and wife earning £20,000 each to pay less tax than an unmarried couple earning £20,000 each. The married couple's allowance is a throw back to the married man's allowance which was born out of the premise that a man needed to support his wife as well as himself.

In deciding what is horizontally equitable, it is necessary to make arbitrary distinctions and distinguish choice from necessity. In the UK it is considered that those who have bought houses need assistance. However, a person buying a house does so through choice. It may be said that those with children need more assistance than those buying a house, but the UK tax system does not give allowances for children, although the benefit system does pay a child allowance which might be seen as a negative income tax.

1.4.3   Certainty

For a tax to be certain it is necessary to know not only the amount of the tax liability, but also when and how it is to be paid. A tax which is uncertain leads to disputes and opens up opportunities for avoidance and even evasion (the distinction is discussed in Chapter 3). The Pay As You Earn system (PAYE) appears to produce certainty, in that employees know what tax they pay because it is deducted from their salaries or wages. PAYE removes a large potential for dispute because most employees do not question the amount of tax deducted. The fact that most employees assume that the amount of tax deducted is correct shows a great deal of faith in a system which is prone to error. Hence, the PAYE system provides great certainty of collection, but perhaps at the expense of certainty of liability.

A tax is convenient if it can be paid easily. Again, the PAYE system would appear to be convenient. Although most employees would have sufficient foresight and restraint to put some money aside each month to pay a tax bill at the end of the year, it is certain that some would be tempted to spend each month's earnings with a view to paying their tax liability out of the following month's salary. The obvious problem here is that by the end of the year a large proportion of the last month's income would be needed to pay the tax due. Those in self employment do, in fact, face the problem of having to finance their tax some time after their income was earned.

1.4.4 Convenience

A tax which has a high administrative cost does not provide good value for money with regard to the related benefit to the public. The money paid to the Exchequer should be commensurate with the value of the corresponding supply of services. In determining the cost of a tax there are two aspects to be taken into account. First, the cost to the government in administering the tax system, and second, the cost to the taxpayer complying with the tax system. The former includes the salaries of those employed to collect the tax and administer the system, together with items of capital plant such as computer systems. The latter includes such costs as the employment of an accountant to deal with the tax affairs of the taxpayer, the cost of time that taxpayers spend on their tax affairs which could be spent on earning profits. There are also costs imposed on independent third parties such as banks that have to administer schemes such as the MIRAS scheme (see Chapter 6) and there is also a cost when a tax is uncertain because taxpayers will tend to employ people either to advise on the amount of the liability or to find ways of avoiding the tax altogether.

1.4.5 Economy

A tax is said to be efficient or neutral if its imposition does not affect the behaviour of the taxpayer. A tax which distorts behaviour is inefficient because, first, the tax will not raise as much as was originally thought because the taxpayer's preferences will alter, and second, the alteration of behaviour is considered an unwarranted intrusion by the State into the lives of individuals. An example of such a tax is the window tax which was introduced in 1696. The tax was calculated by reference to the number of windows in a house, which was probably a reasonable measure of the wealth of the owner. To

1.4.6 Efficiency/neutrality

reduce the liability, taxpayers bricked up their windows and new houses were built with fewer windows. There was consequently a detriment to the taxpayer without any increased yield to the Exchequer.

| 1.5 | Tax classifications – the tax base | To define the tax base is to state that which is taxed. In the UK the primary tax base is income, although value added tax (VAT) charged on expenditure raises increasingly large amounts. The following paras outline a number of different tax bases, not all of which are in operation in the UK. The list is not intended to be exhaustive, but is instead meant to outline the different options available to the legislature. |

1.5.1   Income

The primary tax base in the UK is income, whether of individuals or of businesses. However, this requires an examination of the nature of income. The difficulty of providing an acceptable definition of income is avoided in the UK by stating that something is determined as income by reference to whether it falls within a schedule of the Income Tax Acts (see Chapter 5).

1.5.2   Expenditure

An expenditure tax takes as its measure the consumption of the individual. It is levied on the claim that a taxpayer makes on the community's resources. If the taxpayer chooses to spend, rather than save, she is taxed. Saving includes not only saving in the traditional sense, but also investment. Thus, if the taxpayer invests in a business this would be seen not as expenditure but as saving. An expenditure tax also avoids the need for a distinction between capital and income: a person who spends capital would be taxed in the same way as one who spends income.

Despite the number of studies which have favoured the imposition of an expenditure tax, the imposition of such a tax is rejected on two grounds. First, it would be very difficult to change from an income tax to an expenditure tax because such a change would make the tax yield uncertain. Second, it would be difficult to give credit for and against profits derived in other countries because other countries do not, generally, have an expenditure tax.

1.5.3   Estate duties

The UK imposes taxes on the estates of deceased persons. An estate duty taxes by reference to the value of assets at death. The UK's inheritance tax is really an estate duty.

1.5.4   Accessions tax/ inheritance tax

An accessions tax is a levy on gifts and legacies which is cumulative over a lifetime or a period of years. It is imposed on the recipient, not on the donor, and is calculated by reference to the aggregate taxable accessions of the recipient. It can be graduated so that the greater the cumulative total the higher the rate of tax. Generally, tax is levied on the cumulative total less a credit for the tax paid on the cumulative total prior to the accession. Obviously, tax can be avoided by making gifts to a large number of people rather than a large gift to one person. Not surprisingly, those who advocate an accessions tax argue in favour of a redistribution of wealth.

In 1974, the Labour government published a Green Paper (Cmnd 5704, *Wealth Tax*), with a view to introducing a wealth tax. The basic principle was that the taxpayer's assets would be valued each year; if the value exceeded an exempt limit, tax would be levied on the value of those assets. The tax was to increase as wealth increased (ie it was to be progressive, see para 1.6.2).

    A select committee was set up to consider the introduction of the wealth tax. Its deliberations took longer than expected, and were leaked to *The Economist* prior to being published. The report was accompanied by four volumes of materials comprising some 2,000 pages, although the report itself was just two paragraphs in length and stated that the committee was unable to agree on a report. There were a number of minority reports. The failure of the committee to secure a majority was apparently due to two Labour members being abroad when the vote was taken. Since then, nothing has been heard of a wealth tax.

| 1.5.5 | Wealth |

The amount raised by VAT in the UK has increased dramatically in recent years. Generally, VAT is charged on the increase in value at each stage in the chain of production, from the raw materials to the finished product. In the UK, VAT is levied by taxing the full value of the goods supplied at each stage of production. However, credit is given for any tax paid by the supplier on supplies to him, and he accounts to Customs and Excise for the VAT he has charged on his supplies. For example, a carpenter buys wood for £100 and pays tax on it of £17.50. She then makes a table with the wood which she sells for £200 and charges VAT of £35. The person producing the table has added value through her workmanship of £100. She charges tax on the value of the table she sells (£35) but gets credit for the tax on the £100 that she has paid. The net effect of this is that she must account to Customs and Excise for VAT on the value that she has added (ie £17.50).

| 1.5.6 | Value added |

Capital gains tax is not really a tax on capital, it has been referred to as a deferred income tax. One of the problems with the UK tax system is the distinction that is drawn between

| 1.5.7 | Capital gains |

income and capital. For example, X has £10,000 which he puts into a deposit account with a view to leaving it there for ten years. Meanwhile, Y has £10,000 which she uses to buy a painting. The deposit account and the painting both show a return of 10% per annum. X is taxed each year as interest is credited to the account. Y is taxed when she realises her asset. X is subject to income tax. Y is subject to capital gains tax. Each in reality is getting the same return on the investment. If Y is taxed on the annual increase in value, she may have to sell assets to pay the tax. Y has an annual exemption to set against the gain, X has his personal allowances. Unless the annual exemption equals the aggregate of the personal allowances, Y will be more heavily taxed than X. However, to tax Y each year on the increase in value of the asset would require a valuation which would be expensive and thus inefficient.

The UK capital gains tax was introduced to make the system fairer. It taxes realised increases in value over and above increase in the retail prices index.

1.6   Tax classifications – marginal rates

Once the tax base has been chosen, the question arises as to how the burden of tax should be distributed. Should those with more pay more? And should the rate of tax increase as, for example, income increases?

1.6.1   Proportional

A proportional tax takes the same proportion of the tax base from each taxpayer regardless of how much of it the taxpayer owns. A tax levied at a flat rate of 20% is proportional: each taxpayer gives up the same proportion of their income.

1.6.2   Progressive

A progressive tax is one which takes a greater proportion per unit of the tax base owned by the taxpayer. Any tax system which has a nil rate for the first slice of the tax base will, by definition, be progressive once the tax starts to be imposed. As the amount of the tax base increases, a greater proportion of it will be lost in tax. The system can be made increasingly progressive if the rates of tax increase as the amount of the tax base increases.

1.6.3   Regressive

A regressive tax is one which takes a diminishing amount of a particular tax base as the amount liable to tax increases. An example of a regressive tax is tobacco duty. Assuming that most smokers would not increase consumption as their income increases, the amount of income which is expended in tobacco duty will proportionately decrease as income increases. Although VAT is generally seen as a proportional tax being imposed at a flat rate, it can to a certain extent be seen as being regressive, especially since the imposition of VAT on fuel. Individuals will generally spend the same amount on heating regardless of their income. Therefore, if VAT on fuel is considered in isolation, it will take a larger proportion of the income of a poor household than a wealthy one.

Defining the burden of tax is to state who pays it. The traditional distinction is between direct and indirect taxes. However, this distinction does not take account of hidden costs which may mean that a tax is borne by someone else.

1.7   Tax classifications – burden of tax

A direct tax is one which is paid by the people who are intended to bear it. Income tax, capital gains tax and corporation tax are direct taxes.

1.7.1   Direct

An indirect tax is one which is paid by people other than those who bear it. Value added tax is an indirect tax. However, the distinction is not as simple as it sounds. A trader would have a customer believe that they have to charge VAT. They do not. They have to account to customs for VAT, but instead of reducing their profit margins by 17.5%, they choose to pass the cost on to the customer. If they did not do so, they might seek to improve profit margins by reducing overheads, including perhaps wages. It might then be arguable that VAT was being borne by the employees. Similarly, income tax may be partly borne by the employer because, in order to employ people, the employer has to have regard to the after-tax wages of the employees. An increase in the rate of income tax will generally therefore result in an increase in wages, although the employer will probably not bear all the increase because prices will rise as a result.

1.7.2   Indirect

Taxes feature prominently each time a general election is called. There is often a promise that taxes will be reformed and the word 'reform' in this case is meant to imply some change for the better. What it usually means, however, is changing the existing rules either to raise more revenue or to alter the burden of taxation, or both.

1.8   Reform

Recent attempts at reform have centred on tinkering with the existing system. The Inland Revenue has recently introduced 'self-Assessment' and, as a consequence, changes have been made to the existing law. Although this has been done under the guise of making legislation simpler, few would say that it is. If anything, the transitional provisions have made it temporarily more complex.

Definitions, Economics and Policy

Taxes have three characteristics. First, they are compulsory; second, they are unrequited; and third, they are paid to the government or other local authorities. Although a tax is compulsory, there has to be some agreement on the part of those paying. This agreement comes through electing the government. When it is said that a tax is unrequited, it is the value of the benefit that is received by the taxpayer in return for paying the tax that is in question and the main reason for paying a tax is undoubtedly to finance the provision of services by the State through public spending.

Defining taxes

The main purpose of taxation is to raise money for public spending. The State provides public goods eg law and order, and merit goods eg education. Taxation can also be used to correct external costs. For example, smoking increases the cost of health care and a tax on smoking places some of that cost back on to the consumer. Taxation can also be used to redistribute income and this is achieved by raising taxation to finance welfare benefits. The UK has never had a wealth tax. Finally, taxation can be used to control demand; this is primarily an instrument of the political left.

Purpose of taxation

Adam Smith identified four principles, or canons, of taxation. Occasionally a fifth is added. The first canon of taxation is equity. Equity is itself divided into two categories: vertical equity which dictates that people in different circumstances should be taxed differently eg the rich should be taxed more heavily than the poor, and horizontal equity, which means that those in similar circumstances should be taxed equally. In deciding how horizontal equity should apply, it is necessary to identify the unit which is to be taxed. For example, should married couples be taxed the same as a couple living together?

Canons of taxation

The second canon of taxation is certainty. This applies to both the liability, how the tax is to be calculated, and to the payment, how the tax is to be collected. Third, a tax ought to be convenient; it should impose as little burden on the taxpayer as possible. Fourth, the tax ought to be economic; this means that the costs of collection should be commensurate with the benefit provided. The costs of a tax have two aspects: the cost that the government incurs in employing people and acquiring resources to collect the tax; and the cost of the taxpayer in dealing with tax matters. Finally, the tax should be neutral. This means it should not distort behaviour.

The tax base

It is necessary to define the tax base, ie that which is to be taxed. In the UK the primary tax base is income. Numerous people have advocated an expenditure tax, but a change to an expenditure tax would make the tax yield uncertain in the interim and it is therefore thought to be unsatisfactory. Taxes are also levied on assets at death by means of either an estate tax, which taxes by reference to that belonging to the deceased, or by an inheritance tax, which taxes by reference to the value of assets passing to the various beneficiaries. Increasing amounts are raised in the UK by VAT. This taxes the increase in value (ie the value added) at each stage of production. The tax is ultimately borne by the consumer. Capital gains tax taxes the increase in value of an asset over time over and above inflation. It has been referred to as a deferred income tax.

Types of taxes

Taxes can be either proportional, progressive or regressive. A proportional tax will take the same proportion of a person's income regardless of what it is. A progressive tax takes a greater amount from those who earn more than from those who earn less. A regressive tax is one which takes a greater amount from those who own less, and an example of a regressive tax is tobacco duty. This is because a person's consumption does not increase with the amount they earn.

Direct taxes are levied on those who bear it; for example, income tax and capital gains tax. An indirect tax is paid by someone other than the person intended to bear it; for example, value added tax which is accounted for by the shopkeeper but borne by the consumer.

Chapter 2

Judicial Attitudes to Tax Avoidance

The study of judicial attitudes to tax avoidance is probably one of the most difficult areas of tax law. The subject of tax avoidance raises a simple but very fundamental question: can a taxpayer by rearranging his affairs, legitimately reduce the amount of tax for which he would otherwise be liable? Tax tends to generate extreme views in this area and it is difficult to escape the conclusion that the principles which have been applied are, to some extent, coloured by the prejudices of those deciding the cases.

The topic is not made any easier by the lax use of terminology. The subject under discussion is *tax avoidance*: the legal reduction of a liability to tax using the technicalities of the tax legislation. This is often confused with *tax evasion*: the illegal reduction of liability to tax by not complying with tax legislation (eg working for cash and not reporting the income). The former is legal, the latter is not, though the former is increasingly frowned upon by the courts. More recently, the phrase *tax mitigation* has been used to distinguish the less artificial schemes which the courts will permit. The phrase *strategic tax planning* has also been used. Often, tax avoidance has been referred to by members of the judiciary as tax evasion. This is wrong.

Much of the discussion on tax avoidance centres around whether the courts can ignore the legal form of a transaction and, instead, tax the transaction according to its commercial substance. The starting point for this discussion is *IRC v Duke of Westminster*.

The Duke of Westminster had a number of employees. The wages paid to these employees were not deductible by him in computing his liability to sur-tax, long-since abolished. He therefore executed covenants in favour of each employee which provided for the payment of a weekly sum. In all cases but one, the employees were sent a letter stating that the covenant did not mean that the employee could no longer claim his wages. However, each employee was expected to be content with the payment that was being made, with the addition of such sum as would be necessary to bring the total amount received up to the amount which would have been received by way of wages. The employees acknowledged the letter and accepted the arrangement.

The House of Lords held that the payments to the employees were not salaries or wages, but annual payments. As such, they were deductible for sur-tax purposes. The Duke, therefore, reduced his tax liability while continuing to employ his staff with the same outgoings.

It is often said that the decision in *IRC v Duke of Westminster* was that the courts can only look to the form of transaction, not to its substance. The court will, however, look to the legal rights of the parties and the mere labelling of one transaction as another more tax-efficient transaction will be insufficient to reduce a taxpayer's liability. The case was interpreted by many, including the courts, to mean that use of a particular legal form would, as a matter of course, result in a particular tax consequence.

The period following *IRC v Duke of Westminster* saw the advent of many successful avoidance schemes. In retaliation to the ingenuity of the lawyers, Parliament introduced a number of anti-avoidance provisions to stop the greater excesses. However, the sophistication of avoidance schemes and the time needed to enact the legislation against them meant that the tax planners were always a number of steps ahead of the Inland Revenue. This state of affairs changed in the 1980s after a number of cases in the early part of the decade. The judiciary were taking a more active role.

2.3   *Ramsay (W T) Ltd v IRC (1981) – the* **new approach**

The Inland Revenue's first success came in the case of *Ramsay (W T) Ltd v IRC*. In *Ramsay's* case, the taxpayer company had made a gain/profit on which it would ultimately be liable to pay corporation tax. Accordingly, a scheme was entered into with no purpose other than to create a loss which could be set off against that gain/profit, so there would be no liability to tax. The taxpayer bought the shares of Caithmead Ltd for £185,034. The taxpayer then borrowed £437,500 and used it to make two identical loans of £218,750 to Caithmead, each carrying interest at 11%. However, the loans had an unusual feature. The lender had the right to increase the rate of interest on one of the loans and would then be obliged to lower the interest on the other loan by a corresponding amount. One week after the loans had been made, Ramsay exercised the right. The rate of interest on the first loan was increased to 22% and that on the second decreased to 0%. The first loan was then sold for £391,481 realising a gain/profit of £172,731. For certain technical reasons, Ramsay thought this gain/profit would not be liable to tax.

Caithmead Ltd was put into liquidation. Shortly afterwards the 0% loan was repaid, and the shares of Caithmead Ltd were consequently worth only £9,387 because the company still had to repay the 22% loan. Ramsay Ltd claimed an allowable loss of £175,647 (ie £185,034 – the price it had paid for Caithmead Ltd, less £9,387). Through this series of transactions the company hoped to create a non-chargeable gain (on the sale of the 22% loan) and an allowable loss (on the eventual sale of the shares). Commercially, the gain would compensate for the loss, but with the tax result that the loss need not be offset against the non-chargeable gain. Instead, it could be offset against the original gain, on which the company would otherwise have been liable to pay corporation tax.

The House of Lords held that, when considering a series of transactions which were intended to operate as such, regard must be given to the series as a whole rather than to each separate transaction. The court did not, therefore, have to examine each step. If, as a composite transaction, it produced neither a gain nor a loss, it could be treated as a nullity for tax purposes. Therefore, it would be wrong to examine each individual step and isolate that part which gave rise to an allowable loss.

Lord Wilberforce restated the principles which the courts could apply. These were:

- a subject is only to be taxed upon the clear words of a statute, not according to some 'intention' or 'fairness';

- a subject can arrange his affairs so as to reduce his liability to tax. The motive to avoid tax does not invalidate its legal effect;

- it is for the commissioners to find whether, as a question of fact, a transaction is a sham (ie something other than it purports to be); and

- the court cannot go behind a document or transaction which is genuine to look for some underlying substance.

However, in applying these principles the court was not to 'wear blinkers'. If a document was to take effect as part of a series of transactions, it is that series which needs to be considered when considering the tax consequences.

A number of points should be noted. First, there was no contractual obligation to carry each of the steps through. It was found as a fact that the steps would almost inevitably have been carried out, but this is not the same as saying that they had to be carried out. Second, it was also held that the capital gain made on the disposal of the debt would have amounted to a debt on a security and as such it would have been chargeable to capital gains tax. By analysing each step, the court could therefore have rendered the scheme useless because the created chargeable gain would be set against the created allowable loss, still leaving the original gain to be taxed. However, the court chose to adopt what became known as the 'new approach'.

2.4   *IRC v Burmah Oil Co Ltd* **(1981) – circular schemes**

The *Burmah Oil* case involved a scheme which was designed to substitute a loss on a debt transaction, which could not be offset against profits, by a loss on a share transaction, which would be an allowable deduction.

By means of a number of steps, Burmah Oil made a loss of £159m on some shares, which would be allowable, as opposed to a loss of £159m on a debt which would not be allowable. However, the scheme was not self cancelling. It operated by substituting one type of loss for another, and for this reason it was described as circular.

The House of Lords held that if each of the individual steps were looked at in isolation, there would be an allowable loss. However, the scheme, when looked at as a whole, involved no real loss. It was stated (by both Lord Diplock and Lord Scarman) that *Ramsay* marked a significant change in the approach adopted by the House of Lords in cases where there was a preordered series of transactions. This was so regardless of whether or not the series of transactions achieved a legitimate commercial purpose.

Again, however, the House of Lords emphasised that the principle enunciated did not affect the principle in *IRC v Duke of Westminster*. Lord Diplock said that the *Duke of Westminster* case 'was about a simple transaction entered into by two real persons, each with a mind of his own', whereas the type of tax avoidance practised in the *Ramsay* case involved 'interconnected transactions between artificial persons, limited companies without minds of their own but directed by a single mastermind'. In effect, the court was ignoring the separate legal personalities of the various companies.

2.5   *Furniss v Dawson* **(1984) – linear schemes**

The new approach was again applied in the case of *Furniss v Dawson*. However, this case differed from *Ramsay* and *Burmah* in two important respects. First, the scheme was designed to defer tax not to avoid it; although it is not impossible that once the tax had been successfully deferred a further scheme would have been entered into to avoid the tax altogether. Second, the scheme involved the parties making real acquisitions and real disposals. However, notwithstanding its simplicity and its honesty, the House of Lords unanimously held that it was incapable of withstanding the 'new approach'.

The facts of *Furniss v Dawson* are quite straightforward. The taxpayer and his two sons negotiated the sale of the shares in their two family companies to a third party. In order to defer the liability to capital gains tax that would arise because the shares had increased in value, they incorporated a company in the Isle of Man. This new company agreed to purchase from the taxpayer and his sons all the shares in the two family companies. The price was to be satisfied by the issue of new shares to the three of them in the Isle of Man company. By providing shares as consideration, the gain that would have been realised on the sale of the shares had cash been given was deferred until the future sale of the new Isle of Man shares. The Isle of Man company then sold the shares in the family companies to the third party for cash, with the effect that they had acquired the shares in the taxpayers' company for market value and then immediately sold them for market value, realising no gain or loss. The taxpayer and his sons were left holding shares in an Isle of Man company, the only asset of which was the cash which would otherwise have been received by the taxpayer and, if so received, would have been taxable. In the event that the taxpayer sold the shares in the Isle of Man company, the gain would then have been realised and tax would have been due.

The House of Lords held unanimously that there was a disposal of the shares by the Dawsons to the third party for cash, the cash being paid to the Isle of Man company with the concurrence of the taxpayers. It should be noted that the sale between the Dawsons and the third party had been negotiated prior to the interposing of the Isle of Man company. The existence of the Isle of Man company was, therefore, purely to defer the liability to tax. It had no other commercial purpose.

The House of Lords held that the Dawsons were to be taxed as if they had sold their shares in the family company directly to the third party. It is clear that the House of Lords intended to extend the *Ramsay* principle beyond self cancelling schemes. Both the court at first instance and the Court of Appeal had found for the taxpayers.

Although the case of *Furniss v Dawson* left the law in a state of some uncertainty, it was obvious that the House of Lords was unwilling to accept artificial tax schemes and was content to allow the law to develop on a piecemeal basis. The words of Lord Brightman were often recited as some hallowed formula, and it was forgotten that Lord Bridge formulated the test in slightly wider terms. The test was generally stated to be that,

2.6   The aftermath

where a composite transaction comprises a preordained series of steps, some or any of which are inserted for no other reason than the avoidance of tax, the court can ignore those steps and tax the real transaction.

2.7	***CIR (New Zealand) v Challenge Corporation Ltd (1986) – tax mitigation***

In 1986, the Privy Council heard the case of *CIR (New Zealand) v Challenge Corporation Ltd* on appeal from New Zealand. New Zealand legislation had a provision similar to UK law, which allowed the losses of one member of a group of companies to be set against profits of another. The Challenge group had assessable profits of $5.8m. A company in another unconnected group had losses of $5.8m. This second company was sold to the Challenge group for the greater of $10,000, or 22% of the losses which could be set against Challenge group's profits. New Zealand had two sets of anti-avoidance provisions: one a general provision and the other more specific, which was contained in the code that governed the offset of losses. The transaction entered into by the Challenge group could not be contested under the specific provision, but could be contested under the general provision. The question was whether the unavailability of the specific anti-avoidance provisions in the loss relief code precluded the application of the more general provision. The Privy Council held by a majority of 4:1 that the general provision applied.

2.7.1	*Craven v White* (1988) and related appeals – the retreat from *Furniss v Dawson*

Craven v White addressed the question of how preordained a series of transactions needed to be in order for it to be disregarded. The facts were similar to *Furniss v Dawson* but the shares had been sold to the intermediate company before a purchaser had been identified; it could not, therefore, be said who the ultimate purchaser would be at the time of transfer to the intermediate company. (In fact a purchaser had been identified but talks had broken off. Before talks recommenced the shares were exchanged for those of an Isle of Man company.) The House of Lords found for the taxpayer by a majority of three to two. The majority included Lord Oliver who had found for the taxpayer in the Court of Appeal in *Furniss v Dawson*. The minority included Lord Templeman.

Lord Oliver treated the new approach as a rule of statutory interpretation; consequently, the tax avoidance purpose of the transaction or step to be disregarded was relegated to the sidelines. The reason for this was that during the course of argument two conflicting views had emerged. First, *Furniss v Dawson* had decided that, where a transaction has as its purpose or one of its purposes the avoidance of tax, that part of the transaction can be ignored. Second, that it is a rule of statutory interpretation. The two tests had now been separated, were found to conflict, and the latter view was to be preferred over the former.

Craven v White also gave birth to another concept, that of strategic tax planning; the entering into of a transaction with a view to a tax advantage being obtained in the future. Thus, in *Furniss v Dawson*, if the Dawsons had, prior to finding a purchaser, transferred their shares to the Isle of Man company, there would have been no preordained series of transactions. On this analysis, the application of *Furniss v Dawson* depends upon the foresight of the vendors.

In *Shepherd v Lyntress,* a company, Lyntress, which was carrying forward a capital loss was sold to News International. News International then transferred into Lyntress a number of companies on the sale of which there would be a capital gain and Lyntress sold these shares on the UK stock exchange two days later. The gain was set against the loss that was being carried forward. The Inland Revenue challenged the transaction on the grounds that *Furniss v Dawson* applied. Vinelott J held that there was no suggestion the shares were going to be sold at the time they were purchased by Lyntress. There was an intention to sell them; but it was not until after they had been acquired that instructions were given to brokers to sell them on the stock exchange. He therefore applied *Craven v White*; there was no preordained series of transactions.

2.8   Shepherd v Lyntress (1989)

The case of *Ensign Tankers (Leasing) Ltd v Stokes (HMIT)* is interesting for two reasons. First, the argument relied upon by Lord Templeman, who delivered the leading judgment, was one which had not been put to him by counsel for the Inland Revenue, but was one which had been raised because of his own comments during the course of argument in front of him. Second, because Lord Oliver's speech in *Craven v White* expressed the principle as one of statutory interpretation, the insertion of steps for purely tax avoidance reasons receives very little attention.

2.9   Ensign Tankers (Leasing) Ltd v Stokes (HMIT) (1992) – the death knell for tax avoidance?

In the early 1980s, it was possible to get a deduction from profits for the full cost of producing a master film negative. Ensign Tankers (Leasing) Ltd was a company with a large corporation tax bill. It had nothing to do with the film industry until it was introduced to the Victory Partnership, a limited partnership set up for the financing of the film *Escape to Victory*. The essence of the scheme was that Ensign, together with four others, put up 25% of the cost of making the film ($3.25 m). The rest of the cost was put up by Lorimar by way

2.9.1   The facts

of a non-recourse loan, which meant that repayment of the loan could only be made out of receipts from the film. If there were no receipts the partners could not be made liable for the debt. The money borrowed by the partnership was immediately returned to Lorimar. The effect of this was to enable the members of the partnership to claim the full $14m cost against there own tax bills, while at the same time putting only $3.25 m of their own money at risk.

| 2.9.2 | First instance – motive and purpose |

In the High Court the arguments centred around two questions: first, was the company trading; and second, could *Furniss v Dawson* apply?

Millett J held that the decision of the commissioners – that transactions which were entered into with a fiscal *motive* could not be trading transactions – was wrong in law. In order to be a fiscal nullity the transaction had to be entered into for a purely fiscal *purpose.* The motive was irrelevant. A transaction entered into for a purely fiscal purpose was incompatible with the idea of trading. He held that the distribution of the film and its exploitation at a profit were entered into on a commercial basis and therefore the partnership was trading. He then went on to hold that as the transactions were real transactions which were not just entered into for a fiscal purpose, *Ramsay* and *Furniss v Dawson* could not apply.

| 2.9.3 | Court of Appeal – the judge was plainly right |

In the Court of Appeal the argument centred upon whether Ensign Tankers (Leasing) Ltd was truly trading. Vice Chancellor Browne-Wilkinson held that Millet J, at first instance, was correct in holding that motive is irrelevant. However, he went on to say that as far as Ensign's purposes was concerned, this had to be determined subjectively and, where the transaction is equivocal, the motive may become relevant evidence as to the parties' subjective purpose. On this basis he held that the commissioners had erred in law because they had seen the question of whether or not a company was trading as one of law not one of fact. He therefore remitted the case to them to be reheard. On the question of applying the *Ramsay* principle he said that the Inland Revenue had not appealed the decision of Millett J, that the existence of the limited partnership could not be ignored and this was 'plainly right'.

| 2.9.4 | House of Lords – a raid on the Treasury |

In the House of Lords counsel for the Inland Revenue did not argue *Furniss v Dawson*, having conceded the point in the Court of Appeal. However, Lord Templeman raised it in argument.

In all previous cases the House of Lords had been at pains to point out that *Ramsay* and *Furniss v Dawson* had not eroded the *Westminster* principle. Lord Templeman's comments in *Ensign* were tantamount to saying that *Westminster* was wrongly decided. He said there were two rival explanations of that case. First, that the gardener worked voluntarily for the Duke. Second, that the gardener worked full time for full wages and volunteered not to take the annuity until he retired. Lord Templeman said:

> 'I agree with Lord Atkin; gardeners do not work for Dukes on half wages.'

However, he went to distinguish the *Duke of Westminster* case. Accordingly, it would appear that it is still good law, whatever remains of it (see para 2.13).

Lord Templeman also returned to the subject of tax mitigation first broached in the *Challenge* case. He said that a tax avoidance scheme is recognisable by the 'apparently magical result'.

In *Ensign*, Lord Templeman states that mitigation is where the taxpayer suffers a loss or incurs an expense. For example, there is a real tax liability but the tax legislation specifically makes it exempt. If the taxpayer has already used the exemption, tax on the disposal is due. However, in *Furniss v Dawson* the taxpayers were using a specific exemption, one which said that if shares were exchanged for shares there would be no tax until the new shares were disposed of. Where then is the distinction? Bed and breakfast arrangements have been used by many small investors to avoid tax since the tax was first introduced. Briefly, a bed and breakfast transaction allows the taxpayer to retain the shares whilst realising a loss inherent within them by selling them and immediately buying them back. Consequently, it is accepted practice. Whether this makes them tax mitigation rather than tax avoidance is debatable.

Lord Templeman went on to discuss the application of *Furniss v Dawson* to the *Ensign* case. He held that the real transaction was one in which the partnership expended $3.25m. It was not money borrowed and returned in a self-cancelling transaction. Allowances were therefore to be given on the $3.25m, not the $14m claimed.

Four points are to be noted. First, in applying Lord Keith's dictum in *Craven v White*, the idea of a step having been interposed for purely tax avoidance reasons has been lost. The test was expressed to involve identifying the real transaction and then applying the relevant statutory provisions to it. Lord Oliver's reinterpretation of *Furniss v Dawson* in *Craven v White* effectively gave the new approach a new direction. Second, Lord Templeman dismissed the decision in *Craven v White* referring to it as 'a difference of judicial opinion'. Third, he said that the Victory Partnership was trading by producing and exploiting a commercial film; this was not withstanding the fact that the commissioners had found that the company was not trading. Finally, considering the appeal had found its way to the House of Lords, he thought that, 'the facts are undisputed and the law is very clear'.

The question of whether the partnership had been trading had occupied the minds of all those in the lower courts; this question was vital if no transaction could be ignored under the *Furniss v Dawson* principle. Once the business purpose test was eliminated and the focus became the real transaction, the importance of whether the partnership was trading took a back seat. Lord Templeman found that the partnership was trading, but that its real trading expenditure was the $3.25m not the $14m claimed.

Lord Templeman said that the transactions were nothing more than a raid on the Treasury using as weapons the technicalilties of revenue and company law.

2.10   *IRC v Fitzwilliam & Others* (1993) – a return to orthodoxy

IRC v Fitzwilliam & Others involved a complex scheme to avoid capital transfer tax. It may be thought that, in the light of preceding case law, it would be foolhardy to enter into such a scheme. However, the scheme was entered into in 1980, just as *Ramsay* was coming to the House of Lords. Fourteen years later, the *Fitzwilliam* case appeared in the House of Lords in a totally different climate to that prevailing when the scheme was originally entered into.

The scheme comprised five steps. At step three, one of the participants took separate advice, in order to bolster the argument that the steps were not preordained.

Lord Keith, with whom Lords Ackner and Mustill agreed, held that the plan was 'strategic tax planning' although he also referred to it as a 'pre-planned tax avoidance scheme'. Lord Keith's view was that, because two of the steps gave rise to an income tax charge, there were enduring legal consequences which meant the argument that the series of transactions was a composite transaction 'could not be regarded as an intellectually possible view of the matter'. The enduring legal consequences of an interposed transaction was what prompted the Court of Appeal to dismiss the Inland Revenue's argument in *Furniss v Dawson*. This argument was firmly rejected by the House of Lords. Lord Keith went on to hold that the series of transactions undertaken entitled the taxpayer to an exemption from tax. However, it was only the individual steps which gave rise to the exemptions, in the same way that, when viewed individually, the steps in the *Burmah* case gave rise to an allowable loss but, when viewed as a whole, there was a liability to tax.

Lord Templeman found for the Inland Revenue. In what is a scathing judgment he held that 'tax avoidance schemes of the kind invented and implemented in the present case are no better than attempts to cheat the Revenue'. He said that the new approach had in fact spawned two tests, one for the self-cancelling scheme of which the *Ramsay* case is an example, and the other for the scheme whereby one transaction was split into a number of transactions of which *Furniss v Dawson* is an example. The *Fitzwilliam* case contained both devices. In his opinion, steps two to five were a preordained series of transactions, the steps could be ignored and the fiscal result should then be taxed.

Lord Browne-Wilkinson held that the scheme comprised steps one to five. As it was admitted by the Inland Revenue that the scheme was not implemented until step one had taken place, there was no preordained series of transactions to which the new approach could be applied.

Considering the number of cases that have now been before the House of Lords, there is still a divergence of views as on how the principle is to be applied. The view of the majority would take the principle back 10 years to before the House of Lords in *Furniss v Dawson*. Lord Browne-Wilkinson would appear to be more in keeping with the principle as subsequently developed to *Craven v White*. Lord Templeman's view takes the principle a little further, allowing the court to extract parts of a preordained scheme and then to apply the new approach to these parts.

2.10.1 Conclusions on *Fitzwilliam*

The *Matrix Securities* case involved an application for judicial review of a decision by the Inland Revenue to withdraw a clearance. As such, the merits of the case were not in question and four of the Law Lords expressed no opinion on the tax scheme for which clearance was sought. Lord Templeman, however, took the opportunity to discuss the scheme which he said was, 'a sophisticated tax avoidance scheme designed to plunder the Treasury of £38m'. It involved a trick or a pretence, the results of which were too good to be true.

Of the *Fitzwilliam* case he said 'the majority failed to take account of the nature of and effect of the transaction regarded as a whole', so he continued to dismiss decisions with which he did not agree notwithstanding that he was in the minority. However, he did reiterate the business purpose test; the scheme involved certain steps which had been inserted to

2.11 *Matrix Securities –* **Templeman's final bow**

obtain a tax advantage. Lord Templeman retired soon after the *Matrix* case.

2.12   Judicial tension

The underlying impression is that the application of the new approach varies with the judiciary and their understanding of the principle. The development of principle in the early 1980s was effectively halted in *Craven v White*, after which it went off in a new direction as a result of Lord Templeman's views which have dominated. However, he has recently faced some stiff opposition and has had a few defeats. Undeterred, in subsequent cases he has taken the opportunity to play down the importance of contrary judicial opinion. The *Ensign* decision itself may have been decided differently but for an accident of history. *Ensign* was originally listed for Autumn 1991, but this coincided with the State Opening of Parliament and the case was moved to January 1992. Lord Oliver resigned on 1 January 1992. If he had heard the case, Lord Templeman may have had a more difficult time discussing his views in *Craven v White* as a mere difference of judicial opinion.

The new approach is now firmly established, although not quite as robust as it once was. It remains to be seen whether the 'enduring legal consequences' test gains any more ground. With new judges hearing the cases there may yet be a re-emergence of the motive/purpose test. Lord Browne-Wilkinson who applied it in the Court of Appeal is now in the House of Lords and sat in both *Fitzwilliam* and *Matrix*. Millet L J is now in the Court of Appeal.

2.13   *Duke of Westminster*

What then remains of the *Duke of Westminster* case? Lord Templeman has disapproved of it without actually saying it was wrong – 'gardeners do not work for Dukes on half wages', he said. It certainly does not fulfil Lord Templeman's criteria for tax mitigation. Millet L J, the architect of the new approach, considered that it was correctly decided, although this may have been an attempt to calm the hysteria which followed *Furniss v Dawson*. However, he applied his views consistently in *Ensign* and there is no reason to suppose that his view has changed.

Judicial Attitudes to Tax Avoidance

In 1936 the case of *IRC v Duke of Westminster* laid down the principle that a person is entitled to arrange their affairs such that the tax attaching is less than otherwise would be the case. Following the *Duke of Westminster* case, a number of schemes were devised which sought to exploit the technicalities of the tax legislation in order to reduce the taxpayer's tax liabilities.

In the case of *Ramsay v IRC* (1981) the House of Lords held that where a number of transactions are entered into which are intended to achieve a given result, those steps which were inserted purely for the avoidance of tax could be ignored and the 'real transaction' should be taxed. The *Ramsay* case was followed by that of *IRC v Burmah Oil Co Ltd* (1981), in which an allowable loss was sought to be substituted for a otherwise non-allowable loss. The House of Lords held that although each individual step looked at in isolation gave an allowable loss, the scheme, looked at as a whole, was circular and therefore involved no real loss. The House of Lords therefore held that those parts of the scheme which were circular could be disregarded and that the taxpayer was taxable in full.

In the case of *Furniss v Dawson* (1984) the House of Lords held that even where the parties entered into a genuine transaction, a step inserted purely for tax avoidance reasons could be ignored and the 'real transaction' was to be taxed.

In the case of *CIR (New Zealand) v Challenge Corporation Ltd* (1986), the Privy Council introduced the concept of tax mitigation. A tax is mitigated by a taxpayer who reduces his income or incurs expenditure in circumstances which reduce assessable income or entitle him to a reduction in tax liability.

In the case of *Craven v White* (1988) the House of Lords held that where the last step of a series of transactions had not been entered into, ie the ultimate sale, then the principle in Furniss v Dawson did not apply. This case gave birth to the concept of strategic tax planning, that is entering into transactions with a view to the final transaction before the final transaction became certain.

In the case of *Ensign Tankers (Leasing) Ltd v Stokes (HMIT)* (1992) the judge at first instance, Millet J found in favour of the taxpayers. He found that the taxpayers entered into the transaction for a commercial purpose, notwithstanding that its motive was to avoid tax. It was only when a transaction was entered into for no commercial purpose that the *Furniss v Dawson* principle could apply. The Court of Appeal agreed with Millett J. However, the House of Lords found for the Inland Revenue. On this basis the taxpayer was allowed a deduction of $3.25m not the $14m which was claimed.

In the case of *IRC v Fitzwilliam & Others* (1993) the House of Lords had to apply the *Furniss v Dawson* principle to a scheme designed to avoid inheritance tax. The scheme comprised five steps. The majority felt that the five steps comprised strategic tax planning and therefore could not be disregarded.

Notwithstanding the fact that the *Furniss v Dawson* principle has been around for over 10 years, there is still no consistent application of the principle by the judiciary. The recent cases, if anything, show a return to the principles applied when *Furniss v Dawson* was first decided. Until recently the judiciary were at pains to point out that the *Duke of Westminster* case has not be overruled.

Chapter 3

Statutory Interpretation –
Pepper v Hart

All taxation has its foundations in statute. It is therefore necessary to examine the way in which the taxing statutes are interpreted by the courts in order to determine whether or not a liability arises. The approach taken by the courts has at times been erratic, though it is still possible – without particularly tortuous reasoning – to discern the principle that the courts have striven to uphold the will of Parliament. This principle, which was once embodied in a literal approach to interpretation, has undergone a fundamental change in recent years in response to a more mature commercial world. The courts now tend to adopt a more purposive approach, intended to give more weight to the intention of Parliament in enacting the statute. This chapter examines the courts' approach, how it has changed, and how it may evolve in the future. In particular, it looks at the case of *Pepper v Hart* (1992), a decision which may, as far as taxpayers are concerned, prove to be a double-edged sword. It is to be noted that despite the application of the literal approach by the courts in order to discern the will of Parliament, this often resulted in a decision that went against the express intention of Parliament when enacting the legislation.	**3.1 Introduction**

Tax is an invention of Parliament; the subject can only be taxed if Parliament says so. In an effort to uphold the will of Parliament, the courts adopted a strict analysis of statutory words – a literal interpretation – and held that in order for a liability to arise, the statute had to be clear. Ambiguities were consequently interpreted in favour of the taxpayer. This approach of the courts was based on the presumption that clear words in legislation could be relied upon to confer Parliament's will; it did not mean that the courts would strain to find in favour of the taxpayer. The rule was stated by Rowlatt J in *Cape Brandy Syndicate v IRC* (1921) in the following terms:

3.2   No equity in a tax

> 'There is no equity about a tax. There is no presumption as to a tax. Nothing is to be read in, nothing is to be implied. One can only look fairly at the language used ...'

The rule of literal statutory interpretation could also operate against the taxpayer. If the legislation clearly imposed a charge, the taxpayer was liable, notwithstanding the fact that the result may appear unfair, or that it was not the result intended by Parliament.

3.2.1   Literal interpretation

Broadly, literal interpretation means that plain words will be construed objectively by applying their ordinary meaning. This does not mean that specific provisions should be considered in a vacuum. The courts have developed many rules which are generally applicable. They include the following:

- statutes must read as a whole;

- the *ejusdem generis* rule: where specific words are followed by general words, the later words should be interpreted with reference to the specific words (eg 'dog, cat or other animal' may not include, say, a kangaroo, because dog and cat may be considered domestic animals whereas the kangaroo is not); and

- the *expressio unius est exclusio alterius* rule: where something is specifically expressed, other things are by implication excluded (eg a tax on paperback books would not include hardback books or books on tape).

Such rules may be reconciled with the literal approach in that they do not involve looking outside the particular Act, but involve an examination of Parliament's words without external reference.

In certain circumstances, however, the courts have departed from enforcing the clear statutory words where the result would have been so unreasonable that it could not possibly have been within Parliament's intention. This can be viewed in one of two lights. First, that the courts are doing a laudable job in shunning the literal approach where faced with manifestly bad laws; or second, that the literal approach is still being upheld because it is merely an attempt to determine Parliament's will. Where it is obvious that the particular words cannot be representative of Parliament's will, they, by definition, cannot be clear words. Nevertheless, it has become increasingly untenable in recent years to argue that the courts are still consistently applying a literal approach. Furthermore, we are now in an era of much more aggressive tax planning than took place in the 1920s.

The plain words approach of the courts led to taxpayers devising schemes of tax avoidance based in the knowledge that the courts would apply the literal meaning of an act. This led to the judiciary developing the 'new approach'. However, before the development of the new approach, Parliament had sought to counter the avoidance of tax by enacting some very widely drafted anti-avoidance provisions. Tax statutes became more sophisticated as a consequence, and increasingly complex.

This attitude towards anti-avoidance provisions led to cases being decided against what was the express intention of Parliament at the time the legislation was introduced. This can be demonstrated by two cases which were decided early in the 1970s: *IRC v Greenberg* (1971) and *IRC v Joiner* (1975). Both cases involved the interpretation of what is now s 703 Income and Corporation Taxes Act (ICTA) 1988, an anti-avoidance provision designed to counteract certain 'transactions in securities'. When the legislation was introduced the then Attorney General said in the House of Commons:

> 'An ordinary liquidation is not caught. The reason is that liquidation is not a transaction in securities any more than payment of a dividend on shares. It represents the operation of giving effect to the rights attaching to the securities in the circumstances that have arisen.'

The question in both cases was, what is a transaction in securities? In *Greenberg*, the House of Lords held that the payment of a dividend was a transaction in securities; in *Joiner*, the Inland Revenue argued that so too was a liquidation. This has led one commentator to point out that, in fact, the Attorney General was correct. The fact that both were transactions in securities did mean that one was no more so than the other.

Lord Wilberforce thought the intention behind the section was evident. However, the Attorney General's statement set out above indicates that Parliament's intention was not as evident as it might seem.

In *Pilkington Bros Ltd v IRC* (1981), Nourse J suggested that the approach adopted in *Greenberg*, ie a wide interpretation of general words, should only be applied to s 703 ICTA 1988. In other cases, he thought that the ordinary meaning of the words should prevail.

The more relaxed attitude towards anti-avoidance provisions was not applied in other areas of tax legislation where the meaning of the legislation was plain, and the courts continued to apply a literal approach. Consequently, sections which were apparently introduced for one purpose were used for another. Thus, in the case of *Leedale v Lewis* (1982) beneficiaries of a trust were taxed on amounts that they never received. The beneficiaries were to be taxed on a 'just and reasonable' basis, and this was probably intended to relieve the beneficiaries from taxation in the event that nothing was received. However, it was held that the just and reasonable basis applied to the amount on which they were to be made liable, not to whether they should be made liable in the first place. It was therefore just and reasonable that they were all taxed on an equal amount, notwithstanding that none of them received anything.

3.3   A literal change

This wider approach, in the case of anti-avoidance provisions, was taken one stage further in *Ramsay (W T) Ltd v IRC* (1981) and *Furniss v Dawson* (1984), when the House of Lords introduced the 'new approach' in interpreting a statute, so that one had to ascertain what the relevant transaction had been.

The advent of the new approach has created a dichotomy with regard to understanding the fundamental nature of statutory interpretation. It may be that proponents of the new approach now see tax legislation as malleable in circumstances where there exists a tax avoidance scheme, and that literal interpretation is inadequate to deal with today's sophisticated tax planning. Alternatively, it is arguable that a literal interpretation is still sacred but that the new approach concerns only the finding of 'true' facts to which the plain words of the statute should then be applied.

It is suggested that, where the judiciary so wish, statutory interpretation is becoming more purposive, and that the tax adviser may no longer take comfort in ensuring a scheme falls within a literal interpretation of the statute. Judicial pronouncements on a transaction's commercial substance, or its true facts, merely disguise the fact that a literal approach has been ignored. The facts of a case cannot require interpretation because they do not contain a subjective element; it is the way in which the law has been applied to particular facts which has recently undergone development.

This may be seen in *Craven v White* (1988), where Lord Oliver brought the new approach firmly back into the realms of statutory interpretation. It is now a question of interpreting the statute to see to which transactions it was intended to apply.

3.4   *Pepper v Hart* (1992)

The most radical departure from past practice came in the House of Lords case of *Pepper v Hart*. The taxpayer was the bursar at Malvern College. The college ran a scheme whereby, provided there were sufficient vacant places at the school, a master could have his child educated there at only 20% of the normal fee. The school's fees were calculated by disregarding the master's children and then dividing the total costs between the pupils. The 20% charged to the masters was intended to cover the direct cost of, for example, food, laundry, books and sports equipment (ie the additional cost once overheads had been covered), referred to as the marginal cost.

The Inland Revenue sought to tax the bursar under what is now s 154 ICTA 88, which provides that where a person receives a benefit in kind and the cost of providing the benefit is not otherwise chargeable to tax, that person shall be chargeable to tax on the cost of providing it. Section 156 ICTA 1988 provides that the amount of the benefit is the cost to the employer, less so much as is made good by the employee. The question was therefore: what was the cost to the employer? If it was the additional cost, (marginal cost) then the master had made good this amount and no more tax was payable, but if it was the total cost to the school (average cost) there would have been a further amount to pay. Had this latter view, which was advanced by the Inland Revenue, been accepted, there would have been widely felt repercussions. For example, an airline employee given a free trip on a scheduled flight which was empty would arguably have been chargeable on the cost to the airline of the flight, an amount which was probably far in excess of the normal price of a ticket.

After the merits of the case had been heard, the court invited the parties to make further submissions on whether parliamentary debates should be admissible as an aid to the interpretation of a statutory provision. The reason for this appears to be that counsel for the taxpayer had come across a statement in *Hansard* which stated that it was only the marginal cost that was to be taxed. School teachers had been specifically mentioned during the committee stage: 'He mentioned the children of teachers ... now the benefit will be assessed on the cost to the employer, which would be very small indeed.'

The House of Lords decided 6:1 in favour of the taxpayer. The leading judgment was given by Lord Browne-Wilkinson who held that *Hansard* could be referred to provided that three criteria were satisfied:

- the legislation in question was ambiguous or obscure, or would lead to an absurdity;

- the material which was to be relied upon consisted of one or more statements by a minister or other promoter of the bill together, if necessary, with such other parliamentary material as was necessary to understand such statements and their effect; and

- the statements to be relied on were clear.

Lord Browne-Wilkinson went on to decide that the words of what is now s 156 ICTA 1988 were ambiguous and that the words of the minister were sufficiently clear to resolve the ambiguity.

A professional adviser would now have to check the relevant passages in *Hansard* to avoid allegations of negligence, and in most cases the research would be fruitless. Many professional firms have included in their terms of engagement a provision that they will not research *Hansard* unless a matter goes to litigation. Lord Griffiths considered that if the guidelines set by Lord Browne-Wilkinson were followed, the cost would not be greatly increased. He said that he himself had often researched a point and found it easy. However, it transpires that researching a point amounted to asking the House of Commons library staff to find the relevant passages.

It is unclear, following *Pepper v Hart*, whether a literal approach still exists. It would seem that if a literal approach has its foundation in assuming that the intention of Parliament must be that set out in clear words, the rationale for looking only at clear words is now lost because it is possible with far more certainty to look at the intention of Parliament by referring to *Hansard*. However, on the basis of Lord Browne-Wilkinson's three points, it seems that *Hansard* cannot be referred to otherwise than in cases of ambiguity.

A further problem with the case of *Pepper v Hart* is that when the case was first heard in front of five Law Lords, it was held that the master was taxable on the full cost and that what is now s 154 ICTA 1988 was not ambiguous. It is therefore arguable that the three tests set out by Lord Browne-Wilkinson were not satisfied. There was no ambiguity nor was there an absurd result. Consequently, the facts did not justify reference to *Hansard*. How, then, was the *Hansard* passage introduced? The decision obviously gave effect to the intention of Parliament, but in doing so the House of Lords appear to have lost sight of the principle they were laying down.

3.5 Cases post *Pepper v Hart*	Taxpayers have not been slow to seize the opportunity to use *Hansard*, neither have the Inland Revenue. This demonstrates that the rule in *Pepper v Hart* may be a double-edged sword. There is no reason why it should not be used to resolve an ambiguity in favour of the Inland Revenue. Indeed, the Inland Revenue probably have greater access to the materials than the taxpayer's advisers. And what remains of the rule that ambiguities should be resolved in favour of the taxpayer? Why, on general principles did the House of Lords allow the admission of *Hansard*? If the section was truly ambiguous, should not the case have been decided in favour of the taxpayer in any event? If the section was not ambiguous, Lord Browne-Wilkinson's criteria did not apply and reference should not have been made to *Hansard*. The rule that ambiguities are to be resolved in favour of the taxpayer has probably survived *Pepper v Hart*, but it will presumably only be applied after the relevant ministerial statements, if any, have been considered.

In *Sheppard v IRC (No 2)* (1993) the question of whether a previous House of Lords decision, which was made without reference to *Hansard*, could be overruled was addressed. The Inland Revenue had sought to treat a dividend as a transaction in securities. The taxpayer argued that *Greenberg* should be considered afresh with reference to the Attorney General's statement. Aldous J discussed the taxpayer's case and, in so doing, he made some observations on what amounts to an ambiguity.

3.5.1   *Sheppard v IRC (No 2)*

The type of ambiguity envisaged in *Pepper v Hart* was not, what does the statute mean?, but, do the facts as found fit into the statute as it is known to mean? In *Pepper v Hart* the court knew the facts, but they did not know whether those facts were intended to be covered by the statute. It is therefore arguable that it was the former type of ambiguity that was in issue – the question was whether the statute meant marginal cost, as argued by the taxpayers, or average cost, as argued by the Inland Revenue. Once it was found to mean marginal cost it was obvious how the taxpayers were to be taxed.

Aldous J went on to decide that the statement did not help the taxpayer. This statement, and the case of *Greenberg* has always been quoted as the classic case of a statute being interpreted contrary to the intention of Parliament, but following the case of *Sheppard (No 2)* it is difficult to see when any ministerial statement will be admissible. Similarly, in the non-tax case of *National Rivers Authority v Alfred McAlpine Homes East Ltd* (1994), Simon Brown LJ refused to consider a passage in *Hansard* because the point to be decided had already been ruled on in a previous House of Lords case.

It remains to be seen whether the case of *Pepper v Hart* is as helpful to the taxpayer as was first thought. The rule applies to both taxpayers and the Inland Revenue. In *Griffin (HM Inspector of Taxes) v Craig-Harvey* (1994) Vinelott J held that there was no ambiguity or obscurity in the provisions under consideration. If there had been, passages from *Hansard*, which had been adduced in evidence by the Inland Revenue, would have resolved the matter conclusively in the Inland Revenue's favour. Furthermore, when introducing legislation in the future, it was not inconceivable that the Inland Revenue could prompt ministers to make statements which could be of use to the Inland Revenue.

3.6   Further problems

The relative quality of a statement causes a significant problem. Is a statement made 50 years ago valid today? (In *Massmould Holdings Ltd v Payne* (1992), counsel for the taxpayer sought to introduce a statement made in 1927.) Does a statement as to the meaning of a particular word still hold good when, due to the passage of time and changed economic circumstances, that word may now mean something different? Until 1968, the Finance Bill was debated in a committee of the whole house. Does this therefore give statements made before 1968 any greater validity?

Finally, if the purpose of referring to *Hansard* is to help determine the will of Parliament when enacting legislation, does it necessarily achieve that end? What if, despite a ministerial statement of intention, the rank and file MPs vote in favour because they all think it means something else? Will a reference to *Hansard* provide any more insight to the meaning of the provision than reading the plain words of the statute?

Statutory Interpretation –
Pepper v Hart

Taxation is creature of statute and it is therefore necessary to examine how the judiciary have approached the interpretation of taxing statutes in order to determine whether or not a tax liability might arise.

The basic principle is that the subject can only be taxed if Parliament says so. In early cases it was stated that it was necessary for there to be clear words before the subject would be taxed. However, this did not mean that the statutory provisions had to be interpreted against the Inland Revenue. It merely meant that the subject was to be taxed in accordance with the plain words; this could just as well lead to a taxpayer being taxed when this was not intended as to a taxpayer escaping tax when Parliament's intention was to tax the taxpayer.

As the lengths to which taxpayers would go to in order to avoid tax became more sophisticated, the judiciary adopted a more liberal approach to statutory interpretation. This was especially true of certain anti-avoidance provisions. However, the zeal of the courts to apply such interpretations often led to a tax charge being imposed where none was originally intended. Consequently, in later cases the judiciary tended to restrict the use of the liberal interpretation. Thus, in the case of *Pilkington Bros Ltd v IRC* (1981) Nourse J suggested that the approach adopted in *Greenburg v IRC* (1971), which was a wide interpretation of general words, should only be applied to the section which was under consideration in that case. In other cases he thought that the ordinary meaning of the words should prevail.

Arguably, the 'new approach' introduced in the case of *Furniss v Dawson* (1984) is a principle of statutory interpretation. It was introduced by the judiciary in order to deal with the greater excesses of the tax avoidance industry. Lord Scarman considered that such schemes were 'beyond the power of the blunt instrument of legislation'.

Prior to the case of *Pepper v Hart* (1992), the intention of Parliament could only be discerned from the words used in the legislation and the judges were not allowed to have recourse to any reports of parliamentary debates which might shed light on the reason why the legislation was enacted. In the case of *Pepper v Hart*, the House of Lords held by a majority of 6:1 that, provided certain criteria were satisfied, the judges could have a recourse to other materials as an aid to the interpretation of statutes. These criteria are:

- legislation has to be ambiguous, obscure or lead to an absurdity;

- the material to be relied upon comprised one or more statements by a minister or other promoter of the bill; and

- the statements to be relied upon were clear.

Pepper v Hart may turn out to be a double-edged sword as far as the taxpayer is concerned. It is likely that the Inland Revenue will have greater access to the materials indicating the reasons for the enactment of the legislation. Further, the costs of researching the parliamentary materials will greatly increase the costs of the taxpayer for what in most cases will be a fruitless search.

In the cases since *Pepper v Hart* attempts to introduce materials indicating the purpose behind the legislation in question has met with little sympathy from the judiciary. Where sections have been interpreted by the House of Lords in previous cases, the lower courts have been reluctant to revisit such sections assisted by the parliamentary debates. In such cases the courts have generally held that the point has been decided already.

Other problems created by the rule are that statements made by Parliament some 50 years ago may no longer be relevant to a section as enacted today. In some cases, where it has been shown that the section has been interpreted against the understanding of Parliament, the fact that the section has later been included in a consolidation act without amendment has been taken to show that Parliament approves of the interpretation placed on the section by the courts. The Finance Bill used to be debated by a committee of the whole house. It is now debated by a much smaller committee. Statements made in committee, often in the early hours of the morning, may not accurately reflect the true intention of Parliament when promulgating the legislation.

Chapter 4

Administration, Collection and Fact and Law

This chapter examines the administration of the tax system. It is concerned with the structure of the system; the way in which taxpayers are assessed; the means by which the authorities can obtain the information necessary to assess the taxpayer; and the procedure to be followed if the taxpayer is dissatisfied with an assessment and wishes to appeal.

4.1   Introduction

The administration of the various taxes in the UK is the responsibility of either the Board of the Inland Revenue (the Board) which has 'care and management' of:

4.2   Administration

- income tax;

- capital gains tax;

- inheritance tax;

- corporation tax; and

- stamp duties.

or the commissioners of Customs and Excise which have control of amongst other things:

- VAT; and

- customs duties.

We will deal mainly with the administration of two direct taxes: income tax and capital gains tax, which are under the control of the Board. The Board comprises seven full-time civil servants who report to the Chancellor of the Exchequer.

The Board is empowered to appoint inspectors of taxes and collectors of taxes (s 1 Taxes Management Act (TMA) 1970). The country is divided into districts, each of which is headed by an inspector. The district inspector is assisted by numerous other inspectors of taxes. It is their job to assess the taxpayer and to issue an assessment in respect of the taxpayer's income, capital gains etc. The tax is then collected by a collector of taxes. Every person who is appointed to the Board or to be an inspector or collector of taxes must make a declaration that they shall not disclose any information received by them, except for the purposes of their duties, or for the prosecution of any offence relating to the Inland Revenue, or as is otherwise required by law (Sch 1 TMA 1970).

4.3   Obligation to notify

Every person who is chargeable to tax in any year of assessment must inform the Inland Revenue of that fact before the end of the following year.

4.4   Powers to require information

The Inland Revenue has various powers at its disposal to obtain sufficient information so that it can assess the taxpayer to the right amount of tax.

4.4.1   Returns

A person may be required to make a return providing 'such information a may be required' and to deliver with it 'such accounts and statements, relating to information contained in the return as may be required ...' (s 8 TMA 1970).

The return form also includes the necessary information for the Inland Revenue to give taxpayers the correct personal allowances for the following tax year. A failure to complete the return may result in a denial of the allowances with a corresponding increase in the liability to tax. The loss of allowances is usually a sufficient incentive to persuade the taxpayer to submit the tax return in good time.

4.4.2   People other than the taxpayer

The Inland Revenue also has the power to obtain information from people other than the taxpayer, these include:

- persons in receipt of income belonging to another (s 13 TMA 1970);
- people who have lodgers or inmates (s 14 TMA 1970);
- employers (s 16 TMA 1970);
- people carrying on business (s 16 TMA 1970);
- banks (s 17 TMA 1970);
- any person who pays interest without deduction of income tax (s 18 TMA 1970);
- any lessee or occupier (s 19 TMA 1970).

Information may also be taken from people who are connected with:

- the payment of annual payments (ss 349 and 350 ICTA 1988);
- settlements (ss 669 and 680 ICTA 1988); and
- a deceased's estate (s 700 ICTA 1988).

4.4.3   Power to obtain information

The Inland Revenue has very wide powers to obtain information from the taxpayer and third parties. These powers have been recently extended by the F (No 2) A 1987.

Under s 20(1) TMA 1970, an inspector may by notice in writing require a person to give up any documents in that person's possession or power which, in the inspector's reasonable opinion, contain or may contain information relevant to either any tax liability to which that person is, or may be, subject, or the amount of such liability.

Under s 20(3) TMA 1970 the inspector may, for the purposes of enquiring into the tax liability of any person, require any other person by notice in writing to deliver, or make available for inspection by a named office of the Board, such documents as are in his possession or power and which, in the inspector's reasonable opinion, contain or may contain information relevant to the liability of the taxpayer or the amount of that liability.

Under s 20A TMA 1970, where a tax accountant has been convicted of a criminal offence in relation to tax, or has had a tax penalty imposed on him, an inspector may, if authorised by the Board, require the tax accountant to deliver to the inspector such documents as are in his possession or power, and which in the inspector's reasonable opinion contain information relevant to any tax liability or the amount of such liability of a client.	**4.4.4 Tax accountant papers**

Notwithstanding the authorisation of the Board, the inspector must also seek the consent of a circuit judge who must be satisfied that the inspector is justified in proceeding in the manner proposed.

Where an inspector requires any information as described in paras 4.4.3 and 4.4.4, the person must first be given a reasonable opportunity to provide the information.	**4.4.5 Safeguards**

Where there are reasonable grounds for suspecting that an offence involving serious tax fraud is being, has been, or is about to be committed, and that evidence may be found on certain premises, the inspector – on the approval of the Board – may apply in writing for a warrant which authorises an officer of the Board to enter the premises, by force if necessary, at any time within 14 days from issue of the warrant, and search them.	**4.4.6 Entry into premises**

Once the information has been gathered the inspector will raise an assessment on the taxpayer showing the amount of tax due. Where the inspector is not satisfied that any return submitted is complete, or if no return has been submitted, she may make an assessment to the best of her judgment. If the assessment is not appealed within 30 days, it becomes final and is conclusive of the amount due. A notice of appeal must be given to the inspector or other officer of the Board by whom the notice of assessment was given.	**4.5 Assessment**

Once the taxpayer has appealed the assessment he may, prior to the hearing, come to an agreement with the inspector to settle the appeal. Under s 54 TMA 1970 such an agreement is treated as if the appeal had been determined by the commissioners in the manner agreed.

An assessment cannot be made more than six years after the end of the period to which the assessment relates (s 34 TMA 1970). However, where an assessment is being made for the purpose of making good a loss of tax which is attributable to the fraudulent conduct or negligent conduct of a taxpayer, the assessment can be made up to 20 years after the end of the period to which it relates.

| 4.5.1 | Discovery assessments |

Once an assessment has been made and agreed, the matter can only be reopened if the Inland Revenue 'discover' something which justifies an extra assessment (s 29 TMA 1970). A 'discovery' does not have to be new facts.

| 4.5.2 | Postponement |

In para 4.5, it was stated that the taxpayer has the right to appeal an assessment and that any such appeal must be notified to the inspector within 30 days of issue of the notice of assessment. However, unless the taxpayer applies for a postponement of the tax payable, it will become payable, notwithstanding the appeal, as if there were no appeal (s 55 TMA 1970).

4.6   Making an appeal

If the taxpayer and the inspector cannot agree the amount of tax payable, the matter will be listed for appeal. Notice of appeal must be lodged within 30 days of the date of the notice of assessment. Note that this is not the date upon which notice is received by the taxpayer, but the date on which it is issued. Appeals are heard by either the general commissioners or the special commissioners. Normally, an appeal would be heard by the general commissioners, though s 31(3) TMA 1970, provides for certain cases to be heard specifically by the special commissioners.

Once an appeal has been made it cannot be withdrawn without the consent of the Inland Revenue, notwithstanding that it is the taxpayer who has appealed (s 54(4) TMA 1970). An appeal before the general commissioners can be transferred to the special commissioners if the general commissioners consider that, because of the complexity of the matter and the length of time the case would take to hear, the appeal ought to be brought before the special commissioners (s 43(3A) TMA 1970).

Confusingly, the TMA refers to three types of commissioner: the commissioners of the Inland Revenue; the commissioners for the general purposes of the income tax; and the commissioners for the special purposes of the Income Tax Acts. The former are usually referred to as the Board. When people refer to commissioners, it is usually the general and special commissioners which are being referred to. The general commissioners and special commissioners have nothing to do with the Board.

4.7 The general and special commissioners

The commissioners for the general purposes of the income tax, or general commissioners as they are more usually known, are rather like justices of the peace; they are part time and local to the area in which they sit (s 2 TMA 1970).

4.7.1 General commissioners

The general commissioners for each area have a clerk. The clerk is rather like a clerk to the justices. He has a knowledge of tax law and procedure, and his job is to advise the general commissioners on such matters.

The commissioners for the special purposes of the Income Tax Acts, or special commissioners as they are more usually known, are more akin to stipendiary magistrates. A special commissioner must be a barrister, solicitor or advocate of not less than ten years standing. They are paid, full-time appointees.

4.7.2 Special commissioners

It has already been noted that certain appeals are to be heard only by the special commissioners, and that in other cases the choice lies with the taxpayer. The taxpayer's choice will prevail unless that choice can be overridden because the taxpayer's election was merely for purposes of delay.

4.7.3 Which commissioners?

On 1 September 1994 new rules were introduced governing the procedure before general and special commissioners. The rules are now set out in three statutory instruments:

4.8 Appeals procedure

- the Special Commissioner's (Jurisdiction and Procedures) Regulations 1994;

- the General Commissioner's (Jurisdiction and Procedures) Regulations 1994; and

- the General and Special Commissioner's (Amendment to Enactments) Regulations 1994.

Once a notice of appeal has been served, any party to the proceedings which are to be heard by special commissioners may serve a notice on the clerk that he wishes a date for the hearing to be fixed. The clerk should send notice to each party

4.9 Procedure for the special commissioners

of the place, date and time of the hearing. The date shall not be earlier than 28 days after the date on which the notice is sent to the parties unless they agree otherwise.

A tribunal of special commissioners can comprise either one, two or three special commissioners.

The tribunal may make an order for costs if it is of the opinion that the party against whom the order is made has acted wholly unreasonably in connection with the hearing in question.

The tribunal must record their final determination in a document which must contain a statement of the facts found by the tribunal and the reasons for the determination. The clerk must send a copy of the final determination to each party. If either party is dissatisfied in point of law with the commissioner's determination, that party may appeal to the Chancery Division of the High Court. If the leave of the Court of Appeal has been obtained, the appeal may be heard directly by the Court of Appeal. A further appeal lies to the House of Lords.

| 4.10 | **Procedure before the general commissioners** |

The procedure before the general commissioners is similar in many respects of that before the special commissioners. However, there are a number of significant differences. There is no provision for general commissioners to either give directions or to have a preliminary hearing. Unlike the special commissioners, who can sit either singularly, in pairs, or threes, a tribunal of general commissioners should, where possible, comprise at least three general commissioners; However, where it comprises only two, the validity of the proceedings cannot be challenged on that basis.

The hearings of the general commissioners are held in private.

Although the general commissioners must notify the parties of their final determination, there is no provision for them to set out the facts upon which that determination was made or the reasons for coming to the conclusion that they did. The facts as found by the commissioners are conclusive and the parties can only appeal on a point of law. Where a party wishes to appeal, that party must within 30 days after the final determination, serve a notice upon the clerk to the tribunal requesting the tribunal to state and sign a case for the opinion of the High Court. This is the appeal by way of case stated which was mentioned in the previous paragraph.

Within 56 days of the receipt of a notice requiring a case to be stated, the clerk must send a draft of the case to the party who required it to be stated and to all other interested parties.

There is then a further 56 days during which any party may make representations on the draft to the clerk to the general commissioners in writing and must send a copy of the representations to other interested parties. Within a further 28 days after the latest date on which any representations have been made, a party may make further representations in response to representations made by the other party, again sending such representations to the other interested parties. Following the making of representations the tribunal, having taken account of any representations made, shall state and sign the case. The clerk to the tribunal must then send it to the party who required the case to be stated. That party must subsequently transmit the case to the High Court within 30 days of receiving it. A failure to transmit the case stated to the High Court in the prescribed time would deprive the High Court of jurisdiction to hear the case.

The strictness of the 30 day rule and the absurd consequences that can follow are highlighted by the recent case of *Petch v Gurney* (1992) in which both the Inland Revenue and the taxpayer wished to appeal against the decision of the commissioners. The Inland Revenue transmitted the case stated within the 30 day period, the taxpayer did not. Notwithstanding the fact that the documents were identical, the Inland Revenue's appeal was heard but the taxpayer's was not.

It will be noted from the above paragraphs that an appeal from the decision of the general or special commissioners may only be made if a party is dissatisfied with the decision as being erroneous in law.	**4.11 Fact or law?**

This does of course mean that on the facts a judge may have come to a different conclusion from the tribunal but is unable to disturb the tribunal's decision.

It is consequently possible for two different tribunals, on the same facts, to come to opposite conclusions. When looking at a tax case as a precedent, it is therefore important to establish what the facts were and whether the judge was merely upholding the tribunal's decision, or whether he had reversed the decision.

As there is no appeal on a question of fact, it is important to establish whether the question involves one of fact or one of law.

A conclusion which is drawn from primary facts may also be a finding of fact. However, if that conclusion requires the application of some legal principle the conclusion is a conclusion of law.

4.12   Statements of practice and extra-statutory concessions

From time to time the Inland Revenue issues statements of practice which state how they will interpret certain provisions of the Taxes Acts. They also operate a system of extra-statutory concessions. An extra-statutory concession mitigates the harshness of a statutory provision.

The availability of an extra-statutory concession will be denied in cases where it has been used to avoid tax.

The operation of the system of extra-statutory concessions and the ability of the Inland Revenue to deny their operation in certain circumstances could be said to lead to a system of taxation at the discretion of the Inland Revenue.

Administration, Collection and Fact and Law

Taxes in the UK are administered by the Board of the Inland Revenue (the Board) and the commissioners of Customs and Excise. The following notes deal primarily with the administration of income tax and capital gains tax.

The Board appoints inspectors of taxes and collectors of taxes. Such people are required to take an oath note of secrecy on their appointment and should not disclose the affairs of a taxpayer accept in certain specified circumstances.

A person who is chargeable to tax has a duty to notify the Inland Revenue of that fact. The Inland Revenue can also require people to make returns of information to enable them to assess the right amount of tax. The Inland Revenue also has the power to enter premises to seize documents which may be required to enable them to assess the right amount to tax.

Once the information has been given, an assessment will be issued. If the inspector has insufficient information he can issue an estimated assessment. If the taxpayer wishes to appeal against the assessment, the appeal must be made within 30 days of the assessment being issued. Unless the assessment is being made for the purpose of making good a loss of tax attributable to fraud or neglect, an assessment cannot be made more than six years after the end of the period to which it relates. Once an assessment has become final it can only be reopened if the Inland Revenue make a discovery.

Pending hearing of the appeal, a taxpayer can make an application to have the tax postponed. Only the disputed amount can be postponed. An appeal will be heard by either the general commissioners or the special commissioners. The general commissioners are like justices of the peace; they are part time and local to the area in which they sit. The special commissioners are more akin to stipendiary magistrates. A special commissioner must be a barrister, solicitor or advocate of not less than 10 years standing. They are paid, full-time appointees. In general, the taxpayer can choose which commissioners the appeal is to go to, although certain matters must go before the special commissioners.

Special commissioners' hearings are now in public unless one party to the proceedings applies for the hearing to take place in private.

Proceedings before the general commissioners are held in private. The general commissioners do not have to state the reasons for the decision nor do they have to set out the facts upon which they based that decision. The parties to the proceedings before the general commissioners must appeal against that decision within 30 days. Once the general commissioners have stated a case and transmitted it to the parties, the parties have 30 days in which to transmit it to the High Court. Failure to transmit to the High Court will result in the High Court not having jurisdiction to hear the appeal.

An appeal from the commissioners cannot be made on a point of law. The facts are conclusive. It is therefore necessary to distinguish between what is a question of fact and what is a question of law. Primary facts are those observed by witnesses, by testimony or by production of the thing itself. A question of law is one which requires the application of legal principle to the facts that have been found.

The legislation is backed up by statements of practice and extra-statutory concessions which are published by the Revenue and which indicate how the Inland Revenue is going to apply certain provisions.

An extra-statutory concession usually mitigates the harshness of a statutory provision. However, where an extra-statutory concession is used for the purposes of tax avoidance, its application will be denied.

Chapter 5

Income Tax – The Source Doctrine and Schedular System

Income tax is based on a schedular system, and this chapter examines its origins, its operation and the consequences of its application. There are some fundamental assumptions which are often taken for granted regarding the workings of the scheduler system, and the text will go on to question those.

5.1 Introduction

Income tax is an annual tax. This means that Parliament must reimpose it each year if it is to be effective. Income tax is imposed by the annual Finance Act. The income tax year runs from the 6 April to 5 April. The reason for this is historical. It can be attributed in the main to the change from the Julian to the Gregorian calendar in 1750, with the result that the rent payable on the March quarter day (March 25) became payable 11 days later.

5.2 Characteristics of income tax

If the annual Finance Act has not become law by the beginning of the tax year, there would be no power to charge income tax and, to avoid the administrative chaos this would produce, a number of provisions have been enacted to ensure the smooth transition from year to year.

The Provisional Collection of Taxes Act 1968 provides that where a resolution of the House of Commons is passed in November or December in any year, the resolution has statutory effect expiring on 5 May in the next calendar year. In the case of a resolution passed at any other time, it will have statutory effect expiring at the end of four months after the date on which it is expressed to take effect or, if no date is expressed, four months after the date on which it is passed.

The annual budget is held in November. Consequently, a budget resolution passed immediately after the budget will enable tax to be collected until 5 May. The Finance Act must therefore be enacted before 5 May. The 1995 Finance Act received royal assent on 1 May.

In *Attorney General v London County Council* (1901) Lord McNaughten stated: 'Income tax, if I may be pardoned for saying so, is a tax on income.' However, so simple a statement hides a number of problems, not least of which is: what is income? In *Longsdon v Minister of Pensions and National Insurance* (1956) Havers J said, quoting the American case of *People v Niagara Board of Supervisors* 'income is what comes in'. But not everything that comes in is income for the purposes of

5.2.1 Income tax and income

income tax. Much ink has been spilt by economists in the argument over what is, and what is not, income. There is no statutory definition.

For tax purposes much of the problem is avoided because s 1 ICTA 1988 provides that income tax shall be charged in respect of all property, profits or gains described or comprised in the five schedules labelled A–F (Schedule B was abolished by s 65 and Sch 14 Finance Act (FA) 1988). Provided that the receipt is one described in the schedules, it will be income for the purposes of income tax.

However, it is still necessary in some cases to determine whether a particular payment exhibits the characteristic of income.

5.3 Characteristics of income – the source doctrine

Although the UK tax system does not seek to define income but instead seeks to identify it by use of description, the courts have identified certain features which help to distinguish income from capital; a major distinction in the UK tax system.

Central to the system of income tax has been the doctrine of the source. This has two aspects. First, it states that all income must have a source and that, if the payment does not have a source, then it is not income. Many reported cases make references to fruit and tree; the income is the fruit, the source is the tree. Second, as income is an annual tax, it follows that the source has to exist in the year of assessment if it is to be taxable in that year.

The application of the source doctrine meant many receipts escaped tax, notably, post cessation receipts. For example, if a trader ceased trading and, in the following tax year received a payment for goods delivered when trading, the receipt escaped tax because the source no longer existed in that tax year. To counter this problem, specific provisions were introduced to tax receipts notwithstanding that the source had ceased to exist. Thus, s 104 ICTA 1988 taxes post-cessation receipts 'not being sums otherwise chargeable to tax'.

However, as recently as 1989 the application of the source doctrine allowed a payment to go untaxed. In the case of *Bray v Best* (1989) Peter Best, who had been employed by Gallenkamp and Co Ltd, was transferred with all the other employees to the parent company, Fisons plc, following a takeover. A trust fund had been established for the benefit of the employees of Gallenkamp which was wound up on 21 December 1979. The transfer of the employees to the parent company occurred on 1 April 1979, in the tax year preceding the winding up of the trust. There was therefore no source of income in that year; neither could the £18,111 received by Mr

Best be attributed to any previous year or years of assessment. As a result, the payment escaped tax. The result in *Bray v Best* was reversed by statute in 1989 (although not the actual decision itself). Section 19(1) para 4A ICTA 1988 taxes payments received after employment has ceased as payments in the last year of assessment in which the employment was held.

It is often easy to identify a source. For example, land is the source of rent, a bank deposit is the source of interest and a business is the source of profit. An example of a payment which does not have a source (at least for income tax purposes) is a gift of cash. However, should the donor enter into a legally binding covenant, the covenant will become a source for the purposes of income tax.

Although the schedules talk of 'annual profits', the courts have held that another quality of income is that profits need to possess the quality of recurrence or, at least, be capable of recurrence. Thus, in *Moss' Empires Ltd v IRC* (1937) an obligation to pay variable sums for a period of five years was held to be an annual payment and consequently it was income, because the payment could recur. There does, however, appear to be some conflict between the fact that income tax is an annual tax reimposed each year and the fact that, to be income, there has to be a quality of recurrence.

5.3.1   Characteristics of income – recurrence

Before dealing with the schedules in any detail, it is interesting to look at their history and why, if they are contained in the body of the Act, they are known as schedules. A succinct explanation was given by Lord McNaughton in *Attorney General v London County Council*. When income tax was first introduced in 1799 the act imposing it divided income into four divisions set out in descending order of importance: (a) income from land; (b) income from personal property and trades; (c) income arising outside Great Britain; and (d) income not falling within (a) (b) or (c).

5.4   The schedules

The form of tax return was given in a schedule to the act.

The four heads of income were represented by 19 cases. The taxpayer had to return his total income under each of the cases. Certain deductions were allowed from total income. However, the single return required was considered to be highly objectionable, disclosing the entire means of the taxpayer. In those days, a person was assessed by someone local and such a return would therefore disclose an individual's entire wealth (or lack of it).

When income tax was reintroduced in 1803, instead of the general return, different specific returns were required for each of what had now become five different sources, each being represented by a different schedule. The schedules were divided into 19 different cases and a return in respect of each case was submitted to a different surveyor taxes. Consequently, no one surveyor of taxes had a complete picture of the person's income. Income tax was reintroduced in 1842 and again, the various schedules were included. When income tax was consolidated in 1952 the schedules were incorporated into the main body of the act. The modern income tax return is made to one inspector who therefore has full knowledge of the taxpayer's income. However, it is unlikely that the inspector would know the taxpayer or indeed would reside in the same part of the country. Inspectors must also take an oath of secrecy.

5.4.1   Schedules A–F

Set out below are the schedules and the various types of income taxed under them.

Schedule A	Income from land situated in the UK eg rents.
Schedule C	Public Revenue Dividends, eg interest on UK government stock.
Schedule D	
Case I	Profits of a UK trade.
Case II	Profits of a UK profession or vocation.
Case III	Interest, annuities or other annual payments (not taxed under Schedule C).
Case IV	Income on non-UK securities not charged under Schedule C.
Case V	Income from non-UK possessions not being income from employment.
Case VI	Annual profits or gains not charged under any other case of Schedule D and not charged under Schedule A, C or E.
Schedule E	
Case I	Emoluments from an office or employment of a person resident or ordinarily resident in the UK.
Case II	Emoluments in respect of duties in the UK of a person who is not resident in the UK or if resident is not ordinarily resident.
Case III	Emoluments from an office or employment of a person resident in the UK whether those emoluments are received in the UK.
Schedule F	Dividends and other distributions of companies resident in the UK.

The schedules are mutually exclusive. This means that any one source of income can only be taxed under the one schedule to which it is properly attributable. There is no question of a choice of schedules. This rule is said to derive from the case of *Fry v Salisbury House Estates* (1930), in which the taxpayer was assessed to tax under Schedule A for a building it owned and which it let to tenants. At that time (the assessments were for the four years ended 5 April 1928), the Schedule A charge was not on the rental income derived from the property but on the 'annual value' of the land, which was approximately half the aggregate amount of rent payable by the various tenants. The taxpayer also provided the tenants with extra services such as porterage and cleaning. Having assessed the taxpayer to tax under Schedule A, the Inland Revenue then raised a second assessment under Schedule D, claiming that the taxpayer was carrying on a trade. The profits assessed included the whole rental income and the income from the ancillary services, but provided for a deduction for tax already charged under Schedule A. The taxpayer agreed that the ancillary services should be taxed under Schedule D.

At first instance, Rowlatt J decided in favour of the Inland Revenue. The Court of Appeal was unanimous in finding for the taxpayer, so too was the House of Lords. Lord Tomlin, paraphrasing Lord McNaughton in *Attorney General v London County Council*, said: 'Now income tax is one tax. There is not a separate tax under each schedule.'

It was held that having assessed a source of income, that source had been 'exhausted' and could not be assessed under another schedule.

Although the decision in *Fry v Salisbury House Estates* was that the taxpayer could not be assessed twice in respect of the same income, the case does not necessarily lend support to the conclusion that the schedules are mutually exclusive.

The view that property letting is not a trade could be said to lend support to the mutually exclusive rule because the court is identifying the type of income in order to identify the correct source, which then decides the correct schedule, ie letting (Schedule A) or trade (Schedule D). However, it is submitted that this may not be correct in the light of the case of *Lowe v J W Ashmore Ltd* (1970) (see para 5.8).

Consequently, if there is another schedule which is more appropriate, that is the one which should be applied. It is arguable, however, that Schedule D is no longer residual. When first introduced Schedule D was the least important because most income was generated through the ownership of land. Since the introduction of income tax there has been much

5.5   The mutually exclusive rule

5.5.1   The mutually exclusive rule – a myth?

movement of different classes of income between the various schedules. Although Schedule D Case VI is the residual case of Schedule D, it is arguable that Schedule D is not, any longer, itself residual to the other schedules. The clear statement of the mutually exclusive rule is only one of five speeches in the case.

Despite this, the fact that the mutually exclusive rule stands upon what might be considered a minority view, it has been applied so often as to be accepted as truth.

Before leaving *Fry v Salisbury House Estate* there are two points to note. The case is cited as authority for two propositions. First, that the schedules are mutually exclusive, and second, that there cannot be a trade of letting. The second point is that the actual decision, that the annual value and not the gross rents were assessable to tax, was reversed by ss 13–18 FA 1940.

5.6	**The consequences of the mutually exclusive rule**	The consequences of the application of the mutually exclusive rule are that once the source, and thus the schedule, has been identified, the issue in question must be dealt with in accordance with the rules of that schedule.

5.6.1   Deductibility of expenses

The difference between the application of the rules of each schedule is exemplified by the case of *Mitchell and Edon v Ross* which concerned a number of doctors who had private practices but who also worked part time within the National Health Service. Their private practices were assessed under Schedule D. In order for expenses to be deductible under Schedule D they need to be 'wholly and exclusively' incurred. However, to be deductible under Schedule E, expenses need to be wholly exclusively and *necessarily* incurred. They claimed to deduct expenses incurred under their NHS appointment from income derived from their private practice. If the part-time NHS appointments were assessable under Schedule E, the more restrictive basis for the deduction of expenses would apply. Counsel for the taxpayers conceded at first instance that the NHS appointments were correctly assessed to Schedule E but sought to argue that their expenses should be deductible under Schedule D rules. The argument succeeded in the Court of Appeal which held that, while the income was assessable under Schedule E, this was an incident of the Schedule D profession. However, it failed in the House of Lords which held that the mutually exclusive rule had to be strictly applied and there was no room for movement between the schedules.

5.6.2   Basis of assessment

The deductibility of expenses is not the only consequence of the schedules being mutually exclusive. Each schedule has its own set of rules determining how the taxable income is to be calculated. The basis upon which tax is assessed under the various schedules was also different until the Finance Act 1994 altered the way in which Schedule D was assessed. Similarly, the Finance Act 1995 altered the way in which Schedule A is assessed. It is now assessed in the same way as Schedule D but there are still specific rules which apply only for Schedule A. Schedule D cases I and II were taxed on a preceding-year basis which meant the profit assessed in the year of assessment was the profit that was actually made in the previous year. This does not offend the source doctrine. The source must exist in the year of assessment, but the assessment to tax was by reference to the income arising in the previous year. In order to simplify matters and so that the tax system can move towards a system of self assessment whereby taxpayers calculate their own tax liabilities, Schedule D has been altered to a current year basis for businesses commencing trading in 1994–95. Businesses already operating are subject to complex transitional rules. Schedule A has also been changed to a current-year basis.

There are also some (what might be called) statutory exceptions to the mutually exclusive rule. However, they are merely cases where the legislature has placed a category of income in a different schedule. For example, any Schedule A business which involves the letting of furnished holiday accommodation is treated as a trade within Schedule D Case I. For corporation tax purposes, income from furnished lettings is also taxable under Schedule D Case VI, unless the taxpayer makes an election, in which case so much of the rental income as in attributable to the rental element is taxed under Schedule A.

5.6.3   Statutory exceptions

The problems created by the mutually exclusive rule can be highlighted by the example of someone who owns a caravan park. At first sight they might be regarded as trading, though their real source of income is from the exploitation of land. They are, therefore, not carrying on a trade; neither would a person who lets out the land for car parking be trading.

5.6.4   Some problems

Although the schedules are mutually exclusive, the cases are not. It was held in *Liverpool and London and Globe Insurance Co v Bennett* (1913) that, where an insurance company had trading income and investment income assessable under Schedule D Case IV and V which, under the law in force at the time would not be taxable if not remitted to the UK, the Inland Revenue could choose to tax it under Schedule D Case I as income of the trade. There are not many examples of instances where the different cases within one schedule may overlap.

5.7   Choosing between cases

5.8 *Lowe v J W Ashmore Ltd* **(1970)**

The distinction, or lack of it, between the schedules and cases is nowhere better exemplified than in the case of *Lowe v J W Ashmore Ltd.* In 1964 the charge under Schedule A was abolished and replaced by a new Case VIII which was introduced to Schedule D.

J W Ashmore Ltd carried on the trade of farming. In 1962 it bought a farm for £15,000. Two contractors offered Ashmore £75 per acre for the right to cut turves from the company's land. As a result, the company received £543 in the year to 31 March 1963, £1,440 for the year to 31 March 1964 and £1,440 for the year to 31 March 1965. The land from which the turves were taken was then ploughed and drilled with corn. The company was assessed to tax on the receipts from the sale of the turves under Schedule D Case I as income from farming, and in the alternative under Schedule D Case VIII as income from land. Ashmore Ltd argued that it had made a capital gain on the basis that it had disposed of an interest in land for a capital sum. Capital gains were at that time not charged to tax and so, if the taxpayer's argument had succeeded, the proceeds would have been tax free.

Megarry J held that the company was assessable both under Schedule D Case I and Case VIII. The Crown therefore had the option of which case to charge under being cases within the same schedule.

In 1970 the various Finance Acts were consolidated into the Income and Corporation Taxes Act 1970. Schedule D Case VIII was abolished and a new Schedule A introduced in identical terms (Schedule 30 ICTA 1988 provides that any reference to Case VIII Schedule D 'whether specific reference or one imported by more general words, in any enactment, instrument or document shall ... be construed as a reference to Schedule A'.) The result of this is that if the facts of *Lowe v Ashmore* were to occur today, the Inland Revenue would no longer have the choice of cases because the income now falls in two different schedules and so the mutually exclusive rule would apply.

So which schedule would apply? It has been held that the cutting of turves is Schedule D Case VIII, which is now A. In *Fry v Salisbury House Estates* it was held that if the choice was between Schedule A or Schedule D, the choice should be A. The schedule to apply is therefore Schedule A. It will be seen that the taxation of the subject and the rules to be applied are arbitrary and depend solely upon which schedule applies. This, in turn, depends upon the label that Parliament has chosen to put upon it.

Income Tax – The Source Doctrine and Schedular System

Income tax is an annual tax which must be reimposed by Parliament each year in order for it to be effective. The income tax year runs from 6 April to 5 April following. As it is an annual tax, there would be no power to charge tax if the annual Finance Act has not become law by the beginning of a tax year. The Provisional Collection of Taxes Act 1968 therefore provides for House of Commons resolutions to be given statutory effect, expiring on 5 May if passed in November or December of the preceding year and, at any other time, to have statutory effect expiring at the end of four months after the date on which the resolution is expressed to take effect.

There is no definition of income in the Taxes Act. However, the problem is obviated by s 1 ICTA 1988 which provides that income tax should be charged in respect of all property, profits or gains described in or comprised in the five schedules labelled A–F (Schedule B was abolished in 1988). Notwithstanding this, the courts have still held that in order for a payment to fall within one of the schedules, it has to have the characteristics of income. Central to the concept of UK income tax is the doctrine of the source. In order for a payment to be income, it must have a source. Income has often been described as the fruit, while the source of income is the tree. Furthermore, as income tax is an annual tax the source must exist in the year in which the taxpayer is sought to be taxed. Consequently, many payments escaped tax and special statutory provisions had to be introduced, eg s 104 ICTA 1988, which taxes post-cessation receipts, ie receipts following the cessation of business. This covers sums which would not otherwise be chargeable to tax. In the case of *Bray v Best* (1989), the application of the source doctrine meant that payments from a trust established for employees were not taxable in the hands of the employee following the winding up of the trust after a transfer of employees to the parent company following a takeover. The result of *Bray v Best* was reversed by statute 1989.

The schedules are as follows:

- Schedule A: which taxes income from land situated in the UK, eg rents;

- Schedule C: which taxes public revenue dividends, eg interest on UK government bonds;

- Schedule D:
    - Case I: profits of a UK trade;
    - Case II: profits of a UK profession or vocation;
    - Case III: interest, annuities or other annual payments;
    - Case IV: income from non-UK securities;
    - Case V: income from non-UK possessions; and
    - Case VI: any other profits or gains not charged under any other case of Schedule D and not being charged under Schedule A, C or E;

- Schedule E:
    - Case I: emoluments from an office or employment of a person resident or ordinarily resident in the United Kingdom;
    - Case II: emoluments in respect of duties in the UK of a person who is not resident in the UK or if resident is not ordinarily resident; and
    - Case III: emoluments or an office or employment of a person resident in the United Kingdom whether those emoluments are received in the United Kingdom.

- Schedule F: dividends and other distributions of a company resident in the United Kingdom.

It has been held that the schedules are mutually exclusive, which means that any one source of income can only be taxed under the one schedule to which it is properly attributable (*Fry v Salisbury House Estates*). The consequence of schedules being mutually exclusive is that each schedule has its own set of rules for, eg the deductibility of expenses. Although the schedules are mutually exclusive, the cases within them are not. So, where income could be taxable under more than one case of, eg Schedule D, the Inland Revenue can choose under which case to tax it (*Liverpool and London and Globe Insurance Co v Bennett*).

Chapter 6

Income Tax – Computation

When taxing the income of individuals, one of the first questions to be addressed is what the tax unit should be: the family; the husband and wife; the individual; or something else? Until 1990 the UK effectively taxed the family unit in the guise of husband and wife by making the husband liable to tax on his wife's income. This was done by deeming the wife's income to be 'her husband's income and not to be her income', a provision which dated back to 1806. Until the passing of the Married Woman's Property Act in 1832, married women were not able to own property and, as recently as 1950, they were classified together with 'incapacitated persons and idiots'. However, children were (and still are) taxed separately unless their income derived from capital given to them by their parents. Since 1990 married women have been taxed independently, although the idea of the family unit has been retained to some extent because what was the married man's allowance has simply been renamed the married couple's allowance.

6.1 **The tax unit**

Nevertheless, the theoretical question still remains: should married couples be entitled to an extra allowance? The value of the allowance was reduced in 1994–95 and is to be reduced further in 1995–96. When separate taxation was introduced in 1988 (it took effect in 1990) the then Chancellor, Nigel Lawson said: '... the tax system will continue to recognise marriage as it should do'. A contrary, but less overt view was put by the Meade report which, in 1978, included amongst its criteria for horizontal equity that:

- the liability to tax should be unaffected by marital status, ie there should be no reward or penalty for being married;

- couples with the same income should pay the same amount in tax; and

- the tax system should not influence the decision as to which one of a couple should earn extra income.

The first criterion suggests that if an unmarried couple are taxed in a certain way then the fact that they get married should not affect that liability. The married couple's allowance clearly does not adhere to this; a married couple get more tax-free income than an unmarried couple.

The second criterion states that one couple should be taxed the same as another couple regardless of how the income is split between the two. In assessing the married couple's allowance in this respect it is necessary to assume that each couple is taxed at the same rate. Before 1990 this criterion was satisfied, but only because the income of the wife was deemed to be that of the husband (although the aggregation of the wife's income with the husband's income may have meant that the husband was liable to higher rates of tax). The allowance is now transferable between husband and wife. The second criterion is not satisfied, not because of the existence of the married couple's allowance, but because personal allowances are not transferable. Consequently, a couple in which only one person works will pay more tax than one in which both work but whose aggregate pay equals that of the first couple. This is because the personal allowance of the non-working partner in the first couple will be wasted.

The third criterion states that it should not matter which person in a couple earns the extra income; again, it is to be assumed that the rates of tax of each couple are equal. The married couple's allowance satisfies this criterion because it is transferable, but again the personal allowance may affect the question.

The answer to the question of whether the married couple's allowance should be retained will depend on whether it is thought that the tax system should be used to encourage marriage. Allied to this is whether couples actually take into account the extra £258 tax-free income they will receive when deciding whether or not to marry. In terms of horizontal equity it is therefore an arbitrary decision as to whether married couples are in different circumstances to unmarried couples.

6.2   *Pro forma*

Table 6.1 shows a *pro forma* calculation for an individual's income tax liability, the details of which are explained in the paragraphs cited in the table.

6.3   Statutory income

The first step is to calculate the individual's income from all sources in accordance with the rules set out in the various schedules. As stated in Chapter 4, it is generally accepted that these schedules are mutually exclusive and it is therefore necessary to first ascertain the schedule into which any particular income falls. If it appears to fall into two schedules, it is that schedule which is most specific to the type of income which applies.

Table 6.1 *Pro forma* calculation of income tax liability

Step	Calculation	Paragraphs			
1	Compute statutory income	6.3			
eg	Schedule D Case I		X		
	Schedule E		X		
	Schedule A	6.4.2	X		
	Schedule F (gross)	6.3.2	X		
	Bank interest (gross)	6.3.1	X		
	Statutory income	6.3.2	X		
				X	
2	Less charges on income	6.4	X		
eg	Annual payments	6.4.1	X		
	Interest	6.4.2	X		
				(X)	
3	Total income			X	
	(statutory income – charges)				
4	Less other deductions	6.5			
eg	Losses	6.5.1	X		
	EIS relief	6.5.2	X	(X)	
				X	
5	Deduct allowances	6.6			
eg	Personal allowances	6.7		(X)	
				X	
6	Compute taxable income				
	£3,200 @ 20%	6.8	X		
	£21,100 @ 25%		X		
	excess @ 40%		X		
				X	
7	Less reductions	6.9			
eg	Interest relief	6.9.1	X		
	Married couple's allowance	6.9.4	X		
				(X)	
				X	
8	Less tax credits				
eg	Tax deducted on interest			(X)	
				X	
9	Add back basic rate on				
	certain charges on income			(X)	
10	Tax liability			X	
11	Less paid under PAYE			(X)	
12	Tax payable			X	

The income, as calculated under the schedules, takes account of the various deductions, thus, trading income under Schedule D Case 1 is the profits chargeable to tax, ie income minus expenses. (Note, however, that the income for a particular year is not necessarily the income *arising* in that particular year. For example, some income which is chargeable under Schedule D is taxed on a preceding year basis; the 1994 Finance Act provided rules to move it on to a current year basis. For the tax year 1995–96 both systems will be in operation.)

Certain income is received after tax has been deducted, and the most common examples are employment income, which has been taxed under the PAYE system, interest on bank accounts, trust income received by a beneficiary, and dividends. Since the Finance Act 1993, the taxation of dividends has been unusual (see Chapter 17).

6.3.1	Building society and bank interest

The interest paid by building societies and banks has had a chequered history. The current regime, referred to as the Basic Rate Tax (BRT) regime, designates certain accounts as 'relevant deposits' and provides that certain defined deposit takers must deduct basic rate tax unless the account holder has signed a declaration stating that they are not ordinarily resident in the UK. The defined deposit takers include recognised banks and the National Giro Bank, but not the National Saving's Bank. A 'relevant deposit' is basically one where an individual (or individuals) is beneficially entitled to the income, thus a company account is not a relevant deposit because, while a company is a 'person' it is not an 'individual'. However, a partnership's account is a relevant deposit because a partnership is a collection of 'individuals'.

6.3.2	Grossing up

Where income has been received which has had tax deducted, it must be entered into the calculation at its gross value. To do this the amount of income must be multiplied by a fraction which is:

$$\frac{100-r}{100}$$

where r is the rate of tax which has been deducted.

In many cases tax is deducted at 25% and therefore the fraction becomes:

$$\frac{100}{75} = \frac{4}{3}$$

A person who receives £75 after deduction of tax at 25% needs to enter the figure of £100 in the computation. Where tax has been deducted under the PAYE system it will be very difficult to ascertain the percentage rate at which the income has been taxed because the PAYE system takes into account personal allowances which will vary from person to person, and because the rate of tax will be variable once a person becomes subject to higher rate tax. It is therefore usual, in any computation, to be given the amount of tax deducted at source under PAYE. On a more practical note, where tax has been deducted under PAYE, the amount deducted will be shown on the employee's pay slip. This will also show a cumulative total over the months. Further, at the end of the year an employee receives a form known as a P60 which shows the total pay for the year and the total deductions including the total amount of income tax deducted. Although tax is deducted, the calculation of an individual's tax liability is therefore shown as the tax on the gross amount. The tax payable, however, is the amount for which the individual is liable after taking account of the PAYE deductions.

A distinction is drawn between earned income and investment income. However, the distinction is not as important as it used to be and its primary importance is now the calculation of pensionable earnings. Investment income over a certain threshold used to be subject to an investment income surcharge of 15%. This is why, under the former Labour government, the top rate of tax was 98%. The top rate of income tax was 83% plus investment income surcharge at 15%.

6.3.3   Investment income

Investment income is all income that is not earned income. Section 833 ICTA 1988 defines earned income as:

- any remuneration from any office or employment held by the individual (including, amongst other things, any pension, superannuation or other allowance, deferred pay or compensation for loss of office);

- any income which is charged under Schedule D and is immediately derived by the individual from the carrying on or exercise by him of his trade, profession or vocation, either as an individual or as a partner.

It was held in *Koenigsberger v Mellor* (1993) that the income must be earned by an individual's personal exertion. Consequently, a Lloyd's name did not receive earned income. Similarly, a limited partner in a limited partnership who cannot participate in the management of the partnership would not be treated as having received earned income for the purposes of these provisions.

Table 6.2 Earned income / investment income

Earned income	Investment income
Employment income	Rents
Profits from a trade, profession or vocation	Interest
Income from furnished holiday lettings (specifically treated as earned income by the legislation	Dividends

---

6.4   Charges on income

A charge on income is an amount which falls to be deducted in computing an individual's total income, and charges on income are not as important as they once were. The theory behind a charge on income is that income of that amount becomes the income of some other person and is therefore to be deducted by the payer. The person to whom the payment is made is taxable on the income as their own. A charge on income is therefore deducted before any other personal allowance because the charge ceases to be the income of the individual in question.

The categories of charges on income have been reduced over the years and those most usually encountered comprise the following:

- annual payments, annuities and certain maintenance payments made under an obligation entered into prior to 15 March 1988;

- interest;

- payments under gift aid;

- private medical insurance;

- vocational training payments; and

- losses on unquoted shares.

6.4.1   Annual payments

A typical example of an annual payment is a covenanted donation to a charity for more than four years. However, notwithstanding that it is a charge on income, the individual is used as an agent of the Inland Revenue to collect tax at the basic rate. The mechanics of the payment are therefore that the individual is entitled to deduct 25% when making a payment to the charity. The individual is charged tax at the basic rate on the full amount deducted by the payer as a charge. A simple example illustrates this point.

Another way to look at it is that the payer is taxed at 25% on the charge. This tax is really on the recipient of the charge, as the charge is no longer the payer's income. In order to reimburse the amount of tax charged because a person is under a legal obligation to pay £1,000, that person is entitled to deduct £250 when making the payment, leaving the payee to recover £250 from the Inland Revenue, or using £250 to satisfy his own liability to tax.

6.4.2   Interest payments

The most common interest deduction for individuals is interest that is eligible for relief because it is paid on a loan applied in purchasing an interest or estate in land in the UK or Ireland, and it is the individual's main residence. From 1994 the relief for such interest is given either through the MIRAS system

(Mortgage Interest Relief at Source) or is restricted to tax at 20%. This was further reduced to 15% for 1995. As such, the interest either stays out of the computation because it is within MIRAS, or it enters the calculation at a later stage (it is therefore dealt with in para 6.9.1). The other types of interest which are still dealt with as charges on income are interest:

- on a loan to purchase an interest in a close company;
- on a loan to acquire an interest in a co-operative;
- on a loan to invest in an employee controlled company;
- on a loan to acquire machinery and plant; and
- on a loan to pay inheritance tax.

- **Interest on a loan to purchase a property that is let (formally a charge on income)**

  Relief for interest paid on a loan to acquire a property which is commercially let was previously given as a charge against Schedule A income. With the change to treating rental income as a 'Schedule A business', interest relief is given in the same way as it would be in a trade. It is therefore deducted in computing the actual profit of the Schedule A business and is taken in account in computing the actual Schedule A income.

- **Interest on a loan to acquire an interest in a close company**

  Relief is available where a loan is taken out to acquire an interest in a close company. The company must exist wholly or mainly for carrying on a trade. Those companies are dealt within in more detail in Chapter 18. To qualify for the relief, the borrower must either be a shareholder in the company and work for the greater part of her time for the company in a management position or have a material interest in the company which means that she must control more than 5% of the ordinary share capital of the company. A person with a material interest need not work for the company. Where the borrower recovers any capital from the company she is treated as having repaid a corresponding amount of the loan and the interest relief is reduced accordingly.

- **Interest on a loan to acquire an interest in a co-operative**

  Interest relief is available where a loan is made in order for the individual to acquire an interest in a co-operative. A co-operative is defined as either a common ownership enterprise or a co-operative enterprise as defined by the Industrial Common Ownership Act 1976. The individual must show that, from the time the loan was made to the time the payment of the interest is made, he has worked for the greater part of his time as an employee in the co-operative or as an employee of a subsidiary of the co-operative.

- **Interest on a loan to acquire an interest in a partnership**

  Interest relief is available where an individual borrows money to either acquire a share in a partnership or contribute to the capital of a partnership. Interest relief is also available if money is borrowed in order to make a loan to a partnership. There is a further condition that the money must be used wholly and exclusively for the business purposes of the partnership. The individual must be a partner in the business from the time the loan is made to the time that the interest is payable. Relief is not available to a limited partner. Furthermore, relief is not available on so much of the loan that is represented by a repayment of capital.

- **Interest on loan to invest in an employee-controlled company**

  Interest relief is available where a loan is taken out by an individual to acquire ordinary shares in an employee-controlled company. An employee-controlled company is one in which full-time employees own more than 50% of the ordinary share capital and can exercise more than 50% of the voting rights. The individual must be an employee from the time the loan is taken out to the time when the interest is paid.

- **Interest on loan to acquire machinery or plant**

  Interest relief is available where a partner or a Schedule E employee borrows money to purchase a car or other plant or machinery on which capital allowances are available. Interest relief is available for up to three years after the end of the tax year in which the loan was made.

- **Interest on loan to pay inheritance tax**

  The personal representatives of a deceased person can claim interest relief on a loan which is being used by them to pay inheritance tax which is attributable to property in the UK which was owned beneficially by the deceased and which is vested in them. The relief is available only for the first 12 months of the estate's administration.

- **Vocational training payments**

  Where an individual pays fees for a qualifying course of vocational training she may claim relief for those payments. Relief is given at the basic rate by the individual deducting that amount from the fees. Relief at the higher rate is given as a charge on income. The fees include both tuition fees and examination fees. Because relief is given by deduction from the fees, a person with no income will get relief.

- **Losses on unquoted companies**

  Where an individual subscribes for shares and then realises a loss on their disposal, that loss can be set against the individual's income for that year or the preceding year. This is an exception to the rule that capital losses cannot be set against income. The shares must be ordinary shares in an unquoted trading company resident in the UK.

- **National insurance contributions**
  One half of the Class 4 national insurance contributions of a self-employed person are deductible in calculating that person's total income.

The amount arrived at by deducting charges on income from statutory income is the individual's total income. Total income is the figure used when determining whether there is any reduction in age-related reliefs (see para 6.7.1). There are two other deductions which can be made before personal reliefs are deducted. These are:

6.5   Deductions from total income

- losses; and

- enterprise investment scheme relief.

Losses arising in a trade, profession or vocation can be used in a number of ways. They are dealt with in detail in Chapter 8, but for present purposes here is a brief description.

6.5.1   Losses

Losses incurred in a trade can be carried forward and set against profits from the same trade for the following year, and profits entered in statutory income for the following year will be reduced accordingly. Where the trade was commenced *on or after* 6 April 1994, the taxpayer may elect instead to set the loss against her *total income* for the year in which the loss was incurred or the previous year. Because the loss is deducted before deducting personal reliefs, it could result in the total income being reduced to an amount less than the personal reliefs and, to the extent that it is less, these reliefs will be wasted. It is not possible to elect for only so much of the loss to be utilised as would take the total income down to the level of the personal reliefs. To the extent that the loss is carried back to the previous year this will entail a recalculation of that year's tax liability and a repayment of the tax overpaid.

For trades commencing *before* 6 April 1994, a loss can be set against total income of that year and, if there is still a loss, against total income of the succeeding year. Transitional relief applies to the years 1994–95 and 1995–96 so that losses will be dealt with in the same way after 1996, regardless of when the trade was commenced.

6.5.2   Enterprise Investment Scheme

The Enterprise Investment Scheme (EIS) replaced the Business Expansion Scheme. It was introduced by s 137 FA 1994 and Sch 15 FA 1994. To be eligible for relief a *qualifying individual* must invest in:

- *eligible shares* in a
- *qualifying company* which carries on
- *qualifying activities.*

(a) Qualifying individuals

A qualifying individual is one who is:

- liable for UK income tax (whether or not resident in the UK); and
- not associated with the company.

(b) Eligible shares

Shares are eligible shares if they:

- are issued after 1 January 1994;
- are irredeemable;
- do not carry preferential rights; and
- are fully paid.

(c) Qualifying company

To be a qualifying company it must:

- be unquoted;
- not be controlled by an unqualifying company;
- only have subsidiaries that are qualifying companies; and
- carry on a qualifying activity.

A company can raise up to £1 million a year through EIS issues. If it exceeds this amount those shares in excess of £1 million do not qualify for relief.

(d) Qualifying activities

To qualify, a company must carry on a trade wholly or mainly in the UK. Certain trades are excluded ie: banking; dealing in shares and securities; dealing in land; legal and accountancy services; and leasing.

The company must commence to carry on the trade within two years of the shares being issued.

- The amount of relief

The individual is entitled to 20% relief on an investment of up to £100,000 in any one year of assessment. On a disposal of the shares, any gain will be exempt from capital gains tax provided the shares have been held for at least five years. If, however, the taxpayer makes a loss, this is allowable for capital gains tax, but the amount of the loss on the shares is reduced by the amount of relief obtained on the original acquisition of the shares.

The taxpayer's personal reliefs is deducted from total income. Until 6 April 1994 all personal reliefs were deducted from total income, but since then certain personal reliefs have had effect to reduce the liability to tax only at a specified percentage. These allowances are not deducted from total income but, instead, the relevant percentage of the allowance is deducted from the final tax bill. The reliefs which are still given against total income are:	**6.6 Personal reliefs**

- personal allowance
  - (a)   standard   £3,525
  - (b)   age related (65–74)   £4,200
  - (c)   age related (74+)   £4,630
- blind person's relief   £1,200

This is available to all UK resident taxpayers including children. It can be set against all forms of income. Because it is a deduction from total income it gives relief to a higher-rate taxpayer at 40%, a basic-rate taxpayer at 25% and a lower-rate taxpayer at 20%. A nil-rate taxpayer cannot use the personal relief. It cannot be carried forward to subsequent years.	**6.7 The personal allowance**

A person is eligible for the increased allowance if they reach the relevant age in the year of assessment. The personal allowance increases with the age of the taxpayer. For 1995–96 the allowance is increased to £4,630 for people over 65 and £4,800 for people over 75. However, the age-related reliefs are restricted if the income of the taxpayer exceeds £14,600. The restriction operates by reducing the allowance by half of the difference between the taxpayer's total income and £14,600. Thus, if the taxpayer earns £14,700 the allowance will be reduced by £50 (ie 50% of 14,700–14,600). Notwithstanding the	6.7.1 Age allowance

reduction, the allowance will not be reduced below the normal personal allowance of £3,525.

<table>
<tr><td>6.7.2</td><td>Blind person's allowance</td><td>Where a taxpayer is a registered blind person for the whole or part of a year of assessment, that person can claim an additional allowance of £1,200. Where both the husband and wife are blind each can claim a separate allowance and, in the event that part of the allowance is not used, it can be transferred to the other spouse.</td></tr>
</table>

6.8	**Calculation of the tax due**

Income tax for the tax year 1995–96 is charged at the following rates:

Band	Rate	Tax on band
£0–£3,200	20%	£640
£3,200–£24,300	25%	£5,275
£24,300 +	40%	–

Where the income includes dividend income this will be taxed at 20% until it falls into the higher rate band when it will be taxed at 40% (see Chapter 17). Note also that deductions which are allowable in computing total income, or which are to be made from total income, are treated as reducing income in such a way that it will produce the greatest reduction in the taxpayer's tax liability (s 835(4) ICTA 1988). So, where the taxpayer's income includes dividend income chargeable at 20% because total income does not exceed £24,300, deductions should be made against other income first.

6.9	**Income tax reductions**

As was described in para 6.7, all personal allowances used to be given as a deduction from total income. From 6 April 1994 certain allowances were given by reducing the tax payable by a percentage of the allowance. So too are certain interest payments. For 1995–96 these reductions are:

- Relief for interest on a loan to purchase an interest in land or interest on a loan to purchase a life annuity; maximum relief is the interest on £30,000 @ 15%.

- Married couple's allowance   £1,720 at 15% = £248

- Married couple's allowance   (65–74) £2,995 at 15% = £449

- Married couple's allowance   (75+) £3,035 at 15% = £455

- Widows' bereavement allowance   £1,720 at 15% = £248

- Additional personal allowance   £1,720 at 15% = £248

- Maintenance payments   £1,720 at 15% = £248

Where the loan is to purchase a main residence the amount of relief is restricted to a loan or loans in an amount not exceeding in aggregate £30,000. The interest payments must be paid by the person owning the property and the property must be the only or main residence of the borrower. This is a question of the fact and, where the borrower has more than one residence, the taxpayer cannot elect (unlike capital gains tax) which is to be the main residence.

In the case of *Frost v Feltham* (1981) the taxpayer, who was the tenant of a public house, bought a property in Wales. Because the terms of his employment meant that he had to occupy the public house, he rarely went to visit the house in Wales. He claimed interest relief on the loan to purchase the house in Wales which the Inland Revenue denied on the basis that it was not his only or main residence. In the High Court it was held that the house in Wales was his main residence because, in deciding what is a main residence, one needs to look at the intention of the person in question not just the length of the period of time of occupation. Where the borrower has to go and live abroad because of his job, he can continue to claim interest relief provided a period of absence does not exceed four years. Similarly, where the taxpayer is required as a condition of his employment to live away from his main residence, he can continue to claim interest relief on his main residence.

It used to be that each individual was allowed relief on the first £30,000 of the loan. However, this meant that an unmarried couple living in a house would get more tax relief than a married couple. Interest relief is now given on an individual basis and the £30,000 limit is spread equally between the number of borrowers. Where this results in one borrower having more relief than the amount of the loan, the excess can be allocated amongst other borrowers. A husband and wife are treated as separate people for the purposes of allocating the relief.

From 6 April 1994 the relief was restricted and is now only given at 15%, despite the government's assurances that interest relief will remain. It is obvious that the amount of relief is gradually being restricted and it could eventually be phased out. It is arguable that interest relief should be given on loans to buy property at all. Although interest relief appears superficially to allow a purchaser to buy a more expensive property – because relief for the interest means that the buyer is better able to afford the property – it is likely that the price of properties increased across the board on the introduction of mortgage interest relief, so that the increased availability of money to the borrower as a result of tax relief would probably

6.9.1   Loan to purchase main residence

help purchase the same (higher priced) property as the buyer would have been able to afford at a lower price prior to the introduction of mortgage interest relief.

6.9.2   The MIRAS system

Most interest relief is within the MIRAS system (Mortgage Interest Relief at Source). A payment of interest is within the MIRAS system if:

- the borrower is a *qualifying borrower*;

- the interest is relevant loan interest, which is interest paid after 5 April 1983 on a loan for a *qualifying purpose*; and

- the payment is to a *qualifying lender*.

A qualifying borrower includes most individuals. A loan for a qualifying purpose is a loan to purchase an estate or interest in land in the UK which is used as the only or main residence of the individual. The term qualifying lender covers most building societies, banks etc who make loans to purchase properties.

If a loan is within the MIRAS system, tax relief is given by reducing the amount paid to the building society or bank. The effect of this is to give the payer a cash-flow advantage. So, a person who would normally pay £100 of interest to a building society deducts tax at the lower rate and pays only £80. The building society recovers the £20 from the Inland Revenue. The effect of this is that payments of interest within the MIRAS system are ignored when calculating a person's income tax. Otherwise the effect would be circular: the interest would be deducted in order to give the tax relief, but as tax relief had been given on making the payment, this amount would have to be added back to previous tax relief being given twice. Consequently, where MIRAS interest is paid these payments are ignored.

6.9.3   Loan to purchase life annuity

Where a person is over the age of 65 they may borrow money secured on their property to purchase a life annuity. The £30,000 limit applies and for 1995–94 the relief is restricted to 15% of the interest. The total income, once the charges on income have been deducted (and as can be seen from the above the number of remaining charges on income are few) the figure remaining is the individual's 'total income'. If the charges on income exceed the statutory, so that a total income is zero, the unused charges cannot be carried forward and are in effect wasted.

6.9.4   The married couple's allowance

This can be claimed in the first instance by a married man whose wife is living with him for any part of the tax year. A couple is considered to be living together unless they are separated by a court order, by deed or in circumstances in which the separation is likely to be permanent. Where a man has two wives he can only claim one allowance (*Nabi v Heaton* (1983)). A common law wife is not a wife for these purposes (*Rignell v Andrews* (1990)).

In previous years the married couple's allowance has been increased by the rate of inflation. However, for 1994, it was frozen at the 1993 rate. It is possible that the government are seeking to phase out the married couple's allowance notwithstanding the comments made by Nigel Lawson in 1988 that the tax system will continue to recognise marriage. With the advent of separate taxation of husband and wife there is little cause to continue it.

This allowance is available to any person who is not married or not living with their spouse throughout the tax year. The relief is dependent upon the taxpayer having a qualifying child who is:

- born in the tax year; or

- under the age of 16 at the start of the tax year; or

- over 16 but attending the full-time education course; or

- undergoing vocational training;

and who is either the taxpayer's own child (which includes a step child), an adopted child under the age of 18, or any other child who is born in, or is under 18, at the beginning of the tax year and who is maintained at the taxpayer's expense. Only one allowance is available regardless of the number of children maintained. Where both parents maintain, the child the allowance should be split between them. Where people are cohabiting and have two or more children they can only claim one allowance in respect of the youngest child.

6.9.5   Additional personal allowance

Where a married man dies leaving a widow, the widow can claim the widows' bereavement allowance in the year in which the husband died, and in the following year. Notwithstanding the liberation of female taxpayers in the move to separate taxation, there is no widowers' bereavement allowance.

6.9.6   Widows' bereavement allowance

Where income tax has been deducted at source, this is now deducted from the total amount of tax payable. Although PAYE is not a deduction of tax at source, it is not generally regarded as a tax credit but rather a payment on account. This is also deducted from the amount of tax payable.

6.10   Tax credits

6.11   Basic rate on charges on income

Where a taxpayer has deducted basic-rate tax on making a payment that is a charge on income (eg a covenant at donation to charity), the amount of the basic-rate tax deducted is now added back to the amount of tax payable. If this were not done the taxpayer would receive relief twice; once when the total amount of the payment was deducted as a charge on income, and a second time when basic-rate tax was deducted on making the payment. The effect of deducting the amount as a charge on income and then adding back the basic rate is to give relief at high rates of tax if the taxpayer is a higher rate taxpayer.

Income Tax – Computation

Until 1990 the tax unit in the UK was effectively the family, in the guise of husband and wife, because the husband was liable to tax on his wife's income. Since 1990 married couples have been tax independently, although the idea of the family unit has been retained to some extent. What was the married man's allowance has continued in the form of the married couple's allowance, albeit that is apparently being phased out gradually.

To calculate an individual's income it is first necessary to calculate their statutory income. An individual's statutory income is their income from all sources, calculated in accordance with the rules set out in various schedules. Following on from the mutually exclusive rule, it is first necessary to ascertain into which schedule the various types of income fall.

Charges on income are deducted from the individual's statutory income. The categories of charges of income have been reduced over the years and those most usually encountered are the following:

- annual payments, annuities and certain maintenance payments;

- interest;

- payments under gift aid; and

- private medical insurance.

Interest on loans to purchase an individual's main residence is no longer treated as a charge on income.

The amount arrived at by deducting charges and income from statutory income is known as total income. Total income can be reduced by losses and payments made under the enterprise investment scheme (EIS). From the resulting total income is deducted the taxpayer's personal reliefs. Until 6 April 1994 all personal reliefs were deducted from total income, but since 6 April 1994 certain personal reliefs have had effect to reduce the liability to tax only at a specified percentage. For the tax year 1995–96 the allowances which can be deducted from total income are:

- personal allowance
  - (a) standard   £3,525
  - (b) age related (65–74)   £4,200
  - (c) age related (created in 1974)   £4,630
- blind person's relief   £1,200

Age-related reliefs are restricted if income of the taxpayer exceeds £14,600. However, the allowance will not be reduced below the normal personal allowance of £3,525.

Income tax for the year 1995–96 is then charged at the following rates:

- £0–£3,200   20%

- £3,200–£24,300   25%

- £24,300+   40%.

Where the income of an individual includes dividend income this would be taxed at 20% until it falls into the higher rate and when it will be taxed at 40%.

Once the individual's tax has been calculated, certain further other amounts can then be deducted. These include the married couple's allowance, the widow's bereavement allowance, the additional personal allowance and maintenance payments. The amount deductible is the amount of the relief multiplied by the percentage at which relief is given. Thus, the married couple's allowance is £1,720 at 15% = £248. As far as relief on interest paid on a loan to purchase the taxpayer's main residence is concerned, tax relief is usually given through the MIRAS system which means that the taxpayer pays a reduced payment to the building society who then claims the difference back from the Inland Revenue. As the relief is given at source, it is not usually necessary to enter such interest into the calculation.

Once the tax liability has been calculated, credit is given for tax deducted at source. For example, the tax credit on dividends and income tax deducted by banks and building societies. The total amount payable is then adjusted to take account of any tax paid under PAYE.

Chapter 7

Schedule D Case I and Schedule D Case II – The Charge to Tax

This chapter is an introduction to the tax charged under Schedule D Cases I and II. It examines the charge to tax and the distinction between trading transactions and investment transactions. It then briefly discusses mutual trading and the question of whether the profits of an illegal trade are subject to tax. The calculation of the profit and the basis of assessment are dealt with in Chapter 8, together with the treatment of losses.

7.1 Introduction

Tax is charged under Schedule D Case I and Case II by s 18 ICTA 1988 which provides for tax to be charged in respect of the annual profits or gains arising or accruing to any person residing in the UK from any trade, profession or vocation, whether carried on in the UK or elsewhere. The profits of a trade are taxed under Schedule D Case I, and those of a profession or vocation under Schedule D Case II.

7.2 The charge to tax

Generally, there is little difference in treatment between profits chargeable under Case I of Schedule D and those chargeable under Case II of Schedule D. The most noticeable differences are:

7.3 Distinction between Case I and Case II

- capital allowances – all capital allowances except those on plant and machinery apply only to income taxable under Schedule D Case I (ie trades);

- the rule in *Sharkey v Wernher* (1955) – this rule (discussed in para 8.5.4) applies only to traders and not to professions or vocations;

- isolated transactions – a one-off transaction may be an 'adventure in the nature of trade' and so taxable under Case I of Schedule D. There is no corresponding charge for a one off transaction of a professional nature;

- companies – a company may trade but cannot carry on a profession; and

- damages – a person carrying on a profession or vocation and receiving damages in respect of it will not be chargeable to capital gains tax in respect of the receipt.

Trade is not defined in the Taxes Act other than in s 832(1) ICTA 1988 which provides that '"trade" includes every trade,

7.4 Trade

manufacture, adventure or concern in the nature of trade'. This definition includes the word it is defining. The definition of the word trade has been left to judicial decision.

A number of points should be noted:

- The authorities do not define the word 'trade' but merely identify characteristics of a trade.

- Many of the judicial pronouncements of the characteristics of a trade are qualified by the word 'normally'. The fact that a transaction does not exhibit normal characteristics would not necessarily preclude a finding that a particular transaction is a trading transaction.

- The question whether a transaction or series of transactions amounts to a trade is a question of fact for the commissioners to decide. They must decide not only the primary facts as to what was done and when it was done, but also, whether those activities amounted to a trade. Although this is an inference, it is treated as a finding of fact. Such findings can only be overturned by the courts if no reasonable body of commissioners could have come to such a finding on those facts (*Edwards v Bairstow and Harrison* (1955)).

7.5 Trading profit or capital gain

Prior to the introduction of capital gains tax it was important to resolve the question whether a transaction was a trading transaction or one on capital account. If the transaction was a trading transaction, it would be subject to tax. If not, it would escape tax altogether. However, it was not always to the Inland Revenue's advantage to argue for a trading transaction. In the event that a loss was incurred, a finding that it was incurred in the course of a trade would mean that loss relief would be available against other income. A finding that it was a capital loss would provide no relief at all.

When capital gains tax was introduced there was still an advantage in claiming that a transaction was not a trading transaction. Capital gains tax was charged at a flat rate of 30%; income was taxed at much higher rates. Since the unification of the rates of tax on capital gains tax with those of income tax, much of the advantage has gone. However, it may still be advantageous to argue that a transaction gives rise to a capital receipt if the person who is sought to be taxed has available the annual capital gains tax exemption or brought-forward capital losses which can be offset against any potential gain.

Cases which look at the distinction between whether a transaction was a trading transaction or a capital transaction must be treated with some caution. In many cases they represent findings of fact which could not be overturned by the courts. The more valuable cases are those where the court did overturn a finding of fact because, in so doing, they have to state why they came to a different conclusion to the tribunal.

A particular problem is that of the 'one-off' transaction, where a person buys an asset and then sells it. What makes that transaction an 'adventure in the nature of trade'? What factors differentiate a trading transaction from the acquisition and disposal of an investment?

7.6   The badges of trade

In 1955 the Royal Commission on the Taxation of Profits and Income in their Final Report (Cmd 9474) identified six 'badges of trade'. These are characteristics which trading transactions tend to exhibit. They are:

* the subject matter of the realisation;

* the length of the period of ownership;

* the frequency or number of similar transactions by the same person;

* supplementary work on or in connection with the property realised;

* the circumstances responsible for the realisation;

* the motive for the transaction.

Each of these will be examined in turn in the paragraphs below. It must be remembered, however, that no one factor is decisive. In the final analysis it is necessary to weigh up all the factors in order to come to a conclusion. It is, therefore, possible for identical cases to be decided in different ways. The courts can only overturn a decision of the commissioners if there is no evidence to support the conclusion. Where there is evidence on both sides, it cannot be said there is no evidence to support a finding either way.

As there are a number of factors to be taken into account, many of the decided cases can be examined under more than one of the above headings.

Certain property is more likely to be the subject of an investment than trade. Assets which are normally treated as investments are:

7.6.1   Subject matter of the realisation

* antiques;

* gold coins;

* fine wines; and

* shares, when dealt in privately.

However, each of these can obviously be the subject of a trading transaction. The people who sell to investors probably do so in the course of a trade. Property which does not provide income or which cannot provide personal enjoyment by ownership is more likely to be the subject of a trade.

The following examples illustrate how in some cases the asset dealt in can colour the nature of the transaction.

- *Routledge v IRC* (1929) – the taxpayer purchased one million rolls of toilet paper and later resold them.

  Held: an adventure in the nature of trade.

  Comment: toilet paper does not produce income nor could a person be said to derive personal enjoyment from one million rolls of toilet paper.

- *Martin v Lowry* (1926) – the taxpayer purchased 14 million yards of government surplus linen which he then sold within a year to numerous purchasers.

  Held: an adventure in the nature of trade.

  Comment: Again, linen does not produce income and the quantity dealt in militated against any personal use.

- *Salt v Chamberlain* (1979) – the taxpayer speculated on the Stock Exchange but was unsuccessful. He claimed relief for the losses incurred.

  Held: not a trading transaction.

  Comment: There is a *prima facie* presumption that speculative trading by an individual is not trading. Shares do produce income and people derive some pleasure from being 'investors'.

- *Wisdom v Chamberlain* (1968) – the taxpayer, Norman Wisdom, purchased silver bullion as a hedge against inflation. He later resold it at a profit.

  Held: an adventure in the nature of trade.

  Comment: Again, bullion does not produce income. This is a case which may now be borderline. It was decided before the introduction of capital gains tax. People may invest in bullion for the long term. However, the taxpayer borrowed the money with which he bought the bullion and this was a further fact on which influenced the finding that he was trading. He was not investing his own money; it was borrowed for the purpose of doing a deal.

- The four previous cases concerned what might be termed normal commodities for a trading transaction. In *Leach v Pogson* (1962) the taxpayer started 30 driving schools over a period of time, which he then transferred to individual companies in exchange for shares and cash. The question arose as to whether the first such transaction was trading ie whether the latter transactions could colour the first.

Held: an adventure in the nature of trade.

Comment: Although the asset was unusual, it is just as likely to be a trading asset as an investment. It should be noted that although he had no intention to start further schools when he set up the first one, he did have that intention when he sold it.

The Royal Commission's report stated that: 'property meant to be dealt in is realised within a short time after acquisition. But there are many exceptions from this as a universal rule'.

This badge is not terribly strong. An asset bought for quick resale may be held for a longer period of time because of problems in finding a buyer. Alternatively, an asset bought for investment purposes may be sold quickly if, for example, the owner's circumstances change and there is a need for ready cash.

- *Wisdom v Chamberlain* (1969) – (see para 7.6.1 above) one of the deciding factors was that the bullion was held for a little less than a year.

- *Eames v Stepnell Properties Ltd* (1966) – land was purchased and was then transferred to an investment company. The land was later sold to the council at a substantial profit. Despite a long delay between acquisition by the company and its sale, the courts reversed the finding of the commissioners that this was not a trading transaction.

  It should also be noted that the company was set up as an investment company, and its objects clause did not state that it could trade. Despite this, the court still held it to be a trading transaction.

There is a presumption that if realisations of the same sort of property occur in succession over a period, or if there are several realisations at about the same time, the transactions are of a trading nature. Again, there must be caution; an investor may often turn over his investments and the fact that this is done on a regular basis does not necessarily mean that the investor is trading.

- *Pickford v Quirke* (1927) – the taxpayer was a member of four different syndicates which asset stripped spinning companies. Apart from the taxpayer, none of the syndicates had members in common.

  Held: the taxpayer was trading, the other members were not.

7.6.2 The length of the period of ownership

7.6.3 The frequency or number of similar transactions by the same person

- *Leach v Pogson* (1962) – (see para 7.6.1 above) having held that the sale of 30 driving schools amounted to trading, the taxpayer appealed arguing that although the last 29 were sales of a trading nature the first sale was not.

  Held: the sale of the first was trading and the later sales could be used to support this finding. Although the taxpayer did not acquire the original school with a view to subsequent resale, he had formed the intention to sell at a profit and to repeat the transaction before the sale took place.

| 7.6.4 | Supplementary work on or in connection with the property realised | Doing work on the property that is the subject matter of a sale to make it more saleable will tend to show an intention to deal, so too will setting up a sales organisation and advertising the property. |

- *Cape Brandy Syndicate v IRC* (1921) – the taxpayers bought a quantity of South African brandy in 1916. Most of it was then shipped to the UK where it was blended with French brandy, recasked and sold in a number of lots, the last being sold in September 1917.

  Held: the transactions amounted to an adventure in the nature of trade.

| 7.6.5 | The circumstances that were responsible for the realisation | The fact that the property in question has been quickly resold after acquisition may tend to show an intention to deal. However, such an intention may be negatived where the circumstances of the taxpayer were such that the realisation of the property was for some other purpose, eg an emergency which required ready money. |

- *The Hudson's Bay Company v Stevens* (1909) – the company acquired certain lands in what is now Canada, by Royal Charter. It surrendered them to the Crown in exchange for other land in the territory. This other land was sold from time to time.

  Held: the company was not trading in land.

  The case can also be looked at as one where the motive for acquisition was not for the purpose of selling in the same way in that a person who acquires by inheritance does not acquire to sell.

- *West v Phillips* (1958) – the taxpayer was a builder. Between 1933 and 1941 he built some 2,200 houses which he held as investments. He also owned some 280 houses which he held for resale. He gave up building in 1942. In 1946 he started to sell the investments because of increased rent control and taxation of rents.

Held: the proceeds of sale of those houses held as investments were not liable to tax.

The motive of the taxpayer may manifest itself in one of three ways.

7.6.6   Motive

- acquisition;

- disposal; and

- profit.

The problem with ascertaining the taxpayer's motive is that it may need to be inferred from the surrounding circumstances.

- **Acquisition**

  If the motive for acquisition is to sell at a profit, this is strong evidence that the transaction is a trading transaction. However, it is not sufficient in itself. In *IRC v Reinhold* (1953), the taxpayer admitted that he had bought four houses with a view to reselling them. In the meantime, however, he had let them to tenants.

  Another example is where the acquisition is made by the seller under a will. The fact that the gift is unwanted and immediately resold will not make the transaction into a trading transaction.

  The taxpayer's motive will not be allowed to alter a transaction which objectively is a sale (for example, in *Wisdom v Chamberlain* (1969) (para 7.6.1) the taxpayer's stated motive was that he had bought the silver bullion as a hedge against inflation because he feared that the pound might be devalued).

- **Disposal**

  If the taxpayer did not acquire the property with a view to making a profit on its resale, the fact that there is an intention to sell at a profit is again not conclusive. However, if, when the sale is made, there is an intention to enter into further transactions then the first can be characterised as trading (*Leach v Pogson* (1962) (para 7.6.1)).

- **Profit motive**

  Although the previous discussion has centred on the taxpayer's design to make money from the acquisition and resale of property, the intention to make a profit is not an essential element of a trading transaction. In *Grove v YMCA* (1903), the profits of a restaurant which was open to the public and run on commercial lines were held to be assessable under Schedule D Case I, notwithstanding that they would 'carry it on even without a profit'.

A transaction or series of transactions which will inevitably make a loss are probably not trading transactions. In the case of *Religious Tract and Book Society of Scotland v Forbes* (1896), it was held that the selling of bibles and the sending out of missionaries – activities which would inevitably produce a loss – were not trading transactions and therefore the losses could not be set against the society's other profits.

A distinction must also be made between the earning of profit and the spending of it. In *Mersey Docks and Harbour Board v Lucas* (1883), the surplus income of the board was put into a sinking fund to pay off the debt incurred on the dock's construction as directed by act of Parliament. It was held that the surplus was taxable notwithstanding the requirement that it be used in a specific way.

| 7.7 | **Trading and tax avoidance** | Where a transaction has been entered into for the purposes of the tax avoidance the courts have held that this is inconsistent with trading. |

| 7.8 | **Land** | Many of the decided cases involve dealings in land. Land causes difficulty because it is not, by its nature, an asset which is obviously a trading asset or an investment. Land can yield an income, it can be traded, it can be occupied for personal enjoyment. A piece of land can be divided into two, one half of which is sold and the other half of which is occupied. Consequently, the question whether a particular transaction is trading or not is a difficult one. Thus, in *IRC v Reinhold*, the taxpayer bought four houses with the *intention* of reselling them. However, it was held that their sale was not a trading transaction. |

In *Taylor v Good* (1974), the taxpayer bid for a large country house at an auction. He did not expect to acquire it but did, for £5,100. He thought about living in the property but his wife refused. He therefore applied for and got planning permission to demolish the house and to build 90 dwellings on the site. He then sold the land to a developer for £54,500. The commissioners held that this was an adventure in the nature of trade. However, in the Court of Appeal, the Crown conceded that the house had not been acquired by way of trade. The Court of Appeal reversed the finding and held that there was no evidence to find a trading transaction. It was further held that although the taxpayer had applied for planning permission, this did not point to a trading transaction. A person is entitled to enhance the value of the property before sale if they can. This case can be compared with that of the

Cape Brandy Syndicate case, where work on the brandy showed an intention to trade. The difference between the two cases is probably that, in the latter case, the brandy was acquired with a view to resale, while in *Taylor v Good*, the land was acquired with the intention that the property would be occupied. It was only later, when the intention, altered that steps were taken to enhance the value.

In *Marson v Morton* (1986) the taxpayers were four brothers who were in business as wholesale potato merchants. They told H, an estate agent that they wished to make a medium-to-long-term investment, and on his recommendation acquired three acres of land for £65,000. A few months later, again acting on the advice of H, they sold the land for £100,000. They were assessed to income tax on the gain. The general commissioners held that the transaction was in the same category as stocks and shares, was far removed from the brothers' normal business and that they intended to make an investment. It was therefore not in the nature of trade and consequently not subject to income tax. The Inland Revenue appealed on the basis that there was only one conclusion that could be drawn from the facts: that the brothers were trading. The Inland Revenue's appeal failed.

It was held that this was a case in 'no-man's-land' in which different minds might come to different conclusions. Browne-Wilkinson VC described the nine factors which point to a trade, in a sense these are an elaboration of the six badges of trade given by the Royal Commission. The nine factors are:

- The transaction in question was a one-off transaction. The lack of repetition shows that there might not be a trade, although a one-off transaction can be a trading transaction.

- Is the transaction in some way connected with a trade which is already carried on?

- The subject matter of the transaction, eg toilet paper.

- Was the transaction typical of a trade in a commodity of that nature?

- What was the source of the finance? If the money is borrowed that is a pointer towards an intention to resell in the short term.

- Was work done on the property?

- Was the item bought and sold as one lot or was it broken up into separate lots for resale?

- What were the purchaser's intentions at the time of purchase?

- Did the item purchased provide enjoyment or pride of possession?

The Vice Chancellor went on to say that this list is not exhaustive, neither was any single item decisive. At the end of the day 'was the taxpayer investing the money or was he doing a deal?' The Inland Revenue argued that the land did not produce income and that this was a decisive factor in showing an intention to trade. The response to this was that, in times of inflation and high rates of tax, an investment may be purchased to make a capital profit at the expense of income yield.

In *Kirby v Hughes* (1993) the taxpayer carried on the business of a builder. In 1978, while living with his parents, he acquired a four-bedroom property which he improved and sold in 1981 for a profit. In 1981 he acquired a site on which he built a four-bedroom property. This was sold in 1984. The commissioners found that the taxpayer was trading. He appealed to the High Court. It was held that the commissioners were entitled to find that he was trading. The facts that he was a builder and that the property was of a size he was accustomed to in his trade were relevant in coming to their conclusion.

7.9   Statutory trades

The Taxes Act 'defines' a trade and taxes those activities under Schedule D Case I. However, certain other activities which do not fall within the definition are also taxed under Schedule D Case I, or treated as if they are. Such activities may be classed as deemed or statutory trades. Typical examples are:

- Furnished holiday lettings – ss 503–504 ICTA 1988 provide for income from furnished holiday lettings to be treated as trading income and chargeable under Schedule D Case I.

- Farming and market gardening – s 53(1) ICTA 1988, provides that 'All farming and market gardening in the United Kingdom shall be treated as the carrying on of a trade ...' Farming could otherwise be considered as the exploitation of land and therefore taxable under Schedule A.

- Mining, quarrying ironworks, gasworks, canals and railways – s 53 ICTA 1988 provides that profits or gains arising out of land in the case of any such concern shall be taxed under Schedule D Case I.

- Income from caravan sites – ESC B29 provides that, where a caravan-site operator carries on activities associated with the site that constitute trading, income from the letting can include as income of the trade.

In *Ransom v Higgs* (1974) Lord Wilberforce said that '... trade moreover presupposes a customer'. To the extent that a person deals with himself there can be no trade. (However, see the case of *Sharkey v Wernher* (1955) discussed in para 8.5.4). Where individuals contribute to a fund and, after applying the fund for whatever purpose it was established, they receive back a surplus, that surplus is not taxable because they are not making a profit; they are merely receiving back part of that which they had contributed. This 'mutuality principle' can be illustrated by the case of *New York Life Insurance Company v Styles* (1889) in which any surplus of premium income over outgoings was held for the members. It was held that this surplus did not constitute a profit.

However, if the members' association allows non members to participate on payment of a fee then any profit made will be liable to tax. Thus, in *Carlisle & Silloth Golf Club v Smith* (1913) fees paid by non members for using the club's facilities were held to be taxable.

In order for the mutuality principle to apply, it is not necessary for each member to contribute the same amount. What is necessary is that what the member receives from the fund must be in proportion to that member's contribution.

In *Doctor's Cave Bathing Beach (Fletcher) v Jamaican Income Tax Commissioner* (1971) a members' club owned a beach. They allowed guests at nearby hotels to use the beach on payment of a fee. It was clear that they were taxable on those fees so they changed the rules so that the hotels became voting members of the club. Such 'hotel members' paid an annual subscription. The hotel was then charged at a further two shillings for each guest during a specified period. The club was assessed to tax on the profits attributable to hotel members. The Privy Council held that it was assessable. Lord Wilberforce said that although it was not necessary to have a uniform fee, if mutuality was to mean anything it was necessary for there to be some relationship between what a member put in and the benefits received. The use which the hotels received was far greater than would be expected from their contributions.

Where the contribution to the fund is tax deductible, a return to the member would not be taxable and hence the member would receive a greater benefit than the cost of the contribution. Section 491 ICTA 1988 provides that, in such cases, the amount returned is subject to tax. Where members receive a distribution which is attributable not to their contribution but to profits made by the association such distributions are assessable to tax under Schedule F s 490 ICTA 1988. The profits of such associations are now subject to tax.

7.10   Mutual trading

| 7.11 | **Illegal trading** | A question which causes some difficulty is whether profits are still taxable if the trade is illegal. |

In *Griffiths v J P Harrison (Watford) Ltd* Lord Denning states that legality is not an essential characteristic of a trade and second, when considering the activities of burglars, there is no detail which their activities lack to preclude a finding that they are not trading; however, it is simply burglary. In order to answer this conundrum it is necessary to examine the nature of the receipts and of the illegality. A burglar does not by his or her actions obtain good title to the asset or, on sale of the stolen asset, to the proceeds of sale. The burglar never makes a profit because a burglar is never beneficially entitled to the proceeds of his or her endeavour. This is the characteristic that it lacks. However, there are other 'trades' which are illegal and, as a result of which, the courts would not enforce a contract on the grounds of policy. If the contract is honoured, the parties to the contract get good title. Thus, in the case of *IRC v Aken* (1990) it was held that the profits of the prostitute, Lindi St Clair, were chargeable to tax. She claimed that, as the profits were the proceeds of an illegal trade, they were not chargeable to tax. It was held that prostitution is not illegal. Even if it was, it is submitted that it would make no difference. Money passing from the customer would become the property of the prostitute and hence assessable.

In *Mann v Nash* (1932) the taxpayer dealt in and provided fruit machines which, at the time, was illegal. He argued that as the business was unlawful he was not chargeable to tax. It was held that the profits were chargeable.

| 7.12 | **Profession** | The term 'profession' is not defined. In *IRC v Maxse* (1919) the taxpayer owned, published and edited a political magazine. He wrote much of it himself. It was held that he carried on a separate profession of journalist and editor and that there should consequently be a deduction from the profits of his publishing business in respect of the time spent while acting on his profession. (The case was an excess profits duty case, and such an argument would be superfluous today.) It was stated that a profession involved either purely intellectual skill, or manual skill controlled by the intellectual skill of the operator, eg a painter, surgeon or barrister. |

| 7.13 | **Vocation** | In the case of *Partridge v Mallendaine* (1886) Denman J said that a 'vocation' is analogous to a 'calling', which means the way in which a person passes his life. |

Over the years, the courts have categorised a number of occupations as either trades, professions or vocations. Some of these may now appear doubtful.

- **Trade**

    (a)   Newspaper reporter: *CIR v Maxse* (1919)

    (b)   Stockbroker: *Christopher Barker & Son v IRC* (1919)

    (c)   Photographer: *Cecil v IRC* (1919)

    (d)   Ophthalmic optician: *Webster v CIR* (1942). His business was selling spectacles; eye testing was ancillary.

- **Profession**

    (e)   Journalist: *CIR v Maxse* (1919)

    (f)   Architect: *Durraint v IRC*

    (g)   Opticians: *Carr v IRC* (1944)

    (h)   Actor/Actress: *Davies v Braithwaite*

    (i)   Land and estate agent: *Escritt & Barrell v CIR* (1947)

- **Vocation**

    (j)   Dramatist: *Billam v Griffith* (1941)

    (k)   Racing tipster: *Graham v Arnott* (1941)

    (l)   Jockey: *Wing v O'Connell* (1927)

Once a trader has made up the accounts, the next question is: how is the trader taxed on them? After all, accounts could be made up to any date in the year of assessment.

The Finance Act 1994 changed the basis of assessment for Schedule D Cases I and II from a preceding-year basis to a current-year basis. The preceding-year basis had been around since 1842 and so the change was a revolution in tax terms. The reason for the change was the more to self assessment, which required a system that people could understand. The preceding-year basis was notoriously difficult. The paragraphs which follow deal only with the new current-year basis. This applies to:

- new businesses, ie trades and professions commencing on or after 6 April 1994;

- existing businesses from 6 April 1997; and

- partnerships, where there is a change in membership of the partnership between 6 April 1994 and 5 April 1997 and no continuation election is made, then a new business is deemed to have started immediately following the partnership change.

7.15.1	Opening years	For the first year of business, a trader is taxed on the profits from the date the business commences to 5 April. If the accounts are not made up to 5 April there will need to be an apportionment.
7.15.2	Continuing assessments	For years after the second year, the trader will continue to be taxed by reference to the accounts made up to a date in the relevant year.
7.15.3	Closing years	For the year in which a trade ceases the final year's assessment is based on the profits from the last accounts date in the preceding year to the date of cessation. If there is an accounts date in the year of cessation this is consequently ignored.
7.15.4	Existing businesses	An existing business will become subject to the current-year basis in 1997. To effect the change from the preceding-year basis, transitional rules will apply for the year 1996–97. In general this will involve taxing the average of the profits between the end of the last accounting period under the preceding-year basis and the end of the first accounting period under the current-year basis. In effect this will mean taking two years profits and halving them. There are numerous anti-avoidance provisions to prevent taxpayers taking advantage of this averaging procedure.

Schedule D Case I and Schedule D Case II – The Charge to Tax

Tax is charged under Schedule D Case I and Case II in respect of the annual profits or gains arising or accruing to any person residing in the UK from any trade, profession or vocation, whether carried on in the UK or elsewhere.

The major differences between Case I of Schedule D and those of Case II are:

- qualification for capital allowances;

- the application of the rule in *Sharkey v Wernher*;

- one-off transactions;

- a company cannot carry on a profession; and

- the taxation of certain damages payment.

The only definition of trade is in s 832 ICTA 1988 which includes the word trade. Case law would suggest that trade involves habitually doing something produces a profit, exchanging goods or services for reward, or dealing with a customer. Trade also involves the intention to trade.

Many of the cases which decide whether there is an adventure in the nature of a trade or a capital gain were decided before the introduction of capital gains tax. It was therefore important for the Inland Revenue to establish that the transaction was of a trading nature.

The Royal Commission on the Taxation of Profits and Income identified six 'badges of trade'. These are:

- the subject matter of the realisation – certain properties are more likely to be the subject matter of an investment, eg antiques, gold coins and shares, when dealt in privately;

- the length of the period of ownership – a trader will normally try and realise a quick profit whereas an investment is usually held for a longer period of time;

- the frequency or number of similar transactions by the same person – the more dealings in a particular type of property that a person has, the more likely that person is to be trading in that type of property;

- supplementary work on or in connection with the property realised – where a person does work on property in order to make it more saleable, it is more likely that that sale would be of a trading nature;

- the circumstances responsible for the realisation – although a trader will usually turn an item to account quickly, the intention to trade may be negatived by the fact that the person needed to realise ready cash for an emergency; and

- the motive for the transaction – if the intention was to acquire and sell it at a profit, it is strong evidence of a trading transaction. However, the profit motive is not a necessary ingredient of a trading transaction.

Land causes difficulty because it is not, by its nature, an asset which is obviously a trading asset or an investment. In the case of *Taylor v Goode* it was held that land did not necessarily have to produce income in order to be an investment; in times of high inflation, an asset could be bought for its capital growth potential.

A person cannot trade with themselves. Therefore, when an individual contributes to a fund and, after applying the fund for whatever purpose it was established, the individual receives back the surplus or their share of the surplus, that surplus is not taxable if these individuals are making a profit they are merely receiving back their excess contributions over expenditure. This is the principle of mutual trading.

The fact that the trade is illegal does not necessarily mean that any profits from it escape taxation. It is submitted that the true distinction here is whether or not property in the money received in exchange for goods and services passes to the person supplying those goods and services. So, a burglar never acquires property in the goods he deals in and cannot therefore be taxed on any resulting profit, whereas a prostitute does acquire good title to the money she receives and is therefore liable to tax.

Profession is not defined by the Taxes Act but usually involves either purely intellectual skill, or manual skill controlled by the intellectual skill of the operator, eg a painter, surgeon or barristers. Similarly, there is no definition of vocation but it has been held to be an analogous to a 'calling' which means the way in which a person passes his or her life.

Schedule D Cases I and II were previously assessed on a preceding-year basis. Where a new business commences on or after 6 April 1994, that business will be assessed on a current-year basis. Existing businesses will be taxed on a current-year basis from 6 April 1997 and transitional rules will apply in the meantime.

Chapter 8

Schedule D Case I and Schedule D Case II – Calculation of Profit and Losses

The last chapter looked at what happens when a person is within the charge to tax under Schedule D Case I or Case II. We will now examine the way in which the profits are calculated. This topic has two specific areas of difficulty. First, the extent to which accountancy evidence can be considered when determining the level of profit (in the last couple of years, there has been by the courts away from accepting accountancy evidence as being merely persuasive to accepting it as conclusive). The second problem is the distinction between capital and income, and recent cases show that the distinction between capital and revenue has become increasingly blurred.

8.1 Profit – introduction

A trader will normally prepare accounts for each year. These will be prepared in accordance with ordinary accounting principles. However, the profit figure shown is by no means conclusive of the profit for taxation purposes. For example, the cost of a capital asset will be written off by means of depreciation over the life of the asset, whereas a deduction for depreciation must be written back for taxation purposes and a more restricted deduction is given by means of capital allowances (see Chapter 9). If the capital asset does not qualify for capital allowances, no deduction will be allowed at all. Similarly, certain other deductions, which may be allowed in the accounts, will not be allowed for tax purposes, eg entertaining expenditure.

8.2 Accounting profits

The profits of a trade are trading receipts minus trading expenses. Whether or not an item of expenditure is a trading receipt will depend upon the nature of the trade. For example, a car dealer buying a car for resale will be buying an item of trading stock, whereas a car which is bought for the use of an employee will be a capital asset.

8.3 Calculation

There is no fixed rule on how a person makes up their accounts. In practice three methods are employed:

- **Earnings basis**

  The earnings basis brings into account sums which have been earned, regardless of whether they have been received, and allows for sums which are owing, regardless of whether they have been paid. There is no requirement for an invoice to have been issued or received.

8.3.1 Types of accounts

- **Bills-delivered basis**

The bills-delivered basis takes into account a receipt when a bill is issued and a payment when an invoice is received. This basis is the one which is used by solicitors and accountants.

- **Cash basis**

The cash basis records a receipt when cash is received and a payment when cash is paid. This basis is used by barristers on account of the fact that they cannot sue for their fees.

8.4 Preparing accounts – accountancy evidence

There is no one proper way to draw up accounts. However, in order to compare one year's profits with another, it is necessary to prepare accounts on a consistent basis. The Inland Revenue will scrutinise accounts where there has been a change in the accounting principles applied if this gives a more favourable tax result.

There appears to be some disagreement in the way the courts treat accountancy evidence. Thus, in the case of *Heather v P E Consulting Group* (1972) Lord Denning MR said: 'The courts have always been assisted greatly by the evidence of accountants. Their practice should be given due weight: but the courts have never regarded themselves as being bound by it. It would be wrong to do so.' In the case of *Gallagher v Jones* (1993), however, Sir Thomas Bingham MR said: '... the ordinary way to ascertain the profits or losses of a business is to apply accepted principles of commercial accountancy. That is the very purpose for which such principles are formulated.'

It is a matter of opinion whether this latter view indicates a change in policy by the courts. It is submitted that the two views do not necessarily conflict. In the first, Lord Denning was talking about determining the legal nature of a payment; for example, the question of whether an item of expenditure is capital or revenue is a question of law (*Beauchamp v F W Woolworth plc* (1989)). So, if an item of capital expense is treated in the accounts as a revenue expense, this will be ignored for tax purposes and it will be recharacterised. However, once the nature of the expense has been identified, its treatment will be in accordance with the ordinary commercial accountancy principles applied to that expense – unless, of course, a different statutory rule is to apply as is the case of depreciation and capital allowances.

8.4.1 Timing

For the purposes of the bills-delivered and cash bases it is generally obvious when a payment is made or an amount is received. However, for the earnings basis it is necessary to

determine when a receipt is earned and when a liability to pay
accrues. In the case of *Willingale v International Commercial Bank
Ltd* (1977), the bank held a number of bills of exchange which
had maturity periods ranging from one to 10 years. To reflect
this they had been bought at a discount and, in its annual
accounts, the bank included part of these discounts as profits
for each year up to maturity. There was evidence to show that
this was in accordance with accepted accounting practice. The
Inland Revenue sought to tax that notional profit which was
brought into account. The bank argued that no account should
be taken of the profit until it was actually realised,
notwithstanding that accountancy principles brought it into
account. It was held in the House of Lords that the bank was
not to be taxed until the profit had finally been ascertained,
which would be on maturity. The majority thought that to
account for the discount would be to violate the 'overriding
principle of tax law' that profit cannot be anticipated. The
decision in the House of Lords was by a 3:2 majority and has
been heavily criticised.

In *Gallagher v Jones* (1993) Nolan LJ said the principle that
profit should not be anticipated was merely a restatement of
the law that a person is to be taxed on the full amount of the
profit arising in any particular year and, in determining profit,
it was necessary to look to accounting principles. The company
had applied accounting principles when drawing up its
accounts.

The courts acceptance of commercial accountancy
principles was further emphasised in the case of *Johnston v
Britannia Airways Ltd* (1994), where it was held that the courts
would be slow to accept that accounts prepared in accordance
with commercial accountancy principles were not adequate for
tax purposes as a true statement of the taxpayer's profits. In
that case there were three different principles which could be
applied, each of which gave a different result. The court held
that no one particular method was correct. It was a matter of
accountancy judgment as to which one ought to be applied in
any one particular case. The fact that one method would show
a higher or lower profit than another was irrelevant.

However, where the application of accountancy principles
would produce only a paper profit, that profit will not be
taxed. In the case of *Pattison v Marine Midland Ltd* (1983) the
taxpayer carried on business as an international banker. It
made loans in dollars and, in order to fund the loans, it
borrowed dollars from sister companies in its group. There
was a profit when these dollar loans were repaid because the
dollar had strengthened against the pound and, when the

loans from the subsidiaries were repaid, there was a corresponding loss. Although the amounts had been translated into sterling for the purposes of the company's balance sheet, the bank had held dollars at all times. The gain and loss were purely paper gains and losses and the Inland Revenue sought to tax the paper gain. However, the corresponding loss was disallowable. The result would have been a wholly artificial tax liability. The House of Lords held that the bank was not taxable on the notional sterling profit which arose because the dollars had never been converted into sterling.

Where the supply of goods or services is conditional, the price is not earned until such time as the condition is satisfied. Therefore, where goods are ordered but payment is to be on delivery, the price is not earned until delivery is made. This is to be contrasted with the situation where payment is deferred. Thus, where goods are delivered but payment is not to take place until some future date, the price is earned immediately and the cash to be received is related back to the period in which it was earned. An expense is deductible when the liability is incurred not when it is paid. The fact that the trader may be taxed on amounts which he has earned but has never received is taken into account by the fact that, once a debt has been proved to be bad, a deduction is allowed at the time of such proof.

8.5 Trading receipts

It has already been stated that the determination of whether a receipt is a trading receipt, and consequently whether it is to be entered in the profit and loss account, may depend upon the nature of the particular trade. Many trading receipts will be obvious, being receipts from the disposal of trading stock. However, certain situations arise where sums are received by a trader which are not directly referable to the trading activities. In such cases it is necessary to determine whether they are trading receipts or some other type of receipt; a capital receipt, for example.

8.5.1 Derived from the trade

It is axiomatic that in order to be a trading receipt the amount received has to be derived from the trade. Thus, where a second-hand car salesman sells his own private car by private sale, the receipt by him of the money – although resembling a receipt of his normal trading activities – would not be a trading receipt because the car was not part of his stock in trade.

8.5.2 The receipt must be income not capital

Determining whether a receipt or payment is income or capital is one of the most difficult areas in revenue law. The cases are not wholly satisfactory and to any rule there always appears to be an exception.

The courts have applied a number of tests. First, there is the fixed capital *versus* circulating capital test. Fixed capital is money which is expended on assets, eg money spent on the acquisition of, or paid on the sale of, plant and machinery. Circulating capital is money which is turned over in the business producing a profit and is, therefore, converted back into cash in the short term, eg money spent on the acquisition of, or received on the sale of, stock. This test is confusing not least because it uses the word capital on both sides of the test. Furthermore, the this test is often applied to determine whether expenditure has been on a fixed asset or stock in trade. To merely identify the receipt as fixed capital circulating capital is to prejudge the issue by saying that the asset was either a capital asset or stock in trade.

Another test which is often applied is the analogy with the fruit and the tree. The tree is capital which bears the income fruit. A disposal of the tree would result in a capital receipt, while disposal of the fruit would result in a revenue receipt.

- **Restriction of activities**

  An amount received by a trader for the restriction on his activities may be capital or revenue, depending upon the extent of the restriction. In *Higgs v Olivier* (1952) Lord Olivier received £15,000 for entering into a covenant not to act in, produce or direct any film for a period of 18 months following the release of *Henry V*. It was held that the £15,000 was not taxable as a receipt of the trade; instead, it was a payment of compensation for the actor agreeing not to carry on his profession. This case can be contrasted with the case of *IRC v W Andrew Biggar* (1982) in which a dairy farmer received compensation from the EEC for converting from dairy farming to beef production. The taxpayer argued that *Higgs v Olivier* (1952) applied and the EEC payment should be tax free. However, the court held that the payment was a trading receipt because the farmer could still continue in business; his activities had not been restricted to such an extent that it could be said that he was no longer carrying on the trade. A similar conclusion was reached on similar facts in *White v G & M Davies* (1979).

  In *Thompson v Magnesium Elektron Ltd* (1943) ICI paid the taxpayer a lump sum to stop them making chemicals which would compete with those produced by ICI. It was held that the receipt was taxable, being a payment to compensate the taxpayer for profits which would have been made if the restriction not been entered into.

  The distinction between these last two cases and *Higgs v Olivier* is that, in *Higgs v Olivier*, it could be said that

Lawrence Olivier was temporarily disposing of his trade to the extent that he could no longer carry it on, whereas in *IRC v Biggar* and *Thompson v Magnesium Elektron Ltd*, the payment was made to compensate the taxpayers for lost profits in a trade that was still being carried on. Should the facts of *Higgs v Olivier* occur again today it is possible that the receipt would be taxable under the capital gains tax legislation as being a capital sum derived from an asset.

- **Sterilisation of an asset**

  If a trader receives a sum for the permanent sterilisation of an asset, the receipt will be a capital receipt notwithstanding that the amount has been calculated by reference to the profits which would otherwise be made had the asset not been sterilised. Receipts in respect of the temporary sterilisation of an asset are trading receipts of a revenue nature. In *Glenboig Union Fire Clay Co Ltd v IRC* (1922) the company received compensation as a result of being restrained from their right to extract fireclay from a neighbour's land. It was held that the receipt was a capital receipt. The permanent sterilisation of an asset can be compared with its disposal which would have given rise to a capital sum.

  In *Burmah Steam Ship Co Ltd v IRC* (1930), an amount received by the steam ship owners for lost profit due to overrunning of a steam ship's repair was held to be a trading receipt. The loss of the asset's use was temporary in nature and, had it been used, sums earned from its use would have been revenue. The compensation received in lieu of these sums was therefore also revenue.

- **Cancellation of business contracts**

  Where a sum is received as compensation for the cancellation of a contract, the question of whether it is revenue or capital will depend upon what part the contract played in the business. The more fundamental a contract is to the business the more likely the sum received is a capital sum. In *Van den Berghs Ltd v Clark* (1935) the taxpayer received the sum of £450,000 as compensation for the cancellation of a contract that defined the territories in which the company could operate and in which a competitor, the other party to the contract, could not operate. It was held that the receipt was capital.

  Where, however, a contract is one of many entered into in the course of the trade, the cancellation of a contract and the receipt of the sum as compensation will give rise to a revenue receipt being compensation for the loss of profit which itself would have been a revenue receipt. Thus in *Kelsall Parsons & Co v IRC* (1938) compensation was received by a firm of manufacturers' agents for the termination of an agency agreement that was to have lasted three years but was terminated a year early. It was held to be a trading receipt.

- **Receipts for the sale of knowhow**

  Section 531(1) ICTA 1988 provides that a payment for knowhow is a trading receipt, provided that the knowhow has been used in the trade and the trade is still being carried on. Where, a person disposes of knowhow as part of the sale of a business, the payment is to be treated as a payment for goodwill and, consequently, it will be treated as capital. However, if the parties to the sale jointly elect, the payment can be treated as a trading receipt.

Under the earnings basis, where a liability is incurred, the trader may take a deduction for that liability even if it has not been paid. Where, in the case of a trading debt, a debt is subsequently released, s 94 ICTA 1988 provides that the release will give rise to a trading receipt in the accounts for the year in which the debt was released. If this were not the case, the trader would receive a deduction and the person to whom the debt is owed would receive a deduction for the bad debt following the release.

8.5.3   The release of a debt

In order for s 94 ICTA 1988 to apply, there must be a release of the debt. Hence, a mere waiver of the debt would be insufficient unless the debt is waived for consideration. Where the doctrine of promissory estoppel operates, this will be insufficient to amount to a release of the debt because promissory estoppel is procedural rather than substantive, ie the debt continues to exist but the creditor is estopped from relying on his legal rights. There is, therefore, no release of the debt.

When a trader makes up accounts on the earnings basis, it is necessary to deduct the value of the trading stock (or work in progress) that is held at the end of the year. The reason for this is that a trader would otherwise be able to contract for the purchase of more stock at the end of the year, deduct this amount as an expense and so reduce the taxable profits. However, to prevent this figure being taxed twice, the same figure is brought in as an expense at the beginning of the following year and the effect of this is to bring into account the actual amount of stock sold during the year.

In the same way that a trader must bring into account the cost of unsold stock as a receipt so a manufacturer must bring into account the cost of work in progress as a receipt.

8.5.4   The rule in *Sharkey v Wernher* (1955)

In the case of *Sharkey v Wernher*, Lady Wernher owned a stud farm, the profits of which were assessable under Schedule D Case I, and she also owned some stables which were not part of the trade. She transferred five horses from the farm to the stables, reducing the stock of the farm. The question arose as to how this transfer of stock from the trade was to be valued and what amount (if any), was to be brought into the accounts. It was held by the House of Lords (4:1) that the value to be brought into account was market value. The House of Lords considered that some value had to be entered into the trading account and they decided upon market value, the same value that would have been entered had the stock been realised commercially.

The case has been criticised on a number of grounds. The actual decision has been criticised because the House of Lords assumed the item had not already been represented in the accounts, although it is clear that it had been represented in the accounts at cost. Until such time as some actual monetary figure was received for the asset, it should remain in the accounts at that value and, if the asset is withdrawn from the trade, then the figure to be withdrawn is the figure which was shown in the accounts, namely the cost.

The question arose as to whether the rule in *Sharkey v Wernher* (1955) applied to professional people, and the answer came in the case of *Mason v Innes* (1967). The taxpayer, Hammond Innes wrote a book called *The Doomed Oasis*. Copyright in the novel was valued at some £15,400 and Innes gave copyright to his father prior to the book's publication. The author incurred substantial expenses in writing the book which had been deducted by him in his accounts. However, in consequence of the copyright having been assigned, no amount was brought into the taxpayer's books in respect of the disposal of the copyright. The Inland Revenue argued that the value of the copyright should be brought into account. The Court of Appeal held that the taxpayer was not assessable on any sum in respect of the assignment.

One reason given for the decision is that a trader prepares his accounts on an earnings basis while a professional person prepares her accounts on a cash basis. However, the method of preparing accounts should not make any difference; the question is really one of valuation.

Writing in the *British Tax Review* prior to the case of *Mason v Innes*, DC Potter QC stated that the point at issue in *Sharkey v*

Wernher was that some figure had to be entered into the trader's accounts because there was an item in the accounts which had been taken out. A professional person does not enter into their accounts the value of services which they may or may not provide; they take no account of opening and closing stock.

The contrary argument is that a professional person should be taxed upon what they are entitled to receive and no account should be taken of the fact that there is no opening stock. It is arguable that, in principle, there is no reason why a professional person should not be assessed on the value of services provided gratuitously, though problems may arise as to the extent to which this rule should apply. An accountant or doctor who gives informal advice at a party may be surprised to learn that the market value of that advice should be chargeable to tax. However, the difficulty in limiting the rule should not affect the question of whether, in principle, the ruling in *Sharkey v Wernher* should apply to professional people.

The principle in *Sharkey v Wernher* can be said to apply to traders and to others who have stock in trade and make up their accounts on an earnings basis. It applies to non-commercial transactions, ie where stock has been transferred at less than market value, though it must be shown that the transaction was 'non-commercial'. The fact that the price is lower than market value because of a commercially negotiated agreement should not bring the rule into play, and the rule applies to dealings with third parties (*Petrotim Securities Limited v Ayres* (1963)) as well as to 'self dealing'.

If the rule in *Sharkey v Wernher* is applied, it applies not only to the accounts of the person disposing of the stock but also to those of the person acquiring the stock, thus a trader receiving stock for nothing can bring it into his accounts at market value (*Ridge Securities Limited v IRC* (1963)). There has to be an appropriation from trading stock, thus, where an asset is only borrowed and subsequently returned the rule does not apply.

Section 770 ICTA 1988 provides that, where one party to a transaction has control over the other and the price paid (price A) is less than would have been expected if the sale had been between independent parties (price B), then the Inland Revenue can substitute price B for the actual price (A). (This section does not apply where the buyer is a trader resident in the UK and the cost of acquisition would be brought into the buyer's accounts. The reason for this is that, if the buyer sells on the item for its full market value, a depressed acquisition

8.5.5   Transfer pricing –
s 770 ICTA 1988

cost would increase the buyer's profits on which he would be liable to tax.) The section applies to transfers at an over value in cases where the over value would not be brought into charge for tax but the over value in the recipient's accounts would give rise to a loss on the subsequent sale of the asset at market value.

8.6 Deductible expenses

In order for an expense to be deductible it must first be of a revenue nature and its deduction must not be disallowed by statute.

8.6.1 Revenue not capital

The comments made in para 8.5.2 regarding the distinction between income and capital for the purposes of trading receipts also apply when distinguishing income and capital for the purposes of expenditure. The starting point in this area is usually the words of Lord Cave in *British Insulated and Helsby Cables Ltd v Atherton* (1925):

> 'Where an expenditure is made, not only once and for all, but with the view to bringing into existence an asset or an advantage for the enduring benefit of a trade, I think that there is very good reason (in the absence of special circumstances leading to an opposite conclusion) for treating such an expenditure as properly attributable not to revenue but to capital.'

However, this test has its difficulties, because not all payments which have an enduring benefit are capital payments. In the case of *Anglo-Persian Oil Company v Dale* (1931) a payment made by one company to another to terminate an agency agreement was held to be a revenue expense notwithstanding that there would be an enduring benefit to the company. Payments made in respect of employees are usually deductible as revenue expenses. Thus, in *Mitchell v B W Noble Ltd* (1927) the sum of £19,200 was paid to a director in order to induce him to resign. It could be said that the director's resignation would be of an enduring benefit to the company, otherwise it would not have been sought. It was held that the sum was deductible.

A different test for determining the distinction was given in *Tucker v Granada Motorway Services Ltd* (1979). This test requires that the asset on which the sum has been spent is first to be identified. If the asset is a capital asset it is then necessary to look at the nature of the expenditure, eg expenditure on acquiring the asset will be capital expenditure, while expenditure on repairing the asset will be revenue expenditure. In the *Tucker* case, a company held a lease for a motorway service area. The rent was calculated in part by reference to the gross takings which would include tobacco duty on cigarettes. The company paid its landlord, the Minister of Transport, £122,220 to vary the lease so that tobacco duty was excluded from the calculation. The House of Lords held that the expenditure was capital, being expenditure on making an asset (the lease) more advantageous.

In *Vallambrosa Rubber Co Ltd v Farmer* (1910), it was held that capital expenditure was something which was to be spent once and for all, while revenue expenditure would recur each year. Consequently, the Inland Revenue's argument that expenditure on weeding a rubber plantation should be disallowed because rubber trees take seven years to mature was rejected. The weeding took place each year and was of a revenue nature.

The difficulty of the distinction between capital and revenue is highlighted by the case of *Lawson v Johnson Matthey plc* (1992). This case shows that, although recurrent expenditure may be revenue, the converse (ie a large one-off payment) is not necessarily capital. In *Lawson v Johnson Matthey plc*, a company dealing in precious metals had a number of subsidiaries, one of which operated a banking business. This particular subsidiary hit financial difficulties and had to be wound up. The Bank of England offered to buy the subsidiary for a pound provided that the parent company injected £50m prior to the sale. The parent company took the view that if the subsidiary was wound up it would probably go into receivership, and so it paid the £50m, seeking to deduct this amount as a revenue expense when calculating its profits. The Inland Revenue argued that the payment was capital because it was made to enable the disposal of a capital asset. The House of Lords held that it was revenue. The motive for the payment was irrelevant. The payment was made to procure the protection of the parent company's business and remove the threat of receivership.

The case is difficult because, having said that the motive is irrelevant, the House of Lords go on to ask what the payment procured. It procured two things. First, the sale of the shares; and second, the protection of the business. In accepting the second reason the House of Lords looked to what the company was trying to achieve, which surely involved looking at the motive for the payment.

Although the item of expense is not revenue under the above tests, it may nevertheless qualify for capital allowances (see Chapter 9).

Once it has been established that the expense in question is of a revenue nature, the deduction must not be disqualified under

8.6.2   The expense must not be disallowed

a statutory provision if it is to be an allowable expense. The main statutory provision disallowing expenditure is s 74 ICTA 1988, and the principal disallowance is in s 74(1)(a), which provides that no sum shall be deducted in respect of: 'any disbursements or expenses, not being money wholly and exclusively laid out or expended for the purposes of the trade, profession or vocation'. This rule is usually transposed into the positive so that expenditure, in order to be deductible, has to be expended wholly and exclusively for the purposes of the trade.

- **Wholly and exclusively**

  In order to be allowed, the sole purpose of the expenditure must be business. Thus, if a person makes telephone calls from his house, a call may be either business use or social use. A business call would be made wholly and exclusively for the purpose of the business, while a social call would not be. Consequently, the cost of the business call would be deductible but the cost of the social call would not. However, the line rental would be paid neither exclusively for business use nor exclusively for social use and it would not therefore satisfy the test. In practice the Inland Revenue will allow an apportionment of line rental as a deductible expense.

  In the case of *Prince v Mapp* (1967), a professional guitarist had an operation on his little finger following an accident. He sought to deduct the cost of the operation and it was held that, because he also played the guitar as a hobby, there was a duality of purpose and the expense was not deductible. In this case the taxpayer admitted before the commissioners that he played the guitar as a hobby. In the case of *Mallalieu v Drummond* (1983), the House of Lords introduced the concept of subconscious motive. The taxpayer was a barrister with a predominantly court practice. She wore black clothes for the purpose and sought to deduct the cost of the clothes when computing here profits. The House of Lords held that in buying the clothes there was a subconscious motive which the commissioners were entitled to take into account; namely, that the clothes also satisfied her personal needs of warmth and decency and therefore the expenditure was not wholly and exclusively incurred.

  Travelling expenses are not allowable if the purpose of the journey is to go to the place of work (*Newsom v Robertson* (1952)). If a journey is made from one place of work to another, these expenses are allowable. In *Sargent v Barnes* (1978), a dentist travelled to work each day by car but stopped off at his laboratory *en route* to pick up dentures. A

claim to deduct the cost of travelling to his place of work
failed. He did not commence work when picking up the
dentures. The journey from the laboratory to the surgery
was therefore made to get to work. In *Horton v Young*
(1971), a bricklayer was entitled to deduct the cost of
travelling from home to building sites as his home was a
place of work.

- **For the purposes of the trade, profession or vocation**

  In the case of *Strong & Co of Romsey Ltd v Woodifield* (1906)
  Lord Davey said:

  '... it is not enough that the disbursement is made in the
  course of, or arises out of, or is connected with, the trade,
  or is made out of the profits of the trade. It must be made
  for the purpose of earning the profits.'

  This is generally seen as an unwarranted gloss on the
  legislation. In that case the chimney of a hotel fell on a
  guest. The hotel owners paid damages of £1,490 and
  sought to deduct this amount in computing profits. The
  House of Lords held that the amount was not deductible as
  it did not arise out of the trade.

Section 74(1) ICTA 1988 contains a number of other expenses
which are not allowable. Each is expressed in the negative and
by implication mean that, to the extent that something is not
disallowed, it may be deducted. The more important expenses
are discussed below.

8.6.3   Other disallowances

- **Rent**

  Section 74(1)(c) ICTA 1988 disallows rent of houses or
  domestic offices unless they are used for the purposes of
  the trade. By implication, therefore, all other rent is
  deductible. For this reason many businesses choose to rent
  premises rather than to buy them because the cost is
  allowable in full, whereas a more restrictive capital
  allowance would be given if a property was purchased.
  Where a premium is paid for a lease a proportion of this
  expenditure may also be allowable under s 87 ICTA 1988.

- **Repairs and improvements**

  Repairs are allowable under s 74(1)(d) ICTA 1988.
  Improvements are not allowed because they enhance the
  capital value of the asset and are therefore capital in nature.
  The difference between a repair and an improvement is a
  difficult question and may depend on the facts in each
  particular case. However, a number of general propositions
  can be advanced:

  (a) Expenditure incurred on an asset to get it into a state of
      repair such that it can be used in capital expenditure. In

Law Shipping Co Ltd v IRC (1924), the taxpayer bought a ship for £97,000. It needed a further £51,000 spending on it before it was seaworthy and it was held that the expenditure was capital in nature.

(b) If the asset is already in a state where it could be used to earn profits, the fact that substantial repairs are done means the expenditure is revenue and will therefore be deductible. In *Odeon Associated Theatres Ltd v Jones* (1973) the taxpayers bought a cinema. Although it was possible to use it at that point, the taxpayers spent money to bring it up to a higher state of repair. They sought to deduct the cost. It was held by the Court of Appeal that the expenditure was revenue. Three points of comparison should be noted. First, in this case, the cinema could have been used at the point when it was purchased. In the *Law Shipping* case, the ship could not have been used. Second, the purchase price of the cinema was not reduced because of the state of repair, while that of the ship was reduced. Third, there was accountancy evidence to show that the expenditure was properly attributable to revenue, whereas no such evidence was adduced in the *Law Shipping* case.

(c) Where the repair includes an element of improvement the expenditure will still be revenue and deductible (*Lurcott v Wakeley and Wheeler* (1911)).

(d) If the degree of repair is such that it amounts to a replacement of the whole, the expenditure will be capital not revenue. In *O'Grady v Bullcroft Main Collieries Ltd* (1932) a colliery chimney which stoved alone was replaced. This was held to be capital, whereas in *Samuel Jones & Co (Devondale) Ltd v IRC* (1951) the replacement of a factory chimney was revenue because it was part of a greater entity. In *Brown v Burnley Football and Athletic Co Ltd* (1980) the question arose whether the building of a stand was repair of a part of the ground or replacement of the whole of the stand. It was held that it was a replacement of a separate entity, and hence capital.

- **Losses**

Section 74(1)(e) ICTA 1988 prohibits the deduction of '... any loss not connected with or arising out of the trade, profession or vocation'. The losses referred to here cannot be the losses arrived at when calculating the profits as these are dealt with in s 393A ICTA 1988. The loss referred to is the type occurring in *Strong & Co of Ramsey Ltd v Woodifield* (see para 8.6.2), when damages were paid to a customer. Another type of loss which might be covered is a loss arising as a consequence of employing dishonest employees. In the case of *Bamford v ATA Advertising Ltd* (1972) a director of the taxpayer company misappropriated £15,000 which then became irrecoverable. It was held that the loss of £15,000 was not an allowable deduction. Where, however, the dishonesty is that of an employee rather than a director, it is thought that any loss may be allowable as arising out of the need for the trader to employ people in the trade.

- **Bad debts**

  The deduction of an amount in respect of amounts thought to be irrecoverable is not allowed under s 74(1)(j) ICTA 1988 unless the debt is proved to be bad. Thus, a general provision for bad debts is not allowable and must be added back when calculating the profit.

- **Interest**

  For individuals (not companies, for which special rules apply) interest is deductible under s 74(1)(n) ICTA 1988 if paid to a UK resident at a reasonable commercial rate.

- **National insurance contributions**

  Under s 617(5) ICTA 1988, an individual carrying on a trade, profession or vocation can deduct half of the total contribution from total income (ie not from the Schedule D1 computation).

8.7   Post cessation receipts

In Chapter 5 we saw that the application of the source doctrine meant that amounts received after a trade or business had discontinued escaped tax because a source, ie the business, had disappeared prior to the receipt. Consequently, ss 103 and 104 ICTA 1988 impose a charge on post-cessation receipts. Section 103 ICTA 1988 deals with the earnings basis and s 104 ICTA 1988 deals with the cash basis.

Under s 103 ICTA 1988 a sum was received after a trade professional vocation has discontinued par taxed under Schedule D Case VI. Where a debt has been released by the discontinuation of a trade it is treated as a receipt under s 103(4) ICTA 1988. Section 104 ICTA 1988 catches amounts which have been invoiced but not paid prior to the discontinuance, and also receipts that would escape tax by a change from the cash to the earnings basis.

It is possible to elect that these receipts instead of being taxed under Schedule D Case VI are instead taxed under Schedule D Case I or Case II as amounts arising at the date of the discontinuance provided the amounts are received within six years of the discontinuance. Such an election might be made if the rates of tax have increased in the intervening period between cessation and receipt.

| 8.8 | **Losses – introduction** | Where the calculation leads to a loss, the legislation gives detailed rules as to how that loss can be used. These rules have altered since the introduction of the current-year basis for Schedule D and this section deals with the new rules. |

| 8.9 | **General** | A Schedule D Cases I or II loss will arise if the allowable expenditure for an accounting period exceeds the taxable income. When this happens there will be a nil assessment for the accounting period. The loss which has been created will be available to the taxpayer for one or two purposes: to set against other income in order to reduce an assessment, or to set against income which has already been taxed which will result in a repayment of tax already paid. |

The two principal uses of losses for an established business are:

- carry forward – the losses are carried forward and used to reduce future profits of the trade (s 385 ICTA 1988); and

- carry across – the losses are used against other income of the taxpayer (s 380 ICTA 1988) and against capital gains (s 72 FA 1991).

Special rules apply on the cessation of a trade either because the trader has ceased trading altogether or the trader has transferred their trade to a limited company. Because of the separate legal personality of a company, losses incurred by a company cannot be used against the income of the shareholder. It is usual, therefore, where it is expected that losses will be incurred in the early years, to run the business until it becomes profitable and then to transfer it to a limited company.

| 8.10 | **Carry forward losses – s 385 ICTA 1988** | Section 385 ICTA 1988 provides that: |

- where a loss is sustained in a trade, profession or vocation,

- and relief for that loss has not been given under any other section,

- then the loss can be carried forward and set against profits of the same trade, profession or vocation, deducting the loss from earlier profits before later ones.

There are a number of points to note:

- The loss must be set against profits of the same trade. In *Gordon & Blair Ltd v IRC* (1962) a brewing company ceased

brewing but continued to sell beer. It was held that the
company had ceased one trade and commenced another.
The losses of the brewing trade could not therefore be
carried forward and used against the new trade.

- There is no time limit. The losses can be carried forward
  indefinitely.

- If the only income a taxpayer has is from the trade, the set
  off of losses may cause the taxpayer to lose her personal
  allowances. A taxpayer cannot choose to set only a
  proportion of the loss off against future profits.

- Where the business's income includes income which has
  been taxed at source, eg dividend income, the loss can be
  set against it and the income tax reclaimed (s 385(4) ICTA
  1988).

- Where a trader makes a loss and also makes annual
  payments wholly and exclusively for the purposes of the
  trade, profession or vocation, the annual payment is
  treated as augmenting the loss.

Section 380 ICTA 1988 provides that:

**8.11   Carry across – s 380
ICTA 1980**

- *where* in any year of assessment a loss is sustained in a
  trade, profession, vocation or employment,

- *and* a claim is made within two years after the end of the
  year of assessment (this will reduce to one year from 1996),

- *then* the amount of the loss can be set against the taxpayer's
  other income,

- *to the extent that* either the taxpayer does not make a claim
  or, having made a claim, there remains an unrelieved loss
  and the taxpayer may claim to set the loss against income
  of the preceding year.

Relief for the current year is given in priority to relief in the
preceding year (s 380(2) ICTA 1988) if a claim is made for both
years. The trade, profession or vocation must be carried 'on a
commercial basis with a view to the realisation of profits' (s
384 ICTA 1988), and the purpose of this restriction is to
prevent a person carrying on a business as a hobby and using
any losses to offset his other income.

Section 384(9) ICTA 1988 provides that, when a trade is
being carried on with reasonable expectation of a profit, that is
conclusive evidence it is being carried on with a view to the
realisation of a profit.

Under s 397 ICTA 1988, a loss incurred in a trade of
farming or market gardening will automatically be disallowed

from relief under s 380 ICTA 1988 if, in each of the five preceding years, a loss was incurred in the trade. In other words, a farmer or market gardener must make a profit at least every sixth year. The restriction does not apply if it can be shown that the trade was carried on in such a way that trader would be justified in a reasonable expectation of the realisation of a profit if they had been undertaken by a competent farmer or market gardener. Again the restriction under s 380 ICTA 1988 does not prevent the carry forward of losses under s 385 ICTA 1988.

Relief is also restricted under s 380 ICTA 1988 where the trader has invested in a limited partnership. Under s 117 ICTA 1988 the amount of the relief is restricted to the amount of capital invested in the business. The purpose of this section is to prevent people effectively buying losses by investing relatively small sums with little work. The section reverses the case of *Reed v Young* (1988) in which the taxpayer successfully claimed relief for £41,423, being her share of the partnership loss under the partnership agreement. Her capital contribution was only £10,068. Again, losses disallowed by s 117 ICTA 1988 for carry across under s 380 ICTA 1988 can be carried forward under s 385 ICTA 1988.

8.12 Extension to capital gains – s 72 FA 1991

In 1988 the rates of income tax and capital gains tax were assimilated. However, while the theory behind this was to make the system fairer by reducing the discrimination between those who lived by earning and those who lived by realising capital assets, there was no equivalent assimilation of losses. An income tax loss could not be set against a capital gain and vice versa. Some measure of relief was given in 1991 by s 72, of that year's Finance Act. This provides that:

- to the extent that the amount of the loss under s 380 ICTA 1988 cannot be set against the taxpayer's income for that year; and

- the loss has not been allowed under any other section; and

- a claim is made in the claim for relief under s 380; then

- so much of the loss as cannot be relieved against income can be treated as a capital loss incurred in the year to which the s 380 ICTA 1988 claim relates.

There are three points to note:

- A claim for capital gains tax relief must be made with a s 380 ICTA 1988 claim. In other words the taxpayer's other taxable income must be reduced before the loss can be set against capital gains.

- The amount to be set against the capital gain cannot exceed
  the amount of the gain. Therefore, to the extent that there is
  a loss over and above the taxpayer's income and capital
  gains, the loss will either be the subject of a s 380 ICTA
  1988 claim for the preceding year or carried forward under
  s 385 ICTA 1988.

- In calculating the amount of the gain, no account is to be
  taken of the capital gains tax annual exemption. In much
  the same way that a s 380 ICTA 1988 claim will waste the
  personal allowances, a claim under s 72 FA 1991 will waste
  the annual capital gains tax exemption (unless the amount
  of the loss is insufficient to relieve the whole capital gain, in
  which case the annual exemption will be set against the
  excess).

Where the taxpayer incurs a loss he can choose which section to use. Where no specific election is made, s 385 ICTA 1988 will apply automatically and the losses will be carried forward. Where the taxpayer elects under s 380 ICTA 1988 or s 72 FA 1991, the loss will be set against the taxpayer's other income and capital gains. To the extent that there is any loss remaining, the balance will be available for carry forward under s 385 ICTA 1988. The application of s 380 ICTA 1988 and s 72 FA 1991 may result in the loss of personal allowances and the loss of the capital gains tax annual exemption, whereas a loss carried forward under s 385 ICTA 1988 will only be set against profits of the same trade. If the taxpayer has other income, this can therefore be used to offset against the personal allowance.	**8.13** **Interaction between ss 380, 385 ICTA 1988 and s 72 FA 1991**
Where a loss is incurred by a taxpayer in the first year of carrying on business or any of the three succeeding years, she can elect, within two years from the end of the year in which the losses occurred, to carry the loss back against her other income in the three years before the loss was incurred. The loss is set against earlier years, before later years, and against earned income before unearned income. The loss which can be offset is the actual loss. If the loss is used in a s 381 ICTA 1988 election, the amount of the loss is reduced by the amount so used. Like loss relief under s 380 ICTA 1988, it will be denied unless it can be shown that the trade, profession or vocation was carried on, on a commercial basis with a view to realising profits (s 381(4) ICTA 1988).	**8.14** **Losses in the early years – s 381 ICTA 1988**

Under s 381 ICTA 1988, where a business is commenced,
makes losses, and continues to make losses, a taxpayer would
be able to extend the relief to eight years by transferring the

business to his spouse. Such a device is prevented by s 381(5) ICTA 1982.

| 8.15 | **Interaction between ss 380, 381 and 385** |

The election under ss 380 and 381 ICTA 1988 are alternatives. The taxpayer may elect under both if she has sufficient losses, but cannot elect to use a loss partially under s 380 ICTA 1988 and partially under s 381 ICTA 1988.

In the case of *Butt v Haxby* (1982) the taxpayer incurred a loss of £41,000 in his first year of trading 1978–79. He had Schedule E income for that year of about £46,000. He elected under both ss 380 and 381 ICTA 1988, arguing that he was able to use £35,000 of the loss against his Schedule E income under s 380 ICTA 1988 and the balance against this other income in 1975–76 under s 381 ICTA 1988. It was held that the loss could not be split. Relief could be claimed under both sections and the taxpayer could specify the order in which they were to apply. However, if the s 380 ICTA 1988 claim was made first, it was only the excess which would be capable of relief under s 381 ICTA 1988. The effect of this would be that the taxpayer's personal allowances for that year would be wasted. The claim would reduce the income to nil and so there would be nothing to set the allowances against.

| 8.16 | **Losses in the closing years – s 388 ICTA 1988** |

Where a business is discontinued, any loss incurred in the last 12 months – so far as it has not been relieved under s 380 ICTA 1988 or s 72 FA 1991 – can be carried back and set against the profits of the business of the three years prior to the year in which the business terminated. It should be noted that it is the loss for the last 12 months of the business. Where the final accounting period is less than 12 months, a proportion of the previous accounting period must be taken into account.

| 8.17 | **Transfer to a company – s 386 ICTA 1988** |

Losses are personal to the person incurring them. A consequence of this is that, where a business is transferred to a company, any losses being carried forward under s 385 ICTA 1988 will remain with the original owner of the business. They will therefore be wasted because the losses can only be set against income of the same trade, and the trade is now being carried on by somebody else, ie the company. To alleviate this problem, s 386 ICTA 1988 provides that where a business is transferred to a company in return for shares in the company, the transferor can offset any losses remaining against income from the company, provided that throughout the year the shares remain held by the taxpayer and the company continues to trade.

Schedule D Case I and Schedule D Case II – Calculation of Profit and Losses

Profit

Tax is charged under Schedule D in respect of the annual profits or gains arising or accruing. A trader will normally prepare accounts for each year and these will be prepared in accordance with ordinary accounting principles. However, the accounting profit is by no means conclusive of the tax profit.

Accounts can be prepared in one of three ways: first, the earnings basis; second, the bills-delivered basis; and third, the cash basis.

There are a number of ways in which accounts can be drawn up. However, accounts from one year to the next must be drawn up on a consistent basis so they can be compared, and so the business's performance can be judged against preceding years. In recent years the courts have been prepared to accept accountancy evidence as to how certain matters ought to be treated in the accounts for the purposes of determining the profit for tax purposes.

In order to decide the case the courts have applied a number of tests. Where a trader receives an amount for the restriction of his activities, it will be the extent of the restriction which decides whether the receipt is income or capital.

Where a trader receives an amount in compensation for the sterilisation of an asset that sum will be capital if the sterilisation is permanent but revenue if the sterilisation is temporary.

Where the sum received is for the cancellation of a business contract it will depend upon what part that contract played in the business as to whether the receipt is income or capital. Where the contract relates to the entire business it will be a capital receipt. However, where it only relates to part of the business it is compensation for profits which would otherwise have been earned under the contract, and is therefore revenue.

Where a trader removes an item of trading stock from the business for the her own personal use, the amount to be entered into the accounts is the market value of that stock (*Sharkey v Wernher* (1955)). The rule in *Sharkey v Wernher* does not apply to professional people (*Mason v Innes* (1967)).

In order for expenses to be deductible they must be of a revenue nature, and the deduction must not be disallowable by statute.

Similar problems arise in determining the revenue/capital status of expenditure as they do in determining whether an item of income is revenue or capital. Again, the courts have used a number of tests. Expenditure will be capital if it is made for all, not just once, and also with the view to bringing an asset or advantage into existence for the enduring benefit of the trade (*British Insulated and Helsby Cables Ltd v Etherton* (1925)). Where the sum expended is on a capital asset it is necessary to identify the nature of the expenditure. A sum expended on the replacement of an asset will be capital and a sum expended on the repair of an asset will be revenue (*Tucker v Granada Motorway Services Ltd* (1979)). Capital expenditure is more likely to be a once and for all payment, while revenue expenditure is more likely to recur (*Vallumbrosa Rubber Co Ltd v Farmer* (1910)). The expense must not be disallowed by statute. Those expenses disallowed are:

- expenditure not being exclusively for the purposes of the trade, profession or vocation;

- rent payment unless the premises are used for the purposes of the trade;

- improvements to capital assets;

- any loss not connected with or arising out of the trade, profession or vocation; and

- bad debts unless they are proved to be bad.

Losses

Where the expenditure exceeds the income, this will lead to a loss. Where there is a loss, this will result in a nil assessment for the year. An assessment is not raised indicating the amount of the loss.

Where a loss is sustained in a trade, profession or vocation, the loss can be carried forward and set against profits of the same trade, profession or vocation, deducting the loss from earlier profits before later ones. A loss can be carried forward indefinitely provided the trade is still carried on.

Where a loss is made in a trade, profession or vocation, the taxpayer can elect within two years from the end of the year of assessment that the amount of the loss is to be set against the taxpayer's other income. To the extent that any of the loss remains unrelieved, the taxpayer can elect to set it against income of the preceding year.

To the extent that there is any loss unrelieved in accordance with the above paragraph, a taxpayer can make a claim to set that loss against capital gains made in the same year as the claim.

Where a loss is incurred by taxpayer in the first year of carrying on a business or in any of the three succeeding years, he may claim within the two years from the end of the year in which the losses occurred to carry the loss back to be used against his other income for the three years before the loss was incurred.

When a business is permanently discontinued, any loss which is incurred in the last 12 months, so far it is not been relieved otherwise, can be carried back and set against profits of the business in the three years prior to the year in which the business terminated.

Where a trader transfers the trade to a company and the trade has been making losses, then, provided that the trader has transferred the trade to the company in return for shares, the transferor can set any unused losses of the trade against income from the company provided that the company's shares are still held and the company continues to trade.

Chapter 9

Capital Allowances

This chapter deals with the way in which the UK tax system gives allowances for depreciating assets. Such allowances are given whether the trade or business is carried on as a sole trader, partnership or company. All businesses are now treated in the same way and the allowances are given as a deduction against income as a trading expense. Transitional rules apply to businesses commenced prior to 1994 but these are not dealt with.

9.1   Introduction

When income tax was first introduced no allowances were given, as the tax was only intended as a temporary measure. The present system of allowances dates back to 1945. The legislation passed since then has recently been consolidated into the Capital Allowances Act 1990. The system of capital allowances is intended to give uniform rates of depreciation to all businesses. To achieve this, the depreciation allowed in the accounts is added back and a 25% writing down allowance is given on a reducing-balance basis for plant and machinery, and a 4% allowance on a straight-line basis is given for industrial buildings. Because there is a large difference between the allowances on plant and machinery and those on industrial buildings, and also because no allowances are given at all if the building is not an industrial building (subject to a few exceptions discussed in para 9.7) there has been a tendency to argue that items included in buildings are plant and machinery. This led to the introduction in 1994 of new provisions whereby the legislature tried to define what was, and what was not, a building. Needless to say, this has only led to further complications rather than to clarifying the issue.

This chapter examines the definition of plant, at how allowances are given and to whom, and then looks briefly at industrial buildings allowances. It should be noted that not all capital assets qualify for allowances and such assets are effectively bought out of taxed income.

To qualify for capital allowances expenditure must be:

- capital in nature

- incurred on a qualifying asset, ie plant or machinery ...

- which belongs to the taxpayer and ...

9.2   Plant and machinery allowances

- which is either used by the taxpayer in a trade or business or, in the case of a lessor produces income which is assessable to tax.

9.2.1   Capital

The distinction between capital and revenue has already been discussed in para 8.5.2. It will be remembered that, for example, the renewal of an asset involves capital expenditure, whereas the repair of an asset involves revenue expenditure. Revenue expenditure is far more beneficial because it means that the whole amount of the expenditure can be deducted in the year in which it is incurred. In many cases it will be a matter of fact and degree whether something amounts to a repair or a renewal.

9.2.2   Plant and machinery

There is no legislative definition of plant and machinery. What is plant will therefore depend on the facts of each individual case. Machinery is perhaps a little easier to identify and that is probably why most of the case law in this area has been concerned with the definition of plant. The starting point for any investigation into whether or not something is plant is the case of *Yarmouth v France* (1887) in which Lindley LJ said:

'There is no definition of plant in the Act: but in its ordinary sense it includes whatever apparatus is used by a businessman for carrying on his business – not his stock-in-trade, which he buys or makes for sale; but all goods and chattels, fixed or moveable, live or dead which he keeps for permanent employment within his business.'

Yarmouth v France was not in fact a capital allowances claim. It concerned a claim under the Employers' Liability Act 1880 for injuries sustained by an employee because of defective plant which, in that case, was a vicious horse.

In the case of *Wimpey International Ltd v Warland* (1988) Hoffmann J analysed the *Yarmouth v France dictum*. He held that there are three distinguishing features to be satisfied:

- items not used in the business cannot be plant;

- stock-in-trade is not plant; and

- plant must be used for permanent employment in the business.

He elaborated on the three tests thus:

'if the item is neither stock-in-trade nor the premises upon which the business is conducted, the only question is whether it is used for carrying on the business. I shall call this the "business use" test. However, under the second distinction, an article which passes the "business use" test is excluded if such use is as stock-in-trade. And under the third distinction, an item used in carrying on the business is excluded if such use is as the premises or place upon which the business is conducted.'

Hoffmann J's analysis was approved by the Court of Appeal.

For many years the problem was to distinguish plant from setting, that is, to distinguish between the plant with which the trade is carried on and the setting in which the trade is carried on. In *Wimpey v Warland*, the plant versus setting test was said to confuse the issue; the question to be addressed is whether the item has become, or is, part of the premises. However, many of the cases have been decided on the plant or setting basis and these need to be looked at.

The case law establishes that, to be plant, an item must not be part of the premises from which the business is carried on unless the premises themselves are an item of plant. Thus, in *IRC v Barclay, Curle & Co Ltd* (1969) a dry dock was held to be plant, and in *Schofield v R and H Hall Ltd* (1975) a grain silo was held to be plant. In a number of cases it has been held that where an item amounts to 'setting' it is not plant. In the following cases the item in question was held not to be plant.

- *St John's School (Mountford and Knibbs) v Ward* (1974) – a prefabricated building used as a chemistry laboratory.

- *Dixon v Fitch's Garage Ltd* (1975) – a canopy over a petrol station (however, this decision has subsequently been doubted).

- *Thomas v Reynolds* (1987) – an inflatable cover over a tennis court.

- *Gray v Seymours Garden Centre (Horticulture)* (1993) – a glasshouse from which plants were sold (the refusal to allow the building as plant was despite its name which was a 'planteria').

- *Bensen v Yard Arm Club Ltd* (1979) – a floating restaurant.

In *Wimpey v Warland* Hoffmann J said that the distinction between setting and apparatus was unhelpful. The real distinction was between business use and premises. If an item passed the business use test it was plant unless it was part of the premises. In the above cases the items in question were part of the premises from which the business was being carried on. In contra distinction, in the case of *Cooke v Beach Station Caravans Ltd* (1974) a swimming pool on a caravan site was held to be plant because it was part of the apparatus with which the business was carried on. It attracted business to the premises but was not part of the premises.

Applying this test, Hoffmann J held in *Wimpey v Warland* that light fittings were plant but that floor files, glass shop fronts and staircases were not. The distinction between the two was that the former had not become part of the building whereas the latter had. In so deciding, he distinguished the case of *IRC v Scottish and Newcastle Breweries* (1982) in which it was held that murals, tapestries, pictures and metal sculptures were all plant on the basis that they were not fixtures and had not become annexed to the building. In *Wimpey v Warland* the light fittings served a purpose in that the amount of light in particular places was considered an important aspect of the fast food business. The case can be compared with *Cole Bros Ltd v Phillips* (1982) in which it was held that light fittings were merely part of the premises because they provided general illumination.

It is in this area that legislation was introduced in 1994 in order to clarify the boundaries. The stated purpose of the legislation was not to change the law but to state which buildings and structures qualify as plant. It appears only to have added confusion, which is disappointing when the aim was to clarify.

9.2.3   Finance Act 1994

To prevent the general erosion of the distinction between buildings and plant, a new schedule, Schedule AA1, was added to the Capital Allowances Act 1990. The schedule excludes from machinery and plant any expenditure on the provision of a building; including any asset which is incorporated into a building or is of a kind normally incorporated into a building. The schedule sets out a table which comprises two columns. The first is a list of items which cannot be plant, the second is a list of items which *may* be plant. The reason why the second column only sets out items which may be plant, is because these items must still pass the case law test, ie they must be used in the business, and not be stock-in-trade etc. The schedule also deals with items which are structures. A structure is something that is a fixed structure other than a building. Again the schedule sets out a table with two columns. The first is a list of items that cannot be plant, the second is a list of items that may be (eg items like grain silos, and swimming pools). Again, inclusion in the second column does not mean the items are plant; they must still pass the relevant tests.

The structure of the legislation is to include in the first column items that have been held not to be plant and to include in the second column items that have been held to be plant. Thus, the legislation precludes any attempt to overturn the former cases but still forces the taxpayer to prove that items are plant in the latter. For those who think this may leave items which do not fall in either list, the list of structures which are not plant in column one ends with: 'Any structure not within any other item in this column', thus any structure not mentioned is included in the list of structures which are not plant.

To claim allowances the asset must belong to the person incurring the expenditure. In the case of *Stokes v Costain* (1984), Costain Property Investments Ltd claimed allowances in respect of lifts and central heating equipment installed in a building for which it had an agreement for lease. The total cost was some £450,000. The Inland Revenue disallowed the claim on the basis that the lifts did not belong to Costain because they had become fixtures in the building. The Court of Appeal found for the Inland Revenue. The lifts were part of the building and could not be disposed of by the tenant. Consequently, they did not belong to the tenant. Neither could the landlord claim allowances because the expenditure was incurred by someone else.

9.2.4   Belongs

Section 51(3) CAA 1990, introduced by the Finance Act 1985 after the *Costain* case, new defines an interest in land as:

- a fee simple estate or an agreement to acquire that estate;

- a leasehold estate or agreement to acquire such an estate;

- an easement; and

- a license.

Section 52 CAA 1990 goes on to provide that where expenditure is incurred by a person having an interest in land on machinery and plant and it becomes a fixture, it shall be treated as belonging to the person incurring the expenditure. Where more than one person would be entitled because there is more than one interest in the land, the plant is treated as belonging to the person with the most subordinate interest.

There appears to be some conflict between this section and the test laid down by Hoffmann J regarding plant becoming part of the premises. Many items which become fixtures will be machinery ie the winding gear in the *Costain* case. For items of plant, it must be shown that, although an item has become a fixture, it has not become part of the premises (an example might be the swimming pool in *Cooke v Beach Station Caravans Ltd*).

Allowances are available on assets used in a business not just a trade, although the most common claim will be one by a trader. Schedule A is taxed as a business, therefore allowances

9.2.5   Which is used by the taxpayer in a trade or business

will be due in the same way as they are to a trader. Consequently, allowances are available to those assessed under schedules A, DI, DII and E. There is no longer any necessity, in the case of an individual, to give allowances to furnished holiday lettings under Schedule D Case VI because these are now brought into Schedule A (see s 503 ICTA 1988) and taxed as if they were a trade under Schedule D Case I. For a company, Schedule D Case VI still applies. Allowances are available to an employee taxed under Schedule E if the plant or machinery is 'necessarily' provided by the employee. In practice this test will be very difficult to satisfy.

In the case of *White v Higginbottom* (1982) a vicar claimed to deduct the cost of a slide projector and on overhead projector which he had bought in order to provide visual illustration for his sermons. This claim was rejected. The test under the capital allowances legislation is as strict as that under the income tax legislation (see Chapter 11). Another vicar would be able to give sermons without the use of this equipment in which case it was not necessary to the job.

9.2.6	Lessors producing income assessable to tax – s 61 CAA 1990

Where machinery or plant is first let, s 61 CAA 1990 provides that the lessor may claim allowances – whether or not it is let in the course of a trade – as if it had been provided for the purposes of a trade carried on by the lessor. This is so even if the plant or machinery is not used in the lessee's trade. This provision applies, for example, to the letting of investment properties. Expenditure on plant and machinery installed is a property which is then let will be allowable for these purposes.

9.3   Qualifying expenditure

To determine the amount of the allowances, it is necessary to ascertain the qualifying expenditure. The qualifying expenditure includes not only the expenditure on the asset but also expenditure on alterations to a building which is incidental to the installation of plant and machinery for the purpose of the trade (s 66 CAA 1990). Normally, the qualifying expenditure will be the expenditure actually incurred and will be ascertainable from invoices and other documents relevant to the acquisition of the plant or machinery or to any alterations necessary for its installation.

9.3.1	Connected persons

To prevent the manipulation of the allowances given, s 75 CAA 1990 provides that where a person incurs capital expenditure on the purchase of plant and machinery, and where he and the seller are connected with each other, the amount of the allowances will be restricted to the smallest of the following:

- the open market value of the machinery or plant;

- the amount of expenditure incurred by the seller on the provision of the machinery or plant; or

- (where capital expenditure was incurred by any person connected with the seller on the provision of the machinery or plant) the amount of the expenditure incurred by that person.

For the purposes of these provisions, 'connected persons' has the same meaning as in s 839 ICTA 1988. 'Open market value' is an amount equal to the price which the machinery or plant would have fetched if sold on the open market (s 76(6)(a) CAA 1990).

The amount of the allowances given has varied from time to time under the capital allowances legislation. However, the only allowance now given on plant and machinery is a 25% writing-down allowance. This is given on the amount of the qualifying expenditure on a reducing balance basis. The allowance is given as a trading expense against the profits of the trade. It is given in full for the period in which the asset is acquired, but no allowance is given in the period during which the asset is disposed of. So, if an asset is bought in year one and sold in year three, the full allowance will be given in years one and two but no allowance will be given in year three.	**9.4 The allowances**
The allowances are given by reference to a 'pool' of qualifying expenditure (ss 24 and 25 CAA 1990). Assets qualifying for capital allowances are therefore pooled and the allowances are given on the aggregate value of the qualifying expenditure of all the assets in the pool. When an item of plant and machinery is acquired its acquisition cost is placed in the pool, and similarly when an item of plant and machinery is sold the disposal proceeds are taken out of the pool. As stated above, the item is placed in the pool in the year during which it is bought, thereby giving full allowances in the year of acquisition (regardless of whether it was bought at the beginning or the end of the year) and the item is taken out of the pool before applying the allowances in the year of disposal. So, no allowance is given in the year of disposal.	9.4.1 The way in which allowances are given
Where an asset is disposed of out of the pool, the price received for the asset is subtracted from the amount in the pool. For example, in year one an asset is acquired for £2,000. The writing-down allowance is 25%, which is £500. In year two the qualifying expenditure is £1,500. If the asset is sold for	9.4.2 The balancing charge and balancing allowance

£1,750, the extra £250 is charged to tax. This is called a balancing charge and it effectively 'claws back' the allowances given over and above the actual depreciation suffered by the asset. Where assets are pooled, the deduction from the pool of the price received by the vendor for the asset disposed of will, in effect, create the balancing charge. This is because, where the amount received is greater than the written-down value of the asset in the pool, the deduction of a greater amount than the written-down value of the sold asset will result in a reduced amount of writing-down allowances for the assets remaining in the pool for that year.

Where the disposal price of the asset is less than the written-down value of the asset in the pool, a writing-down allowance will continue to be given on the difference between the written down-value and the actual disposal value.

9.5 Short-life assets

Under ss 37 and 38 CAA 1990, a taxpayer can elect for certain items to be treated as short-life assets. Such an election is to be made within two years of acquiring the asset and the effect of it is to keep the asset outside the pool. A short-life asset is generally one which is expected to have a useful working life of no more than five years. Certain assets cannot be short-life assets (s 38 CAA 1990), eg ships and motor cars.

The advantage of a short-life asset is that it is not placed in the pool. Consequently, when it is disposed of, a full balancing charge or balancing allowance will be given in the year of disposal. Where a short-life asset has been held for more than four years and has not been disposed of, the written-down value of the asset is placed in the general pool and writing-down allowances are given. The short-life asset election will typically be made on tools and other such items and on computer equipment. The effect is to give a balancing allowance immediately on disposal, if this is less than the written down value, rather than having to claim 25% a year from the balance in the pool.

9.5.1 Motor cars

Allowances on motor cars are restricted because they are often used for private as well as business purposes. Writing-down allowances are given on the full cost of a vehicle if it is unsuitable for use as a private car, eg if it is a lorry or a bus. Vehicles which do not fulfil these criteria qualify for a 25% writing-down allowance, but this allowance is based on an original cost of no more than £12,000. Such vehicles are not pooled and hence a balancing charge or balancing allowance will arise on their disposal.

Capital allowances are given on expenditure incurred upon the construction or purchase of an industrial building or structure, provided it is used for a qualifying purpose. Section 18 CAA 1990 defines in some detail an 'industrial building or structure'. It includes a building in use for the purposes of a trade carried on in a mill, factory, or other similar premises, or for the purposes of a transport, dock, inland-navigation, water, sewerage, electricity or hydraulic-power undertaking. The most important category is a building in use for the purposes of a trade which consists in the manufacture of goods or materials or the subjection of goods or materials to any process. In the case of *Bourne v Norwich Crematorium Ltd* (1968) the taxpayers claimed capital allowances on a crematorium. It was held that a crematorium does not 'subject goods to a process' on the basis that human remains are not goods or 'materials' and the incineration of coffins was not subjecting them to a process.

The allowance given is a writing-down allowance of 4% per annum of a straight-line basis. This allowance is given on either a cost of construction or the purchase price of the building. This latter price excludes the cost of the land.

9.6   Industrial buildings

Certain areas of the country have been designated enterprise zones. Buildings in these zones qualify for a 100% initial allowance. In other words, the whole cost of the building can be written off in the first year. For these purposes, a building in an enterprise zone includes not only an industrial building but also hotels and commercial buildings. Where such a building is sold, it is treated as having a life of 25 years, and any balancing charge of allowance will therefore be calculated by reference to the period for ownership giving a national allowance of 4% each year.

9.7   Enterprise zones

Capital Allowances

There are two main types of capital allowance: those for plant and machinery and those for industrial buildings.

In order for expenditure to qualify for plant and machinery allowances it must be capital in nature, incurred on plant or machinery which, in consequence of the expenditure, belongs to the taxpayer and which is either used by the taxpayer in a trade or business or, in the case of a lessor, produces income which is assessable to tax.

Whether an item is defined as plant depends on the facts in each individual case. Plant has been defined as the apparatus used by a business person for carrying on business, which is not stock-in-trade, but all other goods and chattels that are kept for permanent employment in the business (*Yarmouth v France* (1887)). In the case of *Wimpey International Ltd v Warland* (1988) it was stated that there are three distinguishing features of plant: first, items not used in the business cannot be plant; second, stock-in-trade is not plant; and third plant must be used for permanent employment in the business.

However, where an item forms part of the premises, it will not be an item of plant.

An item can be both plant *and* the premises if the plant itself is the place where the business is carried on, eg a dry dock can be an item of plant even though it is the premises.

Following a number of cases which tried to distinguish between premises and plant, a new schedule was introduced into the Capital Allowances Act 1990 in 1994 which was designed to clarify the issue. The schedule sets out lists of items that are to be considered part of a building and thus are disallowed for plant and machinery purposes.

To claim allowances, the item must belong to the person incurring the expenditure. Where an item becomes affixed to the land, it will cease to belong to the person incurring the expenditure. The capital allowances legislation therefore provides that the person with the lesser interest in land is deemed to own the asset. Thus, where a lessee incurs expenditure, the asset will be deemed to belong to the lessee.

The allowable expenditure includes not only the amount incurred on the asset, but also any amount incurred on making alterations in order to install the asset. When an asset is acquired from a connected person, the expenditure will be adjusted to the lesser of the open market value of the machinery or plant, and the amount of expenditure incurred by the seller on the provision of the machinery or plant. The allowances which can be claimed are 25% of the cost on a reducing balance basis. They are given by reference to a 'pool' of qualifying expenditure. The allowances are therefore given on the aggregate value of the pool. When an item is acquired, it is added to the pool in the year in which it is bought. When an item is disposed of, it is removed from the pool before calculating the allowances. Where the asset is disposed of, the amount subtracted from the pool is the amount received for the asset and where all the assets are disposed of out of the pool, or the business ceases, a taxpayer will receive a balancing allowance for any expenditure remaining in the pool at the time of cessation.

The taxpayer can elect for assets which are expected to have a working life of no more than five years to be treated differently. An election for short-life treatment must be made within two years of acquiring the assets. Short-life assets are not placed in the pool, so when a short-life asset is sold the full balancing charge or balancing allowance is given on each disposal. Where a short-life asset has been held for more than four years and not disposed of, it will be transferred to the general pool at its written down value.

The allowances on cars which are used for private as well as business use is restricted to 25% on an original cost of no more than £12,000. Such cars are not pooled and a balancing charge or balancing allowance will arise on their disposal.

Allowances are given on expenditure incurred upon the construction or purchase of an industrial building. The most important category of industrial building is one that is in use for the purposes of a trade which consists in the manufacture of goods or materials or the subjection of goods or materials to any process. The allowance given is 4% of the cost of the building on a straight-line basis.

Buildings in enterprise zones qualify for a 100% initial allowance. Furthermore, buildings in enterprise zones which qualify for allowances include not only industrial buildings but also commercial buildings.

Chapter 10

Schedule E – The Charge to Tax

10.1   Introduction

Schedule E provisions are those which tax emoluments from offices and employments, and they raise over three-quarters of the total amount raised by income tax each year. The system is made even more efficient by PAYE which reduces the cost of collection and also reduces the scope for avoidance and evasion. The provisions of Schedule E have become increasingly complex over the years as employers have tried to find ways of remunerating employees in more tax-efficient ways. One of the principal methods of doing this was to provide benefits in kind, colloquially known as 'perks'. Non-cash benefits have also been used to avoid wage freezes. Thus, if the law stated that pay rises were to be limited to X%, the employee could be given X% plus a bigger car. In recent years there has been a trend towards taxing benefits on their actual value so as to make them tax neutral, ie so that there is no distortion in the choice between cash or benefit. It is the intention of the present government to tax all employees on the whole of their earnings, whether received in cash or as a benefit in kind. However, there may still be an advantage in receiving a benefit in kind (see Chapter 11).

This chapter looks at the charge to tax. Chapter 11 looks at the benefits in kind legislation and the Schedule E expenses rules.

10.2   The charge to tax

Tax is charged under Schedule E by s 19(1) ICTA 1988. There are three cases of Schedule E:

- Case I taxes those who are resident and ordinarily resident in the UK;

- Case II taxes those who are not resident or, if resident, not ordinarily resident in the UK on emoluments from duties performed in the UK; and

- Case III taxes any emoluments of an office or employment of a person who is resident in the UK so far as the emoluments are received in the UK.

This chapter and the following one deal only with tax chargeable under Case I.

From the words of the charging provision, it will be apparent that, for tax to be charged under Schedule E, there must be:

- an office, or employment; and

- the office, or employment, must give rise to emoluments.

10.3   Office

There is no statutory definition of an office. In the case of *Great Western Railway Co v Bater* (1920) Rowlatt J described an office as: '... a subsisting, permanent, substantive, position which had an existence independent from the person who filled it, which went on and was filled in succession by successive holders ...'

In *Edwards v Clinch* (1981) a civil engineer, whose remuneration was normally taxed under Schedule E, occasionally acted as an inspector in Department of Environment local public enquiries. It was held that there was no office, as the appointment to inspector had no existence independent of the person who held it.

Lord Lowry referred to the *Bater* test as: 'the crude ore which has now by a series of processes ... been refined into something of superior quality.' However, while the legislature has not felt it necessary to alter the wording of Schedule E, the courts in more recent years have held that the quality of permanence is no more than a recognition of the office's separate existence, independent of the person holding it. Provided there is a possibility of a successor being appointed, there is sufficient permanence for there to be an office. Thus, a returning officer at an election holds an office. If the incumbent were to vacate it, there would still be a need for a returning officer and a new one would be appointed. The fact that the office of returning officer would not survive beyond an election does not make it any the less an office.

The idea of permanence and it being filled by successive holders is therefore less relevant than was once thought. The appointment of Mr Clinch was unique to him; there was no question of a successor being appointed. If for some reason he failed to complete an assignment, a new enquiry would have to be held.

10.4   Employment

In *Davies v Braithwaite* (1933) Rowlatt J said that an employment was 'more or less analogous to an office'. However, attitudes have changed and employments are now looked at in the light of the relationship between those doing a task and those requiring them to do it. If the relationship of master and servant exists, ie if it is a contract of service, there will be an employment within Schedule E.

A contract of service is taxable under Schedule E. A contract for services is taxable under Schedule D. A person taxed under Schedule D is in business on their own account. What, then, if the exercise of a profession entails a person taking a number of short appointments which, when viewed separately, could be a number of individual employments? The answer is not an easy one and may depend on how the facts are approached. In the case of *Davies v Braithwaite* (1933) the taxpayer was a professional actress whose activities included work on stage, film, radio and gramophone. She was held to carry on a single profession and was therefore taxable on her worldwide income. It should be noted that the taxpayer was arguing that each was a separate employment and so only those performed in the UK were taxable in the UK. It was held that each appointment was an incident of her profession. *Davies v Braithwaite* is usually compared with the case of *Fall v Hitchen* (1972) in which a ballet dancer who was contracted under a standard-form contract approved by the British Actors' Equity Association was held to be an employee.

10.4.1   Contract of service or contract for services

The fundamental difference between the two cases is that in *Davies v Braithwaite*, the judge looked at the overall activities of the taxpayer and then decided that the constituent parts formed part of the whole, while in *Fall v Hitchen*, the judge looked at the nature of each individual engagement. Once it was decided that each engagement was in the nature of an employment, the matter was settled.

In the case of *Hall v Lorimer* the taxpayer was a freelance vision mixer, who worked on short-term contracts which generally lasted for no more than a couple of days. The Inland Revenue assessed his fees under Schedule E. He appealed, claiming that they should have been assessed under Schedule D Case I. The Inland Revenue argued that because he did not provide his own tools and could not dictate the hours or place he worked, each individual contract was a contract of employment. The degree of control exercised by the employer therefore indicated it was a contract of service and taxable under Schedule E. It was held that he was in business on his own account. He was not dependant on one paymaster but instead worked for 20 production companies during the year in question.

10.4.2   *Hall v Lorimer* (1993)

The Court of Appeal came to the conclusion that Mr Lorimer was not an employee but was instead in business on his own account.

The approach of the Court of Appeal was that the starting point is the overall picture, as in *Davies v Braithwaite*, not the detailed examination of each constituent part as in *Fall v Hitchen.*

Two of the factors which the Court of Appeal appear to have taken into account are the risk of bad debts and outstanding invoices which are not normally associated with employment. Further, the level of expenses incurred by Mr Lorimer from 1 February 1985 to 30 April 1986 amounted to £9,250 out of gross receipts of £32,875.

10.5   Emoluments

Emoluments are defined in s 131 ICTA 1988 as including '... all salaries, fees, wages, perquisites and profits whatsoever'. This definition is wide enough to cover benefits in kind as well as cash (indeed the shortened 'perk' is derived from the word perquisite). However, the courts have had a problem with the application of tax to benefits in kind and consequently, they have not been prepared to impose a liability to tax in circumstances where some monetary value could not be placed on the benefit received by the employee. In order to tax benefits, the legislature has had to introduce, over time, special charging provisions which specifically charge to tax certain benefits that would not otherwise be chargeable. These benefits and the charging provisions are dealt with in Chapter 13. The benefits which the courts would treat as chargeable under the general charging provision (s 19 ICTA 1988) are those which fulfil the following criteria:

• benefits which could be converted into cash; and

• the discharge by the employer of a liability incurred by an employee.

Under the first criterion, the courts would only tax a benefit if it could be turned to account, ie if it could be converted into money. In the case of *Tennant v Smith* (1892) a bank required one of its managers to live on bank premises. The manager was not able to let the premises as he was required to live there for the purposes of security. It was held by the House of Lords that, as the value of the accommodation could not be turned into money or moneys worth, it could not be treated as part of the income of the employee.

Where a benefit can be converted into money or money's worth, the problem arises as to how much value the employee should be taxed on.

In the case of *Wilkins v Rogerson* (1961) it was held, by the Court of Appeal, that the amount to be treated as part of the employee's income was an amount equal to the second-hand value of the benefit received. This was consistent with the idea that, in order to be taxable, the benefit had to be capable of being converted into money. In that case a company arranged for its employees to be supplied with £15 worth of clothing. The mechanism by which the clothes were supplied was that the employees were given a letter which was passed on to a local tailor who then invoiced the company. The court also held that the amount on which the employee was assessable was the second-hand value of the clothing which was appreciably less than its cost (such devices are now prevented by s 141 ICTA 1988 (see Chapter 11)).

The second criterion (the discharge by the employer of a liability incurred by an employee) is exemplified by the case of *Nicoll v Austin* (1935) in which the managing director of the company told his employer that he would have to sell his house in which he had entertained clients. To prevent this, the company maintained the house and garden and also paid the rates, gas and electricity bills. It was held that these amounts paid out by the company were an assessable benefit on the employee and such amounts are now specifically covered by legislation (see Chapter 11).

To be assessable, it is necessary that the payment received by the employee comes as a result acting as an employee, and not for some other reason. In the case of *Hochstrasser v Mayes* (1960) it was held by the House of Lords that to be assessable, a payment must be '... something in the nature of a reward for services past, present or future'. Further, it was stated that 'while it is not sufficient to render a payment assessable that an employee would not have received it unless he had been an employee, it is assessable if it has been paid to him in return for acting as or being an employee'.

10.5.1   Therefrom

In *Hochstrasser v Mayes*, ICI operated a scheme for its employees whereby, if the employee was transferred from one part of the country to another, the company would make good any losses on the sale of their house as a consequence of the transfer. It was held that the benefit arose by virtue of the employee's personal situation as a house owner not by virtue of being an employee, although the opportunity would not have arisen had he not been an employee. This case has led to a distinction being made between the *causa causans* and the *causa sine qua non*. That is, the employment must be a cause of the payment, it must not merely be a condition of the employment. These phrases have been used in a number of cases to explain the conclusion reached.

In the case of *Laidler v Perry* (1966) Lord Reid observed: '... it is well settled that not every sum or other profit received by an employee from his employer in the course of his employment is to be regarded as arising from the employment.' He stated that the question to be addressed was: 'Did his profit arise from the employment?' Notwithstanding these comments, the House of Lords held that £10 vouchers given to employees at Christmas were assessable on the employees because they arose from the employment. It should be noted that in this case every employee received a £10 voucher.

The waters were muddied somewhat by the case of *Hamblett v Godfrey* (1986), in which the Court of Appeal appeared to hold that a payment was taxable because the source of the payment was the employment. This is arguably far wider than the reward-for-services test. In *Hamblett v Godfrey* Miss Hamblett was an employee at the Government Communications Headquarters (GCHQ). She was entitled to join a trade union although she had not been a member of such since 1972. In 1983 the government decided that GCHQ staff should no longer be entitled to membership of a union and it paid £1,000 as compensation for the loss of this right. The Inland Revenue assessed the employees on the £1,000 being an emolument from the employment. It was held that the payments were emoluments. The right now deprived Mrs Hamblett was part of the employer/employee relationship because the employee would not have needed the right to joint the union had there not been any employment. Many considered this decision to mean that a payment could be taxable even though it was not paid as a reward for services but for something else. However, in the case of *Mairs v Haughey* (1993) it was stated that *Hamblett v Godfrey* was consistent with previous authority because the payment was made for Miss Hamblett to continue being an employee at GCHQ. On the basis that the payment was a one-off payment for giving up the right to join a trade union, it is difficult to reconcile this explanation with the reason for the payment. If Mrs Hamblett had resigned four weeks later, she would not have had to give the £1,000 back.

In the case of *Shilton v Wilmshurst* (1991) Peter Shilton, the former England goalkeeper, received a payment of £75,000 from Nottingham Forest on his transfer from Nottingham Forest to Southampton. It was argued on behalf of the taxpayer that the payment of £75,000 by his former club was not a payment for future services because Peter Shilton no longer remained with the club. The House of Lords held that the payment was an emolument because it was made to induce him into becoming an employee of Southampton Football Club. It was therefore a reward for future services, albeit not by his employer.

In *Mairs v Haughey* the House of Lords held that the payment made to relieve distress after employment had ceased (ie a non-statutory redundancy payment) was not taxable as an emolument.

In the preceding two sections it has been assumed that there are two tests to be satisfied: first, that the payment must be an emolument and second, that the emolument must be from the employment. Indeed, in the case of *Shilton v Wilmshurst* this was stated to be the case by the House of Lords.

10.5.2   Emoluments therefrom

The reason for this distinction was that counsel for the taxpayer had argued that, although the payment was an emolument, it was not an emolument from the employment. It is submitted that this argument is false and that it is implicit within the word 'emolument' that it derives from the employment. In the case of *Hochstrasser v Mayes* the words used were 'profit from employment'. The House of Lords was therefore concerned to distinguish between a profit from the employment, ie for acting as an employee, and a profit from something else, ie the personal circumstances of the taxpayer. When the legislation was consolidated the word emolument was introduced. It is submitted that the word emolument was substituted to highlight the distinction between a payment which is made for being an employee and one which is made for some other reason. It is submitted therefore that an emolument has to be from the employment and cannot be from anything else. However, the very fact that the words 'emolument from' are used has allowed the taxpayer to argue that there is such a thing as an emolument which is not from an employment but is from something else. This argument appears to have been accepted by the House of Lords in *Shilton v Wilmshurst*. Similarly, in the case of *Allan v IRC* (1994) it was argued for the taxpayer that, although payments were made as emoluments, they were not emoluments from the employment but were from something else. On the facts of that case it was held that the payments were made from the employment. It is submitted that once a payment is admitted as an emolument this should be sufficient to make the payment taxable because it is inherent within the word emolument that the payment is made in return for being or acting as an employee.

Against this view it could be said that the word emolument has, by judicial interpretation, taken on a meaning other than its usual or everyday meaning. Such a course is not without precedent. It may be that the word 'emoluments' is going through such legal construction. If so, it is probably through ignorance rather than through any conscious effort on the part of the judiciary.

10.6 Inducement payments

A distinction must be drawn between a payment made for future services and a payment made by a prospective employer to a prospective employee as an inducement to give something up. In *Shilton v Wilmshurst* it was held that the payment made to Peter Shilton was for being, or becoming, an employee and it was consequently taxable. However, in the case of *Jarrold v Boustead* (1964) a Rugby Union player was given £3,000 by a Rugby League club as a signing on fee. It was held that the payment was not an emolument but instead was compensation for giving up his amateur status. Consequently, it was not taxable. It should be noted that the giving up of amateur status was a once-and-for-all matter. Under the rules then in existence, once a player had signed up for a Rugby League club, that player would never again be allowed to play for a Rugby Union club.

In the case of *Pritchard v Arundale* (1971) a chartered accountant was given 4,000 shares in a company by another shareholder in order to become its managing director. It was held that he was not taxable on the receipt of the shares because they were given to him as compensation for the loss of his professional practice as a chartered accountant. A number of points must be noted. First, the compensation did not come from his prospective employer, but from another shareholder. Although it is possible for payments from third parties to be taxable as emoluments, it is a factor to be taken into account. Second, the taxpayer was of an age such that should he wish to return to private practice, it would be very difficult for him to resume those activities on the same scale. Third, it was held that, had he died or for some other reason been unable to take up the directorship, the taxpayer would not have had to return the shares (in other words, keeping the shares was not dependent upon the performance of services). Finally, the remuneration which he was going to receive for the directorship was reasonable and there was no presumption that the transfer of the shares was some form of disguised remuneration.

In the case of *Glantre Engineering Ltd v Goodhand* (1983) a chartered accountant claimed that an inducement payment made to him should not be taxed as an emolument. It was held that the accountant in question was merely moving from one Schedule E employment to another and was not permanently giving up anything to which the inducement payment was referable. The payment was therefore held to be taxable.

10.7 Variations

It may be that an employee gives up some right during the course of the employment for which he or she is compensated. It has almost invariably been the case that the courts have treated such payments as emoluments of the employment, being a reward for future services to be performed rather than true compensation for the right that has been given up. Thus, in *McGregor v Randall* (1984) it was held that where an employee was entitled to commission and that right was withdrawn on payment of compensation, the payment was an advance payment for future services not compensation for the loss of commission. It will be remembered that the payment in *Hamblett v Godfrey* was later rationalised in the case of *Mairs v Haughey* as being a payment in respect of future services, not merely compensation for the loss of the right to join a trades union.

In those cases where lump-sum payments have been held not to be taxable, the employee has usually given up some right which would have provided a benefit following termination of the employment. An example is where the employee is given a lump sum for the commutation of pension right (*Hunter v Dewhurst* (1932)). In the recent of *Mairs v Haughey* it was held that an *ex gratia* payment, paid as compensation for loss of rights under a non-statutory redundancy scheme was not taxable. This was because a non-statutory redundancy payment did not fall within the definition of an emolument from the employment and therefore a payment for the waiver of such a right was coloured by the nature of the payment which it replaced. Consequently, the compensation payment was not taxable.

To be an emolument from the employment, the payment does not necessarily have to come from the employee. In the case of *Calvert v Wainwright* (1947) it was held that tips received by a taxi driver were taxable because they were paid in return for the services which had been provided. It was stated that where the tip was paid at Christmas, was particularly generous and was also from a special customer, then it may be considered as something other than an emolument because it was paid in the taxi driver's personal capacity, not as a reward for services. However, where the employer provides a gift to all the employees at Christmas, this would be seen as an emolument being either a reward for services given throughout the year or a reward for services to be given in the future. Thus, in the case of *Laidler v Perry*, all the employees received a £10 voucher in lieu of the turkey they had received in previous years. It was held that the voucher was taxable. In the case of *Blakiston v Cooper* (1908), the taxpayer was a vicar who was entitled to the collection at Easter time. The parishioners knew this and contributed accordingly. It was held that the payments were

10.8   Payments from third parties

taxable because they were paid to the taxpayer in his capacity as vicar of the parish.

Where a taxpayer's contract entitles him to payments made in a voluntarily manner, those sums will also be taxable as emoluments from the employment. In the case of *Moorhouse v Dooland* (1954) a professional cricketer's contract of employment entitled him to have a collection taken each time he scored 50 runs or took a certain number of wickets. The payments were held to be taxable because they were paid to the taxpayer under the employment contract and were therefore paid to him in his capacity as employee.

10.9   Restrictive covenants

Under s 313 ICTA 1988, a payment made in respect of a restrictive covenant to an individual who holds, or has held, an office or employment is now taxable in the hands of the employee and treated as an emolument of the office or employment. It is a deductible expense for the employer. It should be noted that the payment is taxable regardless of whether the restrictive covenant is legally enforceable or not, and it is chargeable to tax in the year it is paid. If paid after the individual has died, it is treated as it were paid immediately before the individual's death.

10.10   Termination payments

The tax treatment of a termination payment will depend upon various factors. The sum will be taxable where there is a contractual right payment, eg under the contract of employment. In the case of *Dale v de Soissons* (1950) the service contract of a director provided that he would receive £10,000 if the contract were prematurely terminated. As the director was contractually entitled to the payment, it was held to be taxable.

Where a payment is paid in lieu of notice, tax will not be payable because it will be a payment of damages for breach of contract, not one in return for services. The payments made under a statutory redundancy scheme are not taxable (s 580(3) ICTA 1988) and by concession payments under non-statutory redundancy schemes are treated in the same way. An *ex gratia* payment is not taxable because it is made to an individual for personal reasons, not in return for services.

Having said that certain payments made on termination are not taxable, this is not strictly true. To the extent that a payment is not taxable under general principles it will be taxable under s 148 ICTA 1988. However, s188(4) ICTA 1988 provides that the first £30,000 of any payment within s 148 ICTA 1988 is tax free. It should be noted that s 188(4) ICTA 1988 only applies to payments within s 148 ICTA 1988 which taxes payments not otherwise chargeable to tax. If a payment is chargeable to tax, eg because the contract of employment provides for a payment on termination, such termination payment will consequently be taxable in full. In these circumstances it may be better to provide for no payment in the contract of employment and instead to pay an amount in lieu of notice, or to make an *ex gratia* payment on termination. In such circumstances, however, the employee is left to rely on the good nature of the employer.

Employees are taxed on a receipts basis. Thus, an employee is taxed on the full amount of emoluments which are received in a year of assessment in respect of the office in employment. There are detailed rules to determine when a payment is received (s 202A ICTA 1988). In general, the rules identify five dates. Where more than one date is applicable to a payment, the earliest date is taken. The dates are:

10.11   The basis of assessment

- the time when the payment is made (s 202(B)(1)(a) ICTA 1988);

- the time when a person becomes entitled to payment (s 202(B)(1)(b) ICTA 1988);

- (where a director of a company has sums credited on account of emoluments in the company's accounts or records) the time when the sums are credited (s 202B(1)(c) ICTA 1988);

- (where a director is voted remuneration for a period before the end of that period) the time when the period ends (s 202(1)(d) ICTA 1988); and

- (where a director is voted remuneration for a period after that period has ended) the time when the amount is determined (s 202B(1)(e) ICTA 1988).

As far as the employer is concerned, a deduction for emoluments can only be made if an amount is paid either during the period for which the accounts are made up or within nine months after that period (s 43 FA 1989).

An obvious problem with the receipts basis arises out of the application of the source doctrine (see Chapter 5). If emoluments are only to be taxed when they are received, an emolument received after the employment has ended would escape tax. To prevent such a result, s 19(4A) ICTA 1988 provides that if emoluments are received by a person and, at the time of receipt, the person does not hold the office or employment to which the emoluments are attributable, then if the office or employment is not yet held, the emoluments will be treated as being received in the first year in which it is held.

If the emoluments are received in respect of a period after an employment has been held, they will be treated as emoluments of the last year for which the employment was held. Further, s 202A(2) ICTA 1988 provides that a person is to be taxed on the receipt regardless of whether the emoluments are for that year or for some other year of assessment and regardless of whether or not the office or employment concerned is held at the time when the emoluments are received.

10.12   PAYE

The Pay As You Earn (PAYE) system of collecting tax applies to Schedule E and is highly complex. Each employee is given a code which the employer uses to determine the amount of tax to be deducted from the employee's emoluments each week or month. A proportion of the employee's allowances are given each month so as to provide for an even collection of tax throughout the tax year. When an employee leaves one employment and starts another, the first employer gives the employee a form P45 which provides the new employer with the necessary information to apply the correct tax code so that collection is continuous from one employment to another.

Benefits in kind are not usually included in PAYE because there is no payment and therefore nothing from which to collect the necessary tax. However, the amount of any benefits in kind received in one year's assessment are usually taken into account when calculating the employee's tax code for the following year of assessment. By reducing the code in the following year the necessary tax is collected, albeit a year late and most employees do not object to such a system. Certain benefits in kind are caught by the PAYE system. These are assets which are given to the employee and which can be immediately 'traded' to provide the employee with cash.

Generally, it is the responsibility of the employer to deduct the correct amount of tax and account for it to the Inland Revenue. If the incorrect amount of tax has been deducted and the employer fails to account for the tax, the Inland Revenue cannot assess the employee unless certain specified circumstances are present eg collusion by the employee with the employer. Late payment by the employer will result in interest and penalties being payable.

Although the PAYE system is said to reduce the cost of collection of tax, it effectively shifts the burden from the government to the employer.

Schedule E – The Charge to Tax

Tax is charged under Schedule E in respect of emoluments from any office or employment.

There is no statutory definition of office. However, the case law would indicate that an office is a post which goes on without regard to the identity of the holder. Offices do not need to be permanent nor must they have a prolonged existence but, if vacated, an office – as it has been defined – would require a successor for as long as it continued.

A contract of employment will exist where there is the relationship of a master and servant, and such contracts are within Schedule E. A contract *of* service must be distinguished from a contract *for* services; the former is taxable under Schedule E, the latter under Schedule D. It appears to be possible that a person may be taxed under Schedule D notwithstanding that she holds a number of short-term appointments that would otherwise be taxable under Schedule E.

Emoluments include all salaries, fees, wages, perquisites and profits. The definition is wide enough to include benefits in kind. However, a benefit will only be taxable if it is convertible into money or money's worth, otherwise it must be taxable under the benefits in kind legislation.

To be assessable to tax, the payment received by an employee must be directly because that person has acted as an employee and not some other reason. The case law shows an increasing tendency on the part of the judiciary to hold that any payment received by an employee is a direct result of the employment.

The legislation refers to 'emoluments therefrom'. It has been argued in a number of cases that even though a payment was an emolument, it was not from the employment. This might be seen as a self-defeating argument. The word emolument means a payment for being an employee, so once it is accepted that a payment is an emolument it should be taxable. However, the House of Lords appears to have accepted the argument where the word 'emoluments' has taken on a different technical meaning in law from that used in everyday speech.

A payment for future services will be taxable, whereas a payment made as an inducement to give something up will not be. Thus, a payment made to compensate the taxpayer for a loss will escape tax. Again, there is an increasing tendency for the judiciary to find that payments are made for future services rather than as an inducement or as compensation.

Where a sum is received in consideration for a variation to the contract of employment, such sums are more often than not treated as payments for future services rather than compensation for the right given up as a consequence to the variation.

A payment from a third party can be an emolument. Hence, tips are taxable because they are payments in return for the services being provided. Where a person's contract entitles them to payments which could have been made in a voluntarily manner, such payments will be taxable because of the contractual right to them.

Payments made under restrictive covenants are treated as an emolument and are deductible by the person making the payment.

Where there is a contractual right to a termination payment, such payments will be taxable as emoluments. Where a payment is made in lieu of notice such payments will not be taxable as damages for breach of contract. *Ex gratia* payments are not taxable on general principles. However s 148 ICTA 1988 taxes termination payments which would otherwise escape tax, but provides for the first £30,000 to be tax free. Employees are taxed in the year during which the emoluments are received. There are complex rules which determine when a payment is received. When more than one date applies the earliest date is taken. To avoid payments escaping tax because of the source doctrine, payments that are received when the employment is not held are related forwards or backwards to the time when the employment commences or ceases.

Tax charged under Schedule E is usually deducted under the PAYE system. Unless benefits in kind can be readily converted into cash, they are not included in the PAYE system. It is the employer's responsibility to deduct the tax.

Chapter 11

Schedule E – Benefits in Kind and Expenses

In the previous chapter, we saw that the courts had difficulty charging benefits in kind if they could not be converted into money or money's worth. Consequently, a whole raft of provisions have been enacted in order to charge benefits in kind to tax. These provisions have been added piecemeal over the years as different anomalies where found and corrected. This chapter looks at the most commonly encountered benefits in kind.

An unusual feature of the legislation is that it distinguishes between those who earn less than £8,500 a year and those who earn more. It also draws a distinction between directors who work full time for a company and those who do not. The origins of this feature are historical.

Another point to note is that, as far as the charging provisions are concerned, many of them apply to benefits which are provided 'by reason of' a person's employment. This phrase is far wider than the 'emoluments therefrom' test and is more akin to the 'source of the payment' test which was applied in *Hamblett v Godfrey* (see Chapter 10). A further point to note is that some of the benefit in kind provisions apply when the benefit is 'not otherwise chargeable to tax'. A benefit is otherwise chargeable if, under the general law, it is convertible into money or money's worth. However, this factor is often ignored and notwithstanding that a benefit may be convertible, the specific statutory charging provision is applied.

11.1 Benefits in kind – introduction

Certain benefits are assessable on all employees regardless of the level of remuneration.

Section 141 ICTA 1988 provides that where a non-cash voucher is provided to an employee by reason of his employment, the employee is treated as having received, in the year of assessment in which the voucher is received, an emolument of an amount equal to the expense incurred by the person at whose cost the voucher and any money, goods or services for which it is capable of being exchanged are provided and any money, goods or services obtained by the employee or other person in exchange for the voucher are to be disregarded.

11.2 Benefits applicable to all employees

11.2.1 Non-cash vouchers (s 141 ICTA 1988)

The expense is deemed to be incurred by the employer, in the case of a cheque voucher, when it is handed over by the employee in exchange for money, goods or services and, in the case of any other non-cash voucher, at the time that the expense is incurred. Any expense incurred by the employer in providing the voucher is treated as reduced by any amount which is made good by the employee to the employer.

By charging the cost to the employer the symmetry of the tax system is preserved. The employer will be entitled to a deduction for the cost incurred (if the employee were taxable at a greater amount than the cost, there would be a mismatch between the deduction and the taxable amount).

The charging section is excluded (s 141(6) ICTA 1988) where the employer is a passenger transport undertaking which provides an employee or employee's relation with a transport voucher (ie a ticket, pass or other document intended to allow travel on passenger transport services) and passenger transport services are provided either by:

- the employee's employer;

- a subsidiary of her employer;

- a body corporate of which her employer is a subsidiary; or

- another passenger transport undertaking.

A non-cash voucher which is given to an employee to obtain the use of a car parking space at or near his place of work is also excluded from the section (s 141(6A) ICTA 1988).

11.2.2   Credit tokens (s 142 ICTA 1988)

One of the shortcomings of the voucher legislation described in para 11.2.1 was that, to apply, the voucher had to be exchanged for goods or services. As a consequence, s 142 ICTA 1988 was introduced. This provides that, where a credit token is provided for an employee by reason of her employment, the employee should be treated as having received an emolument every time she uses the credit token to obtain money, goods or services from her employment of any amount equal to the expense incurred by the person at whose cost the money, goods or services are provided. Further, any expense incurred by that person in or in connection with the provision of the credit token is also included. The value of any money, goods or services which are obtained by the employee by the use of the credit token are disregarded.

Again, to the extent that the employee reimburses the employer any amount on which the employee is chargeable by reason of the employer incurring the expense, the charge on the employee will be reduced accordingly.

Where a cash voucher is provided for an employee by reason of his employment, the employee is treated as having received, at the time when he receives the voucher, an emolument of his employment equal to the sum of money for which the voucher is capable of being exchanged. Such vouchers are chargeable to tax under the PAYE system as having a monetary value at the time they are given. Where such a voucher is handed over, the employer does not account for tax and, unless the employee reimburses the employer before the expiry of a period of 30 days, the employer will be treated as having made a payment to the employee of an amount equal to the tax overdue.

Where living accommodation is provided for an employee or for any member of the employee's family and where that accommodation is not otherwise chargeable to tax, the employee is treated as having received an amount equal to the value (to her) of the accommodation, less so much as is properly attributable to that provision of any sum made good by her to those at whose cost the accommodation is provided. The value of the accommodation to the employee is the rent which would have been payable had the premises been let to the employee at an annual rent equal to the annual value. The annual value is to be ascertained under s 837 ICTA 1988. This provides that the annual value of land is to be taken as the rent which might reasonably be expected to be obtained on a letting from year to year if the tenant undertook to pay the usual tenant's rates and taxes, and if the landlord undertook to bear the cost of any repairs, insurance, and any other expenses, if any, necessary for maintaining the property which is the subject of the valuation in a state to command that rent. However, where the person providing the accommodation pays a rent which is higher than the annual value as ascertained under s 837 ICTA 1988, the value of the accommodation to the employee is to be taken as an amount equal to the rent payable by the employer. There are five exceptions to the charge under s 145 ICTA 1988. These are where:

- the accommodation is necessary for the proper performance of the employee's duties (s 145(4)(a) ICTA 1988);

- the accommodation is provided for the better performance of the duties and the employment is of a kind in which it is customary for employers to provide living accommodation for employees (s 145(4)(b) ICTA 1988);

- there is a special threat to the employee's security, special security arrangements are in force and the employee

11.2.3   Cash vouchers taxable under PAYE (s 143 ICTA 1988)

11.2.4   Living accommodation provided for an employee (s 145 ICTA 1988) resides in the accommodation as part of those arrangements (s 145(4)(c) ICTA 1988);

- the employer is an individual and it can be shown that she makes the provision in the normal course of her domestic, family or personal relationships (s145(7)(a) ICTA 1988); or

- the employee is employed by a local authority and the accommodation is provided by the local authority on the usual terms for local authority tenants (s 145(7)(b) ICTA 1988).

11.2.5 Additional charge in respect of certain living accommodation (s 146 ICTA 1988)

Section 146 ICTA 1988 applies where:

- an employee is provided with living accommodation;

- that accommodation is treated as an emolument by virtue of s 145 ICTA 1988 or would be treated as an emolument if amounts made good by the employee are disregarded; and

- the cost of providing the accommodation exceeds £75,000.

If s 146 ICTA 1988 applies, an additional tax charge is charged on the employee. This charge is calculated by multiplying the cost to the employer of the property over £75,000 by the 'official rate of interest'. The official rate of interest is that which is charged on beneficial loans (see para 11.3.11). Thus, if a company buys a property for £150,000 for the managing director to live in, the managing director will be charged on an emolument of:

- the annual value of the property; plus

- (£150,000 minus £75,000) times the official rate of interest.

Where the employer bought the property more than six years before it was occupied by the employee, the amount of the emolument is calculated by reference to the market value of the property at the time it is occupied, not the cost to the employer. Note, to prevent avoidance, it is provided that, where the property has been owned by someone connected with the employer in the period of six years prior to the occupation by the employee, the market value is substituted. This prevents, for example, a group of companies moving the property around at an artificial low value in order to prevent the £75,000 limit being exceeded.

11.2.6 Miscellaneous benefits assessable on all employees

There are various other benefits or payments which may be received by an employee and which are specifically made chargeable to tax. These are:

- sick pay;

- payments under job release schemes;

- maternity pay;

- statutory sick pay;

- statutory maternity pay; and

- income support.

Section 167 ICTA 1988 provides for specific statutory provisions to apply to certain benefits provided to:

11.3   **Employees earning £8,500 or more and directors**

- directors of a company; and

- employees who earn more than £8,500 a year.

Section 168 (8) ICTA 1988 defines a director as:

11.3.1   Directors

- a member of the board of directors;

- a single person who manages the affairs of a company where there is no board of directors; and

- members who manage the affairs of a company where there is not board of directors.

Where any of the people mentioned in the three categories above act in accordance with the directions or instructions of another person, that other person is deemed to be a director unless that person gives directions or instructions in a professional capacity, eg a solicitor or an accountant.

Where a person falls into one of the above three categories that person will not be treated as a director if they are a 'full-time working director'; that is a director who is required to devote substantially the whole of her time to the service of the company in a managerial or technical capacity (s 168 (10) ICTA 1988) and that person does not have a material interest in the company. A person has a material interest if she is the beneficial owner of, or able, directly or through the medium of other companies or by any other indirect means to control more than 5% of the ordinary share capital of the company. Where the company is a close company the 5% test is applied to the assets that would be available to participators in the event that the company was wound up. For the purposes of ascertaining the 5% holding the interest of associates is taken into account.

It should be noted that, even if a person does not qualify as a director because of the above tests, that person will still be caught by the legislation if their emoluments are more than £8,500 per year.

11.3.2	How is the £8,500 a year calculated?	To determine whether a person earns more than £8,500 a year, the legislation directs that any benefits received by the person in question should be taken into account and any deduction for expenses ignored (s 167(2) ICTA 1988).
11.3.3	Expenses (s 153 ICTA 1988)	The treatment of expenses is dealt with in more detail later on in this chapter. For current purposes, however, s 153 ICTA 1988 provides that where an employee receives amounts which are paid to him in respect of expenses, those amounts are to be treated as emoluments and accordingly charged to tax under Schedule E. Where the expenses satisfy the relevant conditions, a deduction can be made (see later on in this chapter). Sums paid in respect of expenses also include the case whereby an employee is given an expense account and the amounts are paid out by the employee rather than being reimbursed by the employer.
11.3.4	General charging provision and the cash equivalent (ss 154 and 156 ICTA 1988)	The general charging provision for benefits in kind received by directors and persons earning more than £8,500 per year is s 154 ICTA 1988. This provides that where, in any year, a person is employed and by reason of that employment he, or members of his family or household, are provided with any benefit to which s 154 ICTA 1988 applies and the cost of providing the benefit is not chargeable to tax as the employee's income (apart from s 154 ICTA 1988), there is to be treated as an emolument as the employment an amount equal to whatever is the cash equivalent of the benefit. There are three points to note. First, a charge arises if a benefit is provided to the employee '... or for others being members of his family or his household'. It would appear, therefore, that if the employee has 'a bit on the side', the benefit provided by the employee's employer to that person would not be a benefit because that person would not be a member of the employee's family or household. Second, the section applies where the 'cost of providing the benefit' is not chargeable to tax. The cost of providing the benefit is dealt with in s 156 ICTA 1988 (see below). If some other method of ascertaining the benefit would otherwise apply, eg the second-hand value, then that method is excluded and s 154 ICTA 1988 applies. Third, the cost of the benefit is defined by s 156 ICTA 1988. This is an amount equal to the cost of the benefit less so much (if any) as is made good by the employee to those providing the benefit. This is further defined as the amount of any expense incurred in, or in connection with, the provision of the benefit including a proper proportion of any expense relating partly to the benefit and partly to other matters. In the case of *Pepper v Hart* (1992) it was held by the House of Lords that the cost was the marginal cost and not the average cost. The marginal cost is the

additional cost which has to be incurred by an employer in providing the benefit to the employee. The average cost is the total cost in providing the benefit divided by the number of people receiving it.

The difference is exemplified by the case of *Pepper v Hart* (1992) in which the taxpayer was a master at Malvern College. His son was educated at the school and the fee that was charged was substantially less than that charged to other fee-paying children. The Inland Revenue sought to charge the taxpayer to tax on an amount equal to the average cost of providing schooling to all the boys in the school. The taxpayer argued that the cost should be the marginal cost, ie the additional cost of taking on an extra boy. It was argued for the taxpayer that the overhead expenses had already been incurred, that the marginal cost was therefore very small and that as the amount of the fee paid by the master covered the marginal cost, it was therefore argued that no further tax was payable. It was held by the House of Lords that it was indeed the marginal cost which needed to be taken into account.

Pepper v Hart is famous not only for deciding the method of ascertaining the value of the benefit, but also for the House of Lords' decision that references to *Hansard* could be made in interpreting legislation (see Chapter 3).

The benefits to which s 154 ICTA 1988 applies are accommodation (other than living accommodation), entertainment, domestic or other services, and other benefits and facilities of whatsoever nature (whether or not similar to any of those mentioned above). Certain benefits are excluded because they are specifically charged to tax elsewhere.

Under s156 ICTA 1988, where an asset is put at the disposal of an employee or a member of the employee's family or household, the employee is charged to tax on 20% of the asset's market value at the time when it was first applied in the provision of the benefit. However, where the person providing the benefit pays a rent or hire charge for the asset which is greater than 20% of the market value, the higher amount is charged. If the asset is then transferred to the employee, there will be a charge under s 156(4) ICTA 1988. The charge to tax is the greater of either the market value of the asset at that time or the original market value of the asset less amounts which have been charged to tax during the period of use by the employee prior to the transfer ownership.

Section 155 ICTA 1988 excludes from the general charge certain benefits. These include any benefit which consists in the provision for the employee, in the premises occupied by the employer or others providing it, of accommodation,

11.3.5   Exclusions from the general charge (s 155 ICTA 1988)

supplies or services used by the employee solely in performing the duties of his employment. This exclusion prevents any charge arising on the provision of a desk, a chair, or ballpoint pens. Similarly, an employee would not be charged if the employee stipulated for the provision of a south facing office.

Other benefits which are specifically excluded are:

- a car parking space at or near the employee's place of work (s 155(1A) ICTA 1988);

- the provision of any pension, annuity, lump sum, gratuity or other like benefit to be given on the employee's death or retirement (s 155(4) ICTA 1988);

- the provision by the employee's employer of meals in any canteen in which meals are provided for the staff generally (s 155(5) ICTA 1988);

- the provision of medical treatment outside the UK when the need for the treatment arises while the employee is outside the UK for the purpose of performing the duties of his employment (s 155(6) ICTA 1988); and

- the provision of insurance for the employer against the cost of treatment whilst outside the UK (s 155(7) ICTA 1988).

11.3.6   Care for children
(s 155A ICTA 1988)

Where an employer provides child care, the provision will not be a benefit in kind under s 155A ICTA 1988 (inserted by the Finance Act 1990). A number of conditions need to be met. First, the child must be one for whom the employee has parental responsibility, or is resident with the employee, or is a child which the employee maintains at the employee's expense. Second, the care must be provided in premises which are not domestic premises. Finally, all the necessary registration requirements must have been met.

11.3.7   Cars available for
private use (s 157 ICTA
1988)

Under s 157 ICTA 1988, where a car is made available to an employee or to a member of the employee's family and it is made available for private use, the cash equivalent of the car is chargeable to tax. The cash equivalent is calculated in accordance with Sch 6 ICTA 1988 and is 35% of the list price of the car as regards the year of assessment in question. The price of the car is calculated in accordance with the rules in ss 168 A–G ICTA 1988. The rules are complex but in general the price is the list price, if the car has one, or the notional price, if it does not. If accessories are fitted to the car which are not included in the list price, the price of these accessories is added to the list price. Where the car is a classic car, ie the age of the car is 15 years or more, and the market value of the car is more than £15,000, the price of the car is the market value of car for the year. Where the value of any car is more than £80,000, the price of the car is deemed to be £80,000 and not the price as found according to the various sections noted above. Where the car is used for business mileage and the business use exceeds more than 18,000 miles in any year, the assessable benefit is reduced by two-thirds. Where the business mileage exceeds 2,500 miles in any year, the assessable benefit is reduced by one-third.

Where fuel is provided to an employee who is also provided with a car, the benefit of the fuel is determined in accordance with a table depending upon the cylinder capacity of the car and the nature of the engine. In such cases a lump sum is assessable on the employee. Where the employee is required to make good to the person providing the fuel, the whole of the expense incurred by him or the fuel is only made available for business travel then the assessable amount is nil.	11.3.8 Car fuel (s 158 ICTA 1988)
Where the employee is provided with a pool car no liability to tax will be incurred. A pool car is defined as one which is made available and used by more than one employee, of which any private use of the car is incidental to the business use and which is not normally kept overnight at, or in the vicinity of, the employee's home.	11.3.9 Pooled cars (s 159 ICTA 1988)
A flat rate benefit of £200 is assessed on an employee to whom is made available a mobile telephone. Where the employee makes good the cost or the phone is used only for business purposes the charge is nil. Where the phone is only made available for a proportion of the year the charge is reduced on a pro rata basis.	11.3.10 Mobile telephones (s 159 A ICTA 1988)
Section 160 ICTA 1988 provides that, where a loan is made to an employee and either no interest is paid on the loan or the amount of the interest paid is less than interest at the official rate, the cash equivalent of the loan, which is that foregone by the employer, is treated as an emolument of the employee. Under s 161 ICTA 1988 no tax is to be charged under s 160 ICTA 1988 if the amount outstanding on the loan during the year does not exceed £5,000. Further, where the employee uses the cheap loan for a qualifying purpose, ie for purchasing a residence, the loan is chargeable to tax under s 160 ICTA 1988, but the employee is deemed to have paid tax at the official rate on so much of the loan as qualifies for interest relief and the employee is given relief accordingly. Where the loan provided by the employer is at a fixed rate and the interest rate subsequently moves, no charge is made on the difference between the two rates if the charge would arise only because	11.3.11 Beneficial loan arrangements (s 160 ICTA 1988)

of an increase in the official rate since the year in which the loan was made.

11.3.12	Employee shareholders (s 162 ICTA 1988)	Section 162 ICTA 1988 provides that, where an employee acquires shares at an undervalue in a company by virtue of being an employee, the beneficial loan arrangements in s 160 ICTA 1988 will apply as if employee had the benefit of a loan equal to so much of the market value of the shares as has not been charged for tax. Section 162 ICTA 1988 has limited application as the benefit of shares is generally charged to tax under other sections of the legislation.
11.3.13	Expenses connected with living accommodation (s 163 ICTA 1988)	It will be noted that under s 145 ICTA 1988 the charge to tax does not cover the cost of heating and lighting etc. However, where the person receiving the benefit is a director or higher paid employee the provision of such services would be covered by the general charge as being a benefit provided to the employee by reason of that person's employment. Where, under s 145 ICTA 1988, the employee is one who is in one of the three types of 'representative occupation' the amount of the charge is limited to 10% of the amount of the emoluments of the employment. The services are heating, lighting, cleaning, repairs to the premises, maintenance or declaration and the provision of furniture.
11.3.14	Scholarships (s 165 ICTA 1988)	Under s 331 ICTA 1988 scholarship income is exempt from tax. However, where the child of a director or an employee earning more than £8,500 a year receives a scholarship, that scholarship will be taxable on the director or employee unless not more than 25% of scholarships awarded by the fund are to children of employees, regardless of whether those employees earn more than £8,500 or are directors. Further, the award must not be made by reason of the child's parents being employed; it must be made on criteria which are satisfied by the child as an applicant for the scholarship.
11.4	**Expenses – introduction**	Unlike those expenses deductible under Schedule D Cases I and II, which must be wholly and exclusively incurred, Schedule E has an extra component: the expenses must also be necessarily incurred. The way this has been interpreted by the courts has meant that there are very few deductible expenses. Why should there be such a major distinction between these who are self employed and those who are employees?
11.5	**The expenses**	The authority to deduct expenses incurred while in an office or employment is given by s 198(1) ICTA 1988.

There are three types of expense:

- travelling in performance of the duties;

- keeping and maintaining a horse; and

- other expenses wholly, exclusive and necessarily incurred in the performance of the duties.

All three types of expenditure require that they be necessarily incurred. It is this aspect which prevents most types of expense from being deductible. In the case of *Ricketts v Colquhoun* (1925) a barrister who practised from chambers in London was appointed part-time recorder in Portsmouth. The post of recorder was an office and hence assessable under Schedule E. He claimed to deduct his travelling expenses between London and Portsmouth. The deduction was refused. The case came before the House of Lords in which it was stated that the words of s 198 ICTA 1988 are not personal to the individual taxpayer but objective. In other words, one does not look to whether the particular employee was obliged to incur the expense but whether the actual office or employment obliged the office holder or employee to incur the expense. 'The test is not whether the employer imposes the expense but primarily whether the duties do, in the sense that, irrespective of what the employer may prescribe, the duties cannot be performed without the particular outlay.'

In the case of *Brown v Bullock* (1961) a bank manager was required by his employer to join a London club, the purpose being to entertain and thereby to attract clients. He claimed to deduct the club subscriptions. Although the payment of the subscription was required by the employer, it was held that the payment was not necessary. Not every bank manager would be obliged to incur the expense.

In the case of *Elderkin v Hindmarsh* (1988), which concerned the meaning of the words 'in the performance of', the taxpayer inspected the laying of pipes. He was sent all over the country to various sites. The Inland Revenue accepted that the expenses were wholly, exclusively and necessarily incurred but they argued that the expenses were not incurred in the performance of the duties. The employee was not inspecting pipes whilst sleeping in a hotel room.

There is obviously a tension between accepting that the practicalities of employment mean that one employee has to travel because it would be costly and inconvenient and maybe even impossible to employ someone at each site, and applying the test that the office, and not the wishes of the employer or

11.6   Necessarily obliged to incur and defray

the personnel circumstances of the employer, dictates what is necessary.

11.7	**The three types of expense**	There are three types of expense. One of them is now effectively obsolete, although it is still useful for the purposes of comparison.

11.7.1   Travelling

Travelling expenses are allowable if incurred 'in the performance of the duties'. The duties must therefore be performed while travelling, or the travelling must be an inherent part of the job. In the case *Ricketts v Colquhoun*, Lord Blanesborough held that the barrister was not entitled to deduct his expenditure.

The barrister resided in London out of his own choice. Someone appointed recorder and living in Portsmouth would not have had to incur the expense. Therefore, it was not the office which imposed the expense, but the personal circumstances of the taxpayer. In *Ricketts v Colquhoun* not only was it not necessary for the taxpayer to incur the expense, he was not travelling 'in the performance' of the duties but rather in order to perform the duties.

Ricketts v Colquhoun can be compared with the case of *Pook v Owen* (1969) in which a general hospital practitioner, having been phoned at home and having assumed responsibility for the patient, travelled to the hospital. He sought to deduct the cost of travelling between his home and the hospital. It was held that he could. The reason for this was that the doctor took responsibility for the patient at home.

However, it is submitted that it does not follow that travelling was *necessarily* in the performance of the duties. Had he lived next to the hospital the expense need not have been incurred. It could therefore be argued that the expense was not brought about by the office but by the personal choice of the taxpayer. Indeed, this was the decision at first instance where Stamp J said that he was '... very sorry for the taxpayer but the words of the statue are ... very rigid'. In the Court of Appeal, Diplock LJ held that the doctor's position was 'undistinguishable from that of the Recorder of Portsmouth so far as the *ratio decidendi* is concerned'. Edmund Davies LJ said: 'Can it be said that the taxpayer's travelling expenses from Fishguard [home] to Haverford West [hospital] were such as he was "necessarily obliged to incur and defray" out of the emoluments of the office?' He concluded that the taxpayer would be able to 'stroll up the hill to the hospital by the expenditure of nothing except a little shoe leather'.

Only Lord Denning MR in the Court of Appeal found that the expenditure was necessary. The House of Lords found 3:2 in favour of the taxpayer. The basis for the decision was that the taxpayer had two places of work and it was therefore necessary to travel between them. Lord Donovan thought that this distinction was erroneous, stating that there are many taxpayers who are required to obey a summons to work to cope with an emergency. He saw no reason why they should not be allowed on that basis to claim a deduction for travelling expenses.

This may be what Vinelott J was doing when he said in *Elderkin v Hindmarsh* that it would be impossible to find an employee at each site; one must therefore disregard the theoretical possibility and have regard to the realities of the situation.

In *Taylor v Provan* a Canadian was employed by an English brewery company because of his special skills in merging brewery companies. He was not paid by the UK company but was paid his expenses. He was, however, made a director of the company. In the event this was probably the tragic flaw. As explained in the previous chapter, s 153 ICTA 1988 makes expenses paid to a director an emolument of the office. Without the directorship he would have been either an employee, in which case the expenses would not have been assessable, or the expense payment would have been a receipt of his trade or profession against which the expenses would have been deductible. However, as a director he was assessed to tax on the expenses as an emolument and he then sought to deduct the expenses under what is now s 198 ICTA 1988. It was held 3:2 by the House of Lords that the expenses were deductible. The reason being that the taxpayer was such a specialist in his field that it was impossible for the company to get the work done by anybody else. The post he filled was created specially for him and no one else could fill it. It was therefore necessary that the person filling the post should incur the expense.

There appears to be some conflict here between *Taylor v Provan* and *Edwards v Clinch*. If Mr Taylor was so unique, it seems that the post was not an office or employment, in which case there were no emoluments under Schedule E, but instead he would be chargeable under Schedule D Case II, for which travelling would have been a deductible expense. However, because he was a director, the payments become emoluments, even though not every director would have been obliged to incur these expenses and it is therefore difficult to see why they were deductible. A distinction must be made between the duties as a director, for which he was paid nothing and did nothing, and the duties of the post for which he was appointed and for which he was unique. The expenses were paid in this latter capacity, in which case they were Schedule D expenses not Schedule E. The House of Lords held that the mere fact that he was a director brought the expenses within the Schedule E charge and thus confused the issue.

Why then were the expenses deductible? Lord Wilberforce who was in the majority in *Pook v Owen* dissented in *Taylor v Provan* saying:

> 'the question then, in this case, is whether the element of "necessity" in the objective sense existed. Necessity from the personal circumstances of the taxpayer is not enough ... The only necessity which is relevant is an objective necessity arising from the nature of the job itself to travel in the performance of its duties.'

It is therefore necessary to determine the point at which the duties start. If they start before the travelling commenced then the taxpayer will be travelling in the performance of those duties.

11.8	**Keeping and maintaining a horse**	When the Taxes Acts were first introduced certain public officials were obliged to keep horses. The legislation was never altered and so such expenses are still deductible. It is to be presumed that the horse was kept at home not at work. Why then should the expense have been necessarily incurred? When the income tax was first introduced there would have been very few people who would have been within its ambit. A deduction for such expenses would not have reduced the revenue generated to any great extent. Nowadays, the majority of taxpayers are within the Schedule E charge. Consequently, a wholesale allowance of expenses would reduce revenues.

11.9	**Other expenses**	The Schedule E taxpayer may deduct other expenses which are incurred:

- wholly and exclusively;

- necessarily; and

- in the performance of the duties.

11.9.1	Wholly and exclusively	This test is the same as for Schedule D expenditure, so, where there is an element of duality the expense will be disallowed. For example, if the employee seeks to deduct the cost of line rental for her telephone, it will be disallowable because the phone will be available for private use. Similarly, it will be necessary to examine the subconscious as well as the conscious motives of the taxpayer (see *Malilieu v Drummond*).

Again the word necessarily is used. In *Ricketts v Colquhoun* Lord Blanesburgh said of the section '... some of it is repeated apparently to heighten its effect'.

In the case of *Smith v Abbott*, there was a finding of fact that the employer considered it necessary for journalists to read other newspapers in order for them to get ideas for their own jobs. The House of Lords did not upset this finding, although from the cases discussed earlier it would appear to be wrong in law in that it is not what the employer requires but what the actual office ie the job of journalist requires. However, the House of Lords managed to find against the taxpayers on other grounds (see below).

In the same way that travelling expenses are not deductible, if the taxpayer is not actually performing the duties while travelling, ie he is on the way to or from work, a distinction is drawn between expenditure incurred to better enable an employee to perform a task, which is not deductible, and expenditure incurred whilst actually doing a task which is deductible. In the case of *Elderkin v Hindmarsh* the allowance given to the consulting engineer was held not to be deductible because the expenditure on overnight stays was not in the performance of the duties. He was not performing his duties whilst sleeping in a hotel bed.

In the case of *Smith v Abbott* the expenditure incurred by the journalists was not deductible because reading papers only prepared them to do their job; they were not actually preparing an edition of the paper. In the Court of Appeal, Nolan LJ said that the ephemeral nature of the information obtained meant that it did not add to the general qualifications of the journalists, but instead equipped them to prepare the next edition of the paper. In which case he was satisfied that it was expended in the performance of the duties. However, the House of Lords held otherwise by 4:1.

Notwithstanding the stringent tests to be applied to Schedule E expenses, some people do get deductions. Further, certain trade unions have negotiated flat-rate deductions for their members. Therefore, a person in a manual trade may get a deduction of £30 for tools. This concessionary treatment makes the system easier to administer but it prejudices those who have to pay out during the course of the trade. And why should the flat rate deduction be available to those who don't incur the expense?

11.11   **Schedule D and**
              Schedule E

It should further be noted that under Schedule D expenses have to be wholly and exclusively laid out for the purpose of the trade. Expenditure of the most frivolous nature may be for the purpose of the trade. Under Schedule E expenditure has to be wholly and exclusively and necessarily expended in the performance of the duties; as has been seen this is an altogether more stringent test and the cost of staying alive might not be deductible.

Schedule E – Benefits in Kind and Expenses

Benefits in kind fall into two categories. First, those benefits which are assessable on all employees regardless of the level of remuneration, and second, benefits which are assessable only on those earning more than £8,500 a year or who earn less than £8,500 and are not full-time working directors. Many benefits in kind are assessable because they are provided by reason of a person's employment. This is a wider test than for emoluments which must be received as a reward for services.

Benefits in kind

Benefits applicable to all employees include:

- Non-cash vouchers. These are vouchers which can be exchanged for goods or services. The amount assessable is the cost to the employer less so much as is made good by the employee.

- Credit tokens, including credit cards. The amount assessable is the cost to the person providing the credit token this will include any annual fee.

- Cash vouchers. These are taxable under the PAYE system on the amount for which they can be converted into cash.

- Living accommodation. The amount chargeable to tax is the annual value of the land unless so much made good by the employee. The annual value is the amount which the property would fetch if let on the open market. There are exceptions to the charge:

    (a) where the accommodation is necessary for the proper performance of the employee's duties;

    (b) where it is customary to provide the accommodation;

    (c) where it is provided for the security of the employee;

    (d) where the accommodation is provided in the normal course of domestic, family or personal relationships; or

    (e) where the accommodation is provided by a local authority on usual terms.

- Living accommodation – an additional charge. Where the cost of the accommodation is greater than £75,000 the additional charge is levied.

- Sick pay, maternity pay, statutory sick pay, and income support are all taxable as benefits.

Certain benefits are only taxable if the employee earns more than £8,500 a year or is a director of the company providing the benefit. A full-time working director is not subject to the rules unless the director earns more than £8,500. The general charging provision provides that where a benefit is provided to an employee or a member of her family, the cost of providing that benefit will be chargeable to tax. Certain benefits are specifically excluded, including accommodation at work, office supplies, car parking spaces, pensions, meals in any canteen in which meals are provided for the staff generally, medical treatment outside the UK and the cost of insurance against medical treatment outside the UK.

Where the employer provides child care, this will not be a benefit, provided that certain conditions are satisfied. Where a car is made available to an employee or a member of the employee's family, the employee is chargeable on the cash equivalent which is generally 35% of the list price. This amount can be reduced if business mileage exceeds 2,500 miles a year and it can be further reduced if business mileage exceeds 18,000 miles a year.

Where fuel is provided this is taxable if the cost is not reimbursed by the employee or it is not specifically for business use. Pool cars are not taxable. Mobile telephones are assessed at a flat rate of £200 a year. Where loans are made at a lower rate of interest, the interest foregone is taxable. There is an exception where the interest would otherwise qualify for relief ie it is to buy a house.

Scholarship income is generally exempt from tax unless the parents of the person receiving the scholarship are employees of the person providing the scholarship. Where such is the case certain criteria need to be satisfied before the scholarship is exempt.

Expenses

Expenses are deductible under Schedule E if they are 'wholly, exclusively and necessarily' incurred in the performance of the duties. This is far more onerous than the test applicable to Schedule D Cases I and II for which expenses need only to be 'wholly and exclusively' incurred.

It is the word necessarily which causes all the problems. The courts have held that in order to be necessarily incurred the expense must be incurred by every holder of the office or employment, ie the expense must be dictated by the nature of the office or employment not by the personal circumstances of the taxpayer.

Travelling expenses are allowable if they are incurred 'in the performance of the duties'. The cases indicate that the expense of travelling from home to work is not deductible because a person is not travelling in the performance of the duties but in order to perform the duties. Where an employee accepts responsibility for some aspect of the work while at home, there is some authority to say that the cost of travelling to work in such cases will be deductible. Further, the expenditure must be necessarily incurred. It would be possible for an employee to live next door to his place of work and as such it is not necessary to incur a great deal of expense in getting to work.

The 'wholly and exclusively' test is same as that for Schedule D Case I and II. Consequently, the duality rule will apply.

Expenses have to be incurred in the performance of the duties not in order to perform them. Thus, a journalist reading newspapers in the morning is merely preparing himself to perform the duties not actually performing them at the time. Similarly, a teacher who attends lectures is preparing to better do the job.

Chapter 12

Schedule A and Schedule D Case VI

When income tax was first introduced, land was considered to be the most important source of income. Income from land was therefore taxed under the first schedule, Schedule A. The charge under Schedule A has varied over the years and was even abolished for a period when land was taxed under Schedule D Case VIII (although the charge was in almost identical terms to the current Schedule A applicable to companies). In 1995 the charge under Schedule A was reformed for individuals with a view to simplication ready for the introduction of self assessment.

As a consequence of the reform, there are now two Schedule As running parallel; each has the same numbering, ie there are two s 15 ICTA 1988. This chapter deals with the new provisions applicable to individuals.

12.1 Income from land – introduction

Before looking at the Schedule A charge, it should be noted that certain items are specifically excluded.

Section 15(1) para 2 (for individuals) ICTA 1988 provides that certain types of income, although being derived from land, are not chargeable under Schedule A. These are:

* yearly interest;

* profits and gains from mines, quarries, markets, tolls, bridges etc which are taxable under Schedule D Case I;

* mineral rents and royalties which are taxed half as income and half as capital; and

* other income such as wayleaves eg the running of electric wires over land using pylons.

12.2 Income excluded from the Schedule A charge

As was noted above, from 6 April 1995 Schedule A changed for individuals. The reason for this is that the old rules were very complex and consequently, if the Inland Revenue were going to ask individuals to calculate their own tax liabilities there needed to be some simplification. The new Schedule A applies for 1995–96. There are transitional rules for 1994–95; these are dealt with in para 12.3.3.

Section 15 ICTA 1988 (as introduced by s 39 FA 1995) provides for tax to be charged on:

12.3 Schedule A – the charge to tax – individuals

'the annual profits or gains arising from any business carried on for the exploitation, as a source of rents or other receipts, of any estate, interest or rights in over any land in the United Kingdom.'

Although the rules for calculating liability under the new Schedule A are very similar to those for Schedule D Case I, they remain two separate Schedules and consequently income arising under Schedule A is not trading income nor is it earned income. Certain reliefs and benefits available to Schedule D taxpayers are, therefore, unavailable ie pension contributions and CGT business reliefs (although an exception is made for furnished holiday lettings).

Prior to the introduction of the new Schedule A, different types of lettings were taxed differently. Rental income was generally taxed under Schedule A; rental income from furnished lettings was taxed under Schedule D Case VI; and rental income from lettings that qualified as furnished holiday lettings were taxable under Schedule D Case VI but treated as if they were taxable under Schedule D Case I. Following the changes, all rental income is taxed under Schedule A. Another point to note is that previously rental income was treated on a property-by-property basis so that expenditure on a property was deductible only from rentals from that property. Now, the rents from all properties are aggregated and the aggregate expenditure deducted.

12.3.1   Schedule A business

Schedule A charges profits arising from any business carried on for the exploitation of land. Profits implies the amount remaining after expenses have been deducted.

Section 15(1) para 1(2) ICTA 1988, provides that any transaction entered into by a person which is entered into for the exploitation of land by the receipt of rents shall be deemed to have been entered into in the course of a business. This prevents a taxpayer arguing that an isolated transaction is not in the course of a business.

12.3.2   Calculation

Section 21 ICTA 1988 provides that tax under Schedule A shall be computed in the same way as profits or gains chargeable to tax under Schedule D Case I. The Schedule D Case I legislation is therefore applied by s 21(3) ICTA 1988 subject to specified exceptions. The income from all the properties is aggregated and any expenses wholly and exclusively incurred can be deducted; for this purpose, it is necessary to look at s 74 ICTA 1988 which will, for example, disallow capital expenditure on improvements. The accounts may be made up on either an earnings basis or a cash basis; however, s 107 ICTA 1988 which treats post-cessation receipts as earned income is disapplied;

otherwise, post-cessation rents would be treated differently from pre-cessation rents. The income is taxed on an accruals basis; for example, if the rent is £365 a year and a lease is granted halfway through the year, the amount accrued at the end of the year will be £183.

Tax is assessed on a current year basis. The Schedule D rules regarding assessing by reference to accounts ending in the year of assessment are disapplied so that tax is assessed on a tax year basis 6 April – 5 April. The tax is due on 1 January in the year of assessment (s 5 ICTA 1988) or 30 days after the issue of the assessment, whichever is the later. From 1996–97 tax will be payable on 31 January following the year of assessment. The person assessable is the person receiving or entitled to the income. Interest is deductible when computing the amount of profit liable to tax if it is wholly and exclusively incurred. It is, therefore, no longer necessary to identify a loan with the particular property which it was used to buy; nor is it necessary for the interest to be incurred on a loan to acquire a property, interest on money borrowed to improve the property will also be allowable.

Under the old rules income was assessed when it was receivable; under the new rules it is taxable when it accrues. Therefore, on a change from the old to the new rules it will be possible for income to be either charged twice or not at all.

12.3.3   The transitional rules

The Inland Revenue will therefore accept two ways of calculating the tax payable:

- calculate the rent without any adjustment; or

- calculate the 1994–95 tax under the old rules; add any income which falls out of charge and any expenditure which is deductible in the 1995–96 assessment; deduct any income which will be taxed in 1995–96 and any non deductible expenditure.

As Schedule A charges profits and gains, if expenditure exceeds income there will be a loss. Where the loss is made by an individual, the rules applicable to Schedule D apply to the Schedule A business.

12.4   Losses

Schedule A tax could be avoided if, instead of leasing the property at a rack rent, that is a rent at market value, the landlord leased the property at a low rent and charged a premium, that is, a capital sum which is consideration for the grant of the lease. Capital gains tax was introduced in 1965, before then a landlord could have, by this method, avoided tax completely. Accordingly, special rules were introduced which

12.5   Anti-avoidance

deem part of the premium to be rent. 'Premium' is defined as including any sum, whether payable to the immediate landlord, a superior landlord or to any person connected with either of them.

There are now two sets of provisions, one applicable to individuals and one applicable to companies. Although couched in different language the substance of both sets of provisions is the same.

| 12.5.1 | Section 34 ICTA 1988 |

Under s 34 ICTA 1988, where a lease is granted for a period not exceeding 50 years ie 50 years or less, part of the premium is to be treated as rent and is taxable under Schedule A. The method employed is to treat 2% of the premium for each complete year of the lease other than the first as a proper premium. Therefore, for a one year lease, all the premium is treated as rent, for a 50 year lease, 2% of the premium is treated as rent.

The amount chargeable to income tax as rent is taxed in the year of receipt; if, however, the premium is payable by instalments, the landlord can pay the tax by instalments over the shorter of the period over which the premium instalments are payable or eight years, but only if the landlord can show that to pay in a lump sum would cause undue hardship. There is no definition of undue hardship. A claim by the landlord must be made before the end of the tax year following the one in which the first instalment of the premium is payable.

12.5.2 Avoiding s 34 ICTA 1988

There are a number of provisions designed to prevent the avoidance of s 34 ICTA 1988. The five principal situations are

- disguising the length of the lease;

- requiring expenditure instead of a premium;

- delaying the premium;

- schemes involving lease assignments; and

- sale with a right to reconveyance.

12.5.3 Disguising the length of the lease

The Act seeks to tax the landlord by reference to the real length of the lease granted. Therefore, if there are provisions in a long lease which make it likely that it will terminate before the full term, it will be treated as a lease for the shorter period. Conversely, if the lease is likely to exceed the stated term it is the longer period which is to be taken into account.

12.5.4 Requiring expenditure instead of a premium

If the landlord requires the tenant to effect improvements to the property (not repairs), the amount by which the landlord's reversion at the beginning of the lease with the provision for improvements exceeds the value without the provision for improvements is treated as a premium to which s 34 ICTA 1988 applies. The provision does not apply in three circumstances:

- if the tenant is required to make improvements to a property other than the one that is let;

- if the obligation to make improvements is not imposed by the terms of the lease; or

- if the expenditure had been incurred by the landlord it would have been a deductible expense (this is another way of saying the works must be improvements not repairs).

Where either a premium is paid during the currency of the lease or the tenant has to pay a sum for the variation (eg reduction in the rent) or waiver of a term, the amount of the premium is taxed in the year it is received by reference to the unexpired term of the lease. If the tenant pays a sum to surrender a lease, that sum is taxed as a premium for a lease which ran from the date of grant to the date of surrender.

12.5.5   Delaying the premium

The anti-avoidance provisions discussed above only apply if a lease is granted not if it is assigned. It was therefore possible for the landlord to grant a lease to his spouse for no, or nominal, consideration and then for the spouse to assign the lease to the intended tenant for a premium. Section 35 ICTA 1988 therefore charges an associate to tax by reference to the amount the landlord could have charged to the extent that the associate makes a profit. The amount charged is charged under Schedule D Case VI; however, s 34 ICTA 1988 still applies.

12.5.6   Schemes involving lease assignments

Where land is sold with a right to reconveyance at a price below that for which it was sold, the difference in price is treated as a premium on a lease for a period equal to the period between the sale and reconveyance. It is taxable under Schedule D Case VI. Where land is sold with a right to have it leased back a similar provision applies. This taxes the vendor on the difference between the price paid by the purchaser and the aggregate of any premium payable to the purchaser on the leaseback and the value of the purchaser's reversion. Again, the amount is taxed under Schedule D Case VI. In both cases the amount of the premium chargeable to tax is discounted under s 34 ICTA 1988.

12.5.7   Sale with a right to reconveyance

Where a trader pays a premium on the *grant* of a lease of 50 years or less, the trader is allowed a deduction for so much of the premium is taxed under Schedule A in the hands of the landlord. The deduction is spread over the unexpired term of the lease.

12.5.8   Relief for traders

Where a trader pays a premium on the *assignment* of a lease, he can get a deduction only to the extent that the assignor was taxable under Schedule A on any premium received.

12.6   Furnished lettings

For individuals, the income from furnished lettings is now taxed under Schedule A.

Capital allowances are given on furniture and fittings on either:

- a renewals basis; in which case no allowance is given on the initial purchase, but a full allowance is given in the year the item is replaced; or

- a depreciation basis; in which case the landlord is allowed a flat rate deduction of 10% of the gross rental income (less water rates).

12.7   Furnished holiday lettings

For individuals, furnished holiday lets are assessable under Schedule A but treated for many purposes as if they are assessable under Schedule D Case I.

A letting is a furnished holiday letting provided the following criteria are satisfied:

- the property must be available for letting to the public on a commercial basis;

- the property must be furnished;

- it must be available for letting for 140 days in the tax year;

- it must be let for at least 70 days in the tax year; and

- it must not normally be let in any period of seven months, including the 70 day period to one person for more than 31 days.

Where the landlord owns a number of properties and, because of the period for which the properties are let, some qualify and some do not, the landlord can elect to average the number of days. Thus, if one is let for 75 days and another is let for 65 days both can be treated as having been let for the minimum period of 70 days. The consequence of a property being a furnished holiday let is that the income is treated as earned income and certain CGT reliefs apply eg retirement relief.

12.8   Rent a room

Under s 59 F (No 2) A 1992, an individual who rents out a room in their only or main home may receive up to £3,250 of rent tax-free. The room must be furnished. Where the rent exceeds £3,250 the taxpayer may either pay tax in the normal way on income minus expenses or on the excess of receipts above £3,250. This latter, 'alternative method' is designed for a taxpayer where receipts exceed £3,250 by a relatively small amount. Where two or more people in one house each separately rent out a room then the £3,250 limit is halved.

When income was taxed at a higher rate than capital gains there was a strong incentive for taxpayers to 'convert' income into capital. Section 776 ICTA 1988 was introduced to prevent such schemes.

12.9   Section 776 ICTA 1988

Section 776 ICTA 1988 charges a gain made on the sale of land to income tax under Schedule D Case VI. The amount of the gain is so much as is just and reasonable. The section applies where a gain of a capital nature is obtained from the disposal of land; this may include the disposal of shares in a land owning company.

The section does not apply to normal disposals by individuals on an arm's length basis. The critical test is whether the land was acquired with the sole or main object of realising a gain from the land or the land is developed with the intention of realising a gain from its disposal. The motive of the taxpayer is, therefore, all important.

Schedule D Case VI is the residual case of Schedule D. Although there is a general charging provision (s 18 ICTA 1988), many items not otherwise chargeable to tax are specifically charged under Schedule D Case VI for example, a number of anti-avoidance provisions impose a Case VI charge.

12.10   Schedule D Case VI – introduction

Other examples are:

- certain receipts from land (ss 15, 34, 35, 36, 776 and 780 ICTA 1988);

- income from settlements (s 660C ICTA 1988);

- certain transactions in bonds and securities (ss 56, 582, 703, 714, 729, 730, 761 and 786 ICTA 1988);

- intellectual property (ss 524, 531 and 775 ICTA 1988); and

- miscellaneous receipts (eg ss 103, 104, 571, 781 and 821 ICTA 1988).

Section 18 ICTA 1988 provides that tax under Schedule D Case VI shall be charged on:

12.11   The charge to tax

> 'any annual profits or gains not falling under any other case of Schedule D and not charged by virtue of Schedule A, ... C or E.'

Notwithstanding the general nature of the charge not all receipts are chargeable.

12.11.1   Capital receipts

For a receipt to be chargeable to income tax it must be in the nature of income; capital receipts are charged under capital gains tax.

In the case of *Leeming v Jones* (1930) the taxpayer was a member of a syndicate which acquired options over some rubber estates which were then assigned to a company. The taxpayer was assessed under both Schedule D Case I as an adventure in the nature of trade and also under Schedule D Case VI on the profit made on assignment. The commissioners found that the transaction was not an adventure in the nature of trade. The taxpayer appealed the Case VI assessment. It was held by the House of Lords that the profit was not assessable to income tax. Lord Buckmaster approved the words of Lawrence LJ in the Court of Appeal when he said:

> 'I have the greatest difficulty in seeing how an isolated transaction of the kind, if it be not an adventure in the nature of trade, can be a transaction *ejusdem generis* with such an adventure and therefore fall within Case VI. In the case of an isolated transaction of purchase and resale of property, there is really no middle course open. It is either an adventure in the nature of trade, or else it is simply a case of sale and resale of property.'

12.11.2   Trading receipts

If a receipt is from an adventure in the nature of a trade it cannot fall within Schedule D Case VI. Note, there is no equivalent to an adventure in the nature of trade for Schedule D Case II therefore, a one off engagement of a professional nature will be chargeable under Case VI. In the case of *Hobbs v Hussey* (1942) the taxpayer, who was a solicitor's clerk, sold rights to his life story to a newspaper for £1,500 payable by instalments. The taxpayer dictated a number of articles which were then published. He was assessed to the £1,500 minus expenses under Case VI. He argued he had made a capital gain from the sale of copyright. It was held to be a Case VI receipt for the provision of services.

12.11.3   Receipts *ejusdem generis*

The courts have held that not all receipts fall into Case VI; to be chargeable receipts must be of a similar nature to those falling within the rest of Schedule D. It is for this reason that the receipts in *Leeming v Jones* were not assessable. If they were not in Case I they could not be similar to Case I and fall into Case VI. Consequently, gifts and gambling winnings are not within the charge.

Section 18 ICTA 1988 charges 'annual profits or gains'. Unlike annual payments within Case III, annual does not mean recurrent. Annual means occurring within the year.

12.12   Annual profits

Tax under Schedule D Case VI is assessed on a current year basis on sums which are actually received ie on a cash basis rather than a receipts or earnings basis. The use of the word profits implies that expenses are deductible notwithstanding that there is no mention of expenses. This is borne out by s 392 ICTA 1988 which provides for Case VI losses to be carried forward and set against other Case VI profits. If only receipts were to be brought into account, there could be no loss. Losses cannot be set against other types of income. Schedule D Case VI income may be earned or unearned depending upon its source; income from providing services will be earned income; furnished letting income formally taxed under Case VI (now Schedule A) will be investment income.

12.13   Basis of assessment

Schedule A and Schedule D Case VI

Income from land is charged under Schedule A. The Schedule A charge was reformed in 1995 so that there are now in existence two sets of rules one for individuals, and one for companies.

Income from land

Certain income is specifically excluded from the charge under Schedule A. These include:

- yearly interest;
- profits from mines, quarries, markets and tolls;
- mineral rents and royalties; and
- other income such as wayleaves.

Individuals are charged as if their income from land is the income from a business. The income from all Schedule A sources is aggregated and the expenses deducted in order to ascertain the profits. However, there are some differences between a Schedule A business and a Schedule D Case I trade. Schedule A income is not earned income nor are certain CGT reliefs available. The tax is assessed on a current year basis on the income for the period 6 April – 5 April. There are certain transitional rules to provide for the change from tax being assessed on an arising basis as was previously the case. Certain anti-avoidance provisions apply.

A lease premium is treated as rent where the lease is for a period not exceeding 50 years. In such a case two percent of the premium for each complete year of the lease other than the first is treated as a proper premium. Therefore, a premium for a one year lease is all treated as rent and a premium for a fifty year lease is treated as a premium except for 2%. There are certain provisions which have been introduced in order to prevent landlords avoiding the premium rules. There are also provisions intended to prevent the avoidance of the premium rules by the assignment of a lease.

Income from furnished lettings is now treated as part of the Schedule A business. Capital allowances are available on furniture and fittings on either a renewals basis or a depreciation basis.

Furnished holiday lettings are assessed under Schedule A but treated for most purposes as if assessable under Schedule D Case I. Certain conditions need to be satisfied if a property is to qualify as a furnished holiday let. Amongst these are: the property must be available for letting to the public on a commercial basis; it must be furnished; it must be let for at least 70 days of the tax year; and it must not be let in any period of seven months to any one person for a period of more than 31 days.

Provisions were introduced in 1992 to enable individuals to rent rooms in their house and to receive the income tax free. The room must be furnished. The first £3,250 is tax free and after that the individual must pay tax on either the income minus expenses or on the excess of receipts over £3,250.

Section 776 ICTA 1988 provides that where a gain of a capital nature is made on the sale of land, the Inland Revenue can tax the gain as income under Schedule D Case VI on a just and reasonable basis. The section does not apply to disposals by individuals on an arm's length basis. The test is whether the land was acquired with the sole or main object of realising a gain from it.

Schedule D Case VI

Schedule D Case VI is the residual case of Schedule D. There are, therefore, many isolated sections which charge tax and is Schedule D Case VI. Examples are certain receipts from land, income from settlements and intellectual properties.

In order for tax to be chargeable under Schedule D Case VI the profit has to be of an income nature. If the transaction cannot be charged under Schedule D Case I because it is not of an income nature, by definition it cannot be charged in Schedule D Case VI.

Tax is assessed on a current year basis on amounts which are actually received. Expenditure is deductible in computing the profits. Any loss can be carried forward and set against other Case VI profit. The income can be either earned or unearned depending upon its source.

Chapter 13

Schedule D Case III –
Interest, Annuities, Annual Payments and Discounts

This chapter examines income chargeable to tax under Schedule D Case III. This income includes interest and payments such as maintenance payments made on divorce or separation. Schedule D Case III has undergone radical changes in recent years. In 1988 many payments were taken outside the schedule as the use of the covenanted payment by parents to children in higher education was leading to a substantial loss of revenue. In 1994 the preceding year basis of assessment was abolished and the current year basis introduced. This chapter deals only briefly with the preceding year basis and the transitional rules.

13.1 Introduction

Section 18(3) ICTA 1988 provides for tax under Schedule D Case III to be charged on:

13.2 The charge to tax

- any interest of money, whether yearly or otherwise, or any annuity or other annual payment;

- all discounts; and

- income, except income charged under Schedule C from securities bearing interest payable out of the public revenue.

  Notwithstanding the above, ss 347A and 347B ICTA 1988 provide that any legally binding obligation to make annual payments entered into after 15 March 1988 shall *not* be chargeable to tax under Schedule D Case III unless the payment is:

- interest;

- a covenanted payment to charity;

- *bona fide* payments made in connection with an individual's trade profession or vocation; or

- a payment to which s 125 ICTA 1988 applies.

The Finance Act 1994 changed the way in which tax under Schedule D Case III is assessed. Previously, tax was charged on a preceding year basis; however, this general rule had become subject to many exceptions and the most common types of income which were chargeable under Schedule D Case III were chargeable on a current year basis, these included:

13.3 Basis of assessment

- maintenance payments (s 38(2) FA 1988);

- interest on bank and building society accounts; and

- income subject to deduction under ss 348 and 349 ICTA 1988 (s 835(6)(a) ICTA 1988).

From 6 April 1994 any new source of income will be assessed on a current year basis, s 64 ICTA 1988 now provides that tax under Schedule D Case III shall be '... computed on the full amount of the income arising within the year of assessment ...'. Note this is not an accounting period ending in the year of assessment, it is the actual income arising.

Where a source of income arose before 6 April 1994 it will continue to be charged on a preceding year basis; transitional rules will apply for the year 1996–97 and from 6 April 1988 all income chargeable under Schedule D Case III will be charged on a current year basis.

13.3.1   Preceding year basis – opening year rules

The scheme (and complexity) of the old preceding year rules is best explained by way of example.

Example

In year 1, A puts £100 into his Post Office savings account on 6 May. When the account is opened the Post Office pays interest at 12% per annum. In year 2 the rate of interest falls to 8%; in year 3 it rises to 9% and in year 4 it is 10%.

The £100 yields income in the form of interest; it is therefore a new source of income. The £11 interest arising in year 1 is charged to tax on the amount arising in that year. In year 2, A receives £8 interest on the £100; this is also charged on a current year basis. In year 3, however, the amount charged to tax is on the income arising in year 2 ie £8. In year 4 tax is charged on the income arising in year 3 ie £9 and year 5 is on the income arising in year 4 ie £10. The income of year 2 is therefore charged twice. The taxpayer could elect to have the income of year 3 taxed on a current year basis if this was more advantageous with the switch to the proceeding year occurring in year 4. In the example A would not make the election because this would result in £9 arising in year 3 being taxed twice.

There is an exception to the rule that the switch to the preceding year occurs in year 3 and that is if the source first arises on 6 April. Therefore, if A had put his £100 in the Post Office on 6 April he would be charged to tax on the income of the preceding year in year 2. The rationale behind this is that the switch to the preceding year basis occurs as soon as the preceding year has income for the whole period.

Comparison

Year	Interest rate	Income	PYB opening year rules	PYB opening year rules (with election)	CYB new rules
1 (11 mths)	12%	£11	£11	£11	£11
2	8%	£8	£8	£8	£8
3	9%	£9	£8	£9	£9
4	10%	£10	£9	£9	£10

It will be obvious that when an account is closed the source ceases. Because of the source doctrine discussed in Chapter 5, the last year's income would escape tax; in any event, it would be inequitable to charge tax up until the cessation because the income year 2 will have been charged twice under the opening year rules, it would therefore make the taxpayer liable to tax on one slice of income twice. To obviate the problem, the last year is charged on a current year basis; however, all this means is that income of the penultimate year will escape tax. The Inland Revenue is therefore allowed to tax the penultimate year on a current year basis if this gives a higher figure, in which case the pre-penultimate year would escape charge. One year escaping charge in the closing years compensates the taxpayer for having one year charged to tax twice in the opening years.

It will be noted that the example in para 13.3.1 only deals with the interest on the original £100 deposit. If the interest itself was left in the account, it would also bear interest; however, each accretion of interest is a new source and the opening year rules would apply afresh, thus further complicating the calculation. Assessing on a current year basis does away with such complications because it is the income actually arising in each year which is taxed regardless of when the source arose.

The opening year rules will continue to apply to a source of income arising before 6 April 1994.

The closing year rules will continue to apply to a source of income which arose before 6 April 1994 but which ceases before 6 April 1998.

Where a source of income arose before 6 April 1994 but continues beyond 6 April 1998 transitional rules will apply to put the basis of assessment onto a current year basis. In the tax year 1996–97 instead of the individual being taxed on the income arising in the year 1995–96, the individual will be taxed on 50% of the income arising in 1996–97 and 50% of the income arising in 1995–96. In effect the individual is taxed on the average income over those two years so as to effect a roughly

13.3.2 The preceding year basis – the closing year rules

13.3.3 How many sources?

13.3.4 Transitional rules

equitable transition to the current year basis. The following year will be taxed on a current year basis.

13.4   Receipt

Income taxed under Schedule D Case III is taxed when it is received. A payment by cheque is received when it is credited to the payee's bank account (*Parkside Leasing v Smith* (1984)). It is therefore possible to delay receipt by delaying payment into the bank. There is no liability where payment is never received (*Woodhouse v IRC* (1936)). The fact that a payment is receivable does not make the payment income of the payee until it is received; however, the payee does not have to actually receive the income, if it enures to his benefit it will be treated as being received. Thus, in the case of *Dunmore v McGowan* (1978) the taxpayer agreed not to withdraw interest credited to his account whilst he was still liable to the bank under a guarantee. The interest was held to be income of the taxpayer because it reduced his liability under the guarantee. In *Macpherson v Bond* (1985) the taxpayer charged money in his account to secure the debts of a company. He had not personally guaranteed the loan and so the accruing of the interest did not reduce his personal liability. It was held that he never received the interest and was therefore not taxable on it.

13.4.1   Pure income profit

Income chargeable under Schedule D Case III is often referred to as pure income profit. This is because in calculating the amount chargeable to tax no amount is deducted by way of expenses; s 64 ICTA 1988 states that tax shall 'be paid on the actual amount of that income, *without any deduction*'. That which is received is pure profit.

13.5   Interest

There is no statutory definition of interest. The classic case law definition of interest was given by Rowlatt J in the case of *Bennett v Ogston* (1930) in which he said that interest is 'payment by time for the use of money'.

In the case of *Re Euro Hotel (Belgravia) Ltd* (1975) Megarry J described interest as:

'... the return or consideration or compensation for the use or retention by one person of a sum of money belonging to, in a colloquial sense, or owed to, another.'

The payment of interest therefore presupposes the existence of a debt.

However, the label which is attached to a payment will not determine its character. In *Ridge Securities Ltd v IRC* (1963) the payment of a sum shortly after the principal amount had been advanced which exceeded the amount of the principal sum was held not to be interest. Further, the rate of interest must be 'just'; thus, in *Cairns v McDiarmid* (1983) it was held that where the payment exceeded a reasonable amount it could not be interest.

Interest must be distinguished from a premium or a discount. The return on a loan may be made in a number of ways, for example:

- A loans B £100 for 1 year at a rate of interest of 10% per annum. At the end of the year A receives back £110; or

- A loans B £100 for 1 year and promises to pay a premium on redemption of £10. At the end of the year A receives £110; or

- A loans B £110 repayable in 1 year but the principal sum is issued at a discount of £10. At the end of 1 year A receives £110 for an outlay of £100.

The question in each case is: what is the true legal nature of the £10 profit received by A? Further, it is possible for a loan to be issued at a premium and to carry interest. In *Lomax v Peter Dixon* (1943) Lord Greene MR put forward the following rules to ascertain the nature of a payment:

- if there is both interest and a premium or a discount, there is no presumption that the premium or discount is interest if the rate of interest is reasonable considering the nature of the security;

- whether a payment is interest, a premium or a discount is a question of fact not a question of law; and

- factors to be taken into account in deciding what, as a question of fact, the payment is, are:
  - the contract;
  - the term of the loan;
  - the rate of interest; and
  - the nature of the risk involved.

13.6 Annuity

An annuity is:

> 'where an income is purchased with a sum of money and the capital has gone and has ceased to exist, the principal having been converted into an annuity' (Watson B, *Foley v Fletcher* (1858)).

The typical annuity is that obtained by person paying a capital sum to an insurance company in return for regular payments; another type of annuity is that arising under a will.

13.7 Other annual payments

There is no definition of 'other annual payments'; however, in *IRC v Whitworth Park Coal Co Ltd* (1959) it was held that other annual payment had to be read *ejusdem generis* with annuity or yearly interest.

Because an annual payment has to exhibit similar characteristics to interest and annuities, the courts have identified the following criteria for ascertaining whether a payment is an annual payment:

- the payment must be made under a legally binding obligation: this can be a contract, a deed of gift or a court order. A plain gift is not a legally binding obligation;

- the payment must be 'annual'; in the case of *Moss' Empires Ltd v IRC* (1937) it was held that this meant the payment had to have the quality of recurrence. However, having the quality of recurrence does not mean that the payment has actually to recur; for example, in the *Moss' Empires* case a company guaranteed the level of another company's profits; if that other company's profits did not fall below the guaranteed level, nothing would ever have been paid. The obligation which the company entered into still gave rise to annual payments. In order to be annual, the payments have to recur in more than one year, an obligation to pay six monthly instalments falling in one year would not give rise to an annual payment. Where, however, payments are weekly or monthly, each will be an annual payment if the obligation to pay them extends into the following year;

- the payment must be income in the hands of the payee; an annual payment must therefore be distinguished from instalments of capital. If A sells an asset to B for £6,000 to be payable in six annual instalments of £1,000, the six payments of £1,000 will be six instalments of capital (*Foley v Fletcher and Rose* (1858)). If, however, a person were to sell a business and instead of asking for a fixed price the person asked for a percentage of the profits to be paid each year, the payments would be annual payments. However, although the payments are income in the hands of the vendor the payments would probably be capital payments as far as the purchaser was concerned being instalments of the price paid to acquire a capital asset;

- The payment must be pure income profit in the hands of the recipient. Thus, in the case of *Earl Howe v IRC* (1919) the taxpayer mortgaged his life interest in some settlements including certain insurance policies on which he paid the annual premiums. It was held that the payments were not annual payments.

The question therefore arises as to what extent the recipient of the payment can provide a benefit to the payer? If a trader provides a benefit, the cost of that benefit would be an expense deductible against the income received and consequently the payment would not be pure income profit. Where, however, the benefit is provided at no cost to the recipient of the payment, there is nothing to deduct. Thus in *Campbell v IRC* (1968) T covenanted to 80% of its trading profits to the trustees of a settlement for seven years. The plan was to enable the trustees to buy the business from T. It was held that they were not income because first, the trustees were bound to repay the sums to T and, secondly because they were capital receipts in the hands of the trustees.

Another example would be where a charity, which runs a theatre, allows priority booking of seats. However, if as a result of making a payment a person is entitled to a reduction in the price, this may be sufficient to deprive the payment of the character of pure income profit. In *Taw and Torridge Festival Society v IRC* (1959) members of the society paid subscriptions which entitled them to priority booking of seats at a reduced rate. The society claimed to recover the tax deducted on payment by the members. The claim failed because the payments were not annual payments.

There is a statutory exemption to the above rule. Section 59 FA 1989 provides that where a person makes a covenant to a charity the sole or main purpose of which is either the preservation of property for public benefit or the conservation of wildlife for the public benefit, and the donor is thereby entitled to free admission to the properties or to observe wildlife, then the provision of such benefits will not prevent the covenanted payments from being pure income profit.

13.8 Discounts

A discount arises when a security is issued at less than its face value; the difference between the amount for which it is issued and the amount for which it is redeemed is the discount. Thus, if X issues a £100 promissory note for £90, the £10 extra paid when the promissory note is redeemed will be a discount chargeable to tax under Schedule D Case III. In the case of *Ditchfield v Sharp* (1983) the taxpayers were trustees of a settlement which were major shareholders in a company B Ltd. B Ltd had acquired shares and as part of the consideration gave a promissory note payable some four years later. The amount of the note was £2,399,000. It did not carry interest. The trustees sold their shares in B Ltd and used the proceeds to acquire the promissory note for £1,780,000 from a merchant bank which guaranteed it for 75% of its face value. The note was ultimately honoured in full. It was held that the profit made was of an income nature resulting from a discounting transaction; namely, a deduction made from the amount of a bill of exchange by one who gives value for it before it is due. It should be noted that a discount remains the same whenever the note is redeemed. A promise to pay £100 in a year's time which is purchased for £90 will still produce £100 whether or not the note is presented in a year's time on 18 months' time, it is this that distinguishes a discount from interest. However, there is little distinction in the substance between a discount and a premium but a discount is taxed as income and a premium is treated as capital. Consequently, legislation was introduced to prevent the conversion of income into capital. The 'deep discount' and 'deep gain' legislation provide that where the amount payable on redemption exceeds either 15% of the issue price or more than $\frac{1}{2}$% for each year of issue, the amount received is to be treated as income. However, this legislation only applies to securities issued by corporate bodies. The Inland Revenue issued a consultative document in May 1995 with a view to taxing all gains on corporate bonds as income. The discount rules will still apply to persons other than companies. It should also be noted that where a promissory note is traded before redemption, it will amount to a capital transaction. Therefore, if X issues a promissory note to Y for £70 redeemable in three years' time at £100, and Y sells it after one year to Z for £81, the £11 profit is treated as a capital gain. If Z holds the note to maturity and receives £100, Z will be taxed on the discount of £30 notwithstanding that the actual 'profit' is £30–£11 = £19. Although this may seem unfair to Z, the trading of discounted notes continues because there are always people whose circumstances differ and who could benefit from receiving income or capital.

| 13.9 | **Payments within s 347A ICTA 1988** |

As stated in para 13.2 above, notwithstanding the general charging provision in s 18 ICTA 1988, s 347A ICTA 1988 provides that no annual payment which would otherwise be within the charge to tax under Schedule D Case III, shall be taxable in the hands of the recipient or constitute a charge on income of the payer unless, it is:

- a payment of interest;

- a covenanted payment to charity;

- a payment made for *bona fide* commercial reasons in connection with an individual's trade profession or vocation;

- a payment to which s 125 ICTA 1988 applies; or

- a payment made pursuant to an existing obligation.

An 'existing obligation' is defined by s 36 FA 1988 and in general covers:

- a court order made before 15 March 1988;

- a deed of covenant executed before 15 March 1988;

- an oral agreement made before 15 March 1988; or

- a court order made after 15 March 1988 but which varies a court order made before that date.

The significance of 15 March 1988 is that that was the date of the 1988 budget. Section 347A ICTA 1988 was enacted to stop what had become a widespread avoidance of income tax. The making of an annual payments reduced the income of the payer and increased that of the payee. Income was therefore gifted by covenant from higher rate taxpayers to lower rate taxpayers (this was, in effect, the scheme in *IRC v Duke of Westminster* (1935)); the rate of tax on that slice of income was therefore reduced. There were some anti-avoidance provisions which prevented parents covenanting sums to their infant children so as to enable them to use their personal allowances; however, these only applied to infant children. In the 1970s and early 1980s it became popular for parents to covenant sums to children going away to college to supplement the student grant.

Section 247A ICTA 1988 therefore sought to prevent such assignments of income with effect from budget day 1988.

Where a person makes an annual payment after 15 March 1988 and it is not of a type mentioned in s 347A(2) ICTA 1988 or an existing obligation, it will not be deductible by the payer or taxable in the hands of the payee.

Sections 348 and 349 ICTA 1988 provide for a system of deduction of tax at source from annuities and certain annual payments. Because many of the payments to which they applied were taken out of the tax net by s 347A ICTA 1988, their importance is much diminished.

13.10   Sections 348 and 349 ICTA 1988

Sections 348 and 349 ICTA 1988 still apply to the following:

- annuities;

- existing obligations; and

- payments within s 347A(2), ICTA 1988.

The system of deduction also applies to:

- patent royalties;

- certain payments made by quarrying concerns; and

- electric line wayleaves.

Many people find the application of these two sections particularly difficult. When examining their application it is worth remembering what it is they seek to achieve. They seek to make the payer liable for basic rate tax on the payment; however, the payer should not be any worse off as a result. Therefore, the outcome should be that:

- the Inland Revenue receive basic rate tax on the payment;

- the payer is no worse off; and

- the payee receives the payments net of basic rate income tax.

13.10.1   Section 348 ICTA 1988

Section 348 ICTA 1988 applies where any annuity or other annual payment which is charged to tax under Schedule D Case III, and which is not interest, is payable *wholly out of profits or gains brought into charge to income tax* the following consequences follow:

- the person who pays the annuity or annual payment is assessed to tax on the amount paid;

- the payer is entitled to make a deduction from the payment of an amount equal to the income tax on it;

- the payee must allow the deduction; and

- the payee is entitled to a credit for the amount of tax so deducted.

Three points need to be noted:

- Section 3 ICTA 1988 provides that the assessment made on the payer is at the basic rate;

- Section 4 ICTA 1988 provides that the amount of tax the payer is entitled to deduct is tax at the basic rate; and

- Section 276 ICTA 1988 provides that the payer may not set any personal reliefs against the tax liability arising on the annuity or annual payment. There is therefore a flow through in that the payer is taxed on the sum regardless of circumstances but is entitled to recoup this amount by deducting a similar amount from the payment made.

The net result of all this can be shown by way of example:

X pays Y annual payments of £1,000 a year. Assume s 348 ICTA 1988 applies.

(a) X is assessed to tax on the amount of the payment (s 348(1)(a) ICTA 1988). The assessment is at the basic rate (s 3 ICTA 1988).

(b) When X makes the payment he is entitled to deduct an amount equal to the income tax on it (s 348(1)(b) ICTA 1988). The deduction is at the basic rate (s 4 ICTA 1988).

(c) Y has to allow the deduction and X is treated as having paid the full £1,000 (s 348(1)(c) ICTA 1988).

(d) Y receives a credit for the tax deducted. If Y is a nil rate tax payer, the tax will be refunded; if Y is a basic rate taxpayer there will be no further liability; if Y is a higher rate taxpayer X will only have to pay the difference between the higher rate and the basic rate.

It will be noted that the stated objectives are achieved.

• The Inland Revenue receive basic rate tax on the payment.

• The payer has undertaken to pay £1,000 and is out of pocket by £1,000; £250 has gone to the Inland Revenue and £750 has gone to the payee. The payer is under no further liability.

• The payee is deemed to receive £1,000 which has suffered tax at the basic rate.

Section 349 ICTA 1988 serves a similar purpose to that of s 348 ICTA 1988; however, it applies when any annuity or annual payment, charged with tax under Schedule D Case III and not being interest *is not payable or not payable wholly out of profits or gains brought into charge to income tax*. The distinction is that whereas under s 348 ICTA 1988 the profits and gains have been brought within the charge to income tax and can therefore easily be assessed; under s 349 ICTA 1988, the source of funds out of which the payment is made is not readily made subject to tax and therefore assessment is not so easy. Therefore, s 349(1) ICTA 1988 provides that in making the payment the payer *shall* deduct an amount representing the income tax thereon and s 350(1) ICTA 1988 provides that any such person shall forthwith deliver an account to the Inland Revenue and shall be assessable and chargeable to income tax on the payment, or so much of it as is not made out of profits or gains charged to tax.

13.10.2   Section 349 ICTA 1988

The major distinction between s 348 ICTA 1988 and s 349 ICTA 1988 is that under s 348 the payer *may* deduct an amount and under s 349 the payer *must* deduct an amount. The reason for this is that under s 348 the payer will in any event be assessed to tax on the amount of the payment so it does not matter whether the payer deducts or not; the legislation merely gives the payer the legal entitlement so that the payee cannot object if the deduction is made. Under s 349 the payer may not be liable to income tax on the funds out of which the payment is

13.10.3   Distinctions between the two sections

made; therefore, it is necessary to impose a deduction. The payer must deduct and account for the withholding to the Inland Revenue.

A number of questions arise if the rules are not followed what if the payer does not fulfil the obligation to deduct tax at the basic rate?

As between the payer and the payee the answer to this question will depend upon the reason for the failure. The general rule is that a payment made under a mistake of law cannot be recovered. The payer is treated as having made a gift of the excess; therefore, the payer is not entitled to withhold a greater amount from any subsequent payment in order to reimburse the shortfall. This is so even if the payments are later instalments in the same year and therefore, could be viewed as part of the same annual payment (see *Tenbry Investments Ltd v Peugeot Talbot Motor Co Ltd* (1992)). Where the under deduction is caused by a change in the basic rate of tax, the s 348 ICTA 1988 specifically permits a compensating deduction from future payments. If there are no more payments to be made, the over payment can be recovered as a debt. If the mistake is one of fact not one of law, the amount can be recovered. A failure to deduct does not prejudice the right to deduct from future payments.

As between the parties and the Inland Revenue, the answer to the question would seem to depend upon which section applies. Under s 348 ICTA 1988 the payer *may* deduct. A failure to deduct does not affect the Inland Revenue because they can assess the payer in any event. However, notwithstanding the fact that the payer is considered as having made a gift, the Inland Revenue do not allow a repayment claim by the payee because no income tax paid by the payee. Under s 349 ICTA 1988 where no deduction is made, the Inland Revenue may directly assess the payee. The Inland Revenue may treat the payment as a grossed up amount from which a deduction has been made.

Another question is: what if this payment is made late and the rates of tax have changed?

Section 348 ICTA 1988 charges tax by reference to when the payment is due; s 349 ICTA 1988 charges tax by reference to when the payment is made. However, s 348 ICTA 1988 only allows a deduction when the payment is actually made. The Inland Revenue take the view that deduction is by reference to when the payment is made.

13.10.4   Which section?

Where the taxpayer has income and other funds out of which a payment can be made, can the taxpayer stipulate which source and hence choose between the application of s 348 ICTA 1988 and s 349 ICTA 1988? The answer is that if the taxpayer has income out of which the payment could be made then s 348 will apply. Where the taxpayer has insufficient income in one year, he cannot bring himself into s 348 ICTA 1988 by saying that he had an excess of income in the previous year. A payment will fall in s 349 ICTA 1988 if the payer is exempt from income tax notwithstanding that they have income. It is for this reason that an annual payment made by a company will always fall within s 349 ICTA 1988 because companies are chargeable to corporation tax.

With the introduction of s 347A ICTA 1988 maintenance payments no longer come within ss 348 and 349 ICTA 1988. The payer therefore no longer receives a deduction and the payee is not taxable on the amount received. However, under s 347B ICTA 1988 the payer is entitled to a personal relief which is geared to the married couple's allowance. As the married couples allowance is reduced so too will be this personal relief. Thus for the year 1994–95 the amount of the relief was 20% of £1,720. In 1995–96 it is 15%. The payer only gets one relief regardless of the number of former spouses are being supported. The deduction is restricted if the payer's income is insufficient to be covered by the allowance; thus the deduction of the relief cannot give rise to a repayment claim.

13.11 **Maintenance payments – post-14 March 1988 arrangements**

Where the obligation to pay maintenance arose pre-15 March 1988, the payer has no right to deduct the amount of the payment and ss 348 and 349 ICTA 1988 do not apply; however, there is a statutory right of deduction, but the amount deductible is capped at the amount payable in the year 1988/89. From 1994 onwards, the amount of the deduction is further restricted. The first £1,720 is dealt with in the same way as post-15 March 1988 arrangements. The excess is still deductible. The payee is taxable on any amount which is deductible by the payer but the payee is also entitled to a deduction equal to the married couple's allowance.

13.12 **Maintenance payments – pre-15 March 1988**

Schedule D Case III – Interest, Annuities, Annual Payments and Discounts

Income is charged under Schedule D Case III if it is interest; a discount; or income from securities payable out of public revenue and not chargeable under Schedule C.

Certain annual payments made after 15 March 1988 are not chargeable under Schedule D unless they are interest, annual payments to a charity or payments made in connection with an individual's trade, profession or vocation.

Tax is assessed on a current year basis unless the source of the income arose before 6 April 1994, in which case it is assessed on a preceding year basis. Transitional rules apply for the year 1996–97. From 6 April 1988 onwards all income chargeable under Schedule D Case III will be charged on a current year basis.

Income is taxed when it is received. A payment by cheque is received when it is credited to the payee's bank account. There is no liability when a payment is never received. A person will be treated as having received income if it enures to that person's benefit.

Income under Schedule D Case III is referred to as pure income profit. There are no deductible expenses in arriving at the amount of the tax liability.

Interest is 'payment by time for the use of money'. In order for a payment to be interest there must be a debt. Interest needs to be distinguished from a premium or a discount.

A typical annuity is obtained by a person paying a capital sum to an insurance company is return for a regular payment.

In order for a payment to be classified as an annual payment, it has to be similar to an annuity or yearly interest. It therefore has to be capable of recurrence and must be pure income profit in the hands of the payee. Where consideration is received for the payment, it is a question of fact and degree whether the payment is an annual payment. Thus, where a person covenants money to a charity and receives a benefit in return, the nature of the benefit may determine whether the charity receives an annual payment.

Certain payments are taken out of the general charging provision. Such payments are maintenance payments made under a court order after 15 March 1988. Such payments are not taxable in the hands of the recipient nor are they deductible as a charge on income by the payer.

Where a person makes a payment of an annuity or another annual payment, that person is obliged to deduct basic rate tax on making the payment. The person will have been taxed on the amount of the annual payment and the deduction of the basic rate reimburses that person the tax deducted. The payee therefore receives an amount under deduction of tax which can be recovered if the payee is a nil rate tax payer.

Where a person makes a maintenance payment, which is not an annual payment because it is made under an obligation entered into after 15 March 1988, the payer is entitled to a personal relief which is geared to the amount of the married couple's allowance.

Chapter 14

Income Tax –
Trusts and Settlements

In the UK trusts are taxed as a separate entity. Any tax paid by the trust is then imputed to the beneficiaries; this may be when the income arises, if the beneficiary has an interest in the income or, when the income is distributed, if not. Special rules apply when the trust assets are held for the benefit of children. This chapter examines the taxation of trustees, then of beneficiaries and finishes with a brief look at the taxation of the personal representatives of a deceased's estate.

**14.1   Trusts –
          introduction**

There are no specific provisions which impose a charge to tax on trustees. Instead it is necessary to look at the general income tax charging provisions to see whether, by their wording, they can apply to trustees. Thus, s 21 ICTA 1988, which states who is chargeable under Schedule A provides that tax shall be '... charged on and paid by the persons receiving or entitled to the income ...' and s 18 ICTA 1988, which creates the Schedule D charge, applies to the 'annual profits or gains arising or accruing to any person'. Under Schedule F, the tax credit is available to the person receiving the distribution and under company law a company does not have to take notice of any trust but instead must make any distribution to the person named on the company register, which will be the legal owner ie the trustees. It could be said that in each of these cases it is the beneficiary who is really entitled to the income as ultimately it will accrue for the beneficiary's benefit; however, the trustees can sue for the income and it is in this sense that they are entitled to the income and so taxable. If the trustees were not charged to tax on trust income, any accumulation of the income would result in them holding capital which would not be chargeable to income tax.

14.2   Trustees

Trustees constitute a continuing body of persons. In their capacity as trustees they are not individuals and consequently they are not entitled to personal allowances. In any event, the trust income does not belong to them, it belongs to the beneficiaries; however, the trustees are not allowed to deduct the personal allowances of the beneficiaries. Instead, the trust income will be aggregated with any other income belonging to the beneficiaries and their personal allowances will be taken into account when calculating their tax liability in the usual way.

14.2.1   The rate of tax

Generally, trustees are only chargeable to tax at the basic rate. This arises from the fact that they are not individuals (s 1(2) ICTA 1988). (The lower rate and the higher rate apply to individuals only.) Where the income is dividend income, the trustees will be taxable on trust income at 20% the value of the credit passed on to the beneficiary is at 20% (s 207A ICTA 1988). Under s 686 ICTA 1988 a higher charge to tax may be imposed on the trustees, this is considered at para 14.2.5.

| 14.2.2 | Trust expenses |

Trust expenses are not deductible in computing the tax liability of the trustees. The effect of this is that any trust expenses are paid out of taxed income; consequently, the beneficiaries are entitled to less income. Where a beneficiary has unused personal allowances this will result in a loss of a tax repayment.

| 14.2.3 | Trustees not in receipt of income |

It may be that notwithstanding the fact that income arises under a settlement, it is not paid to the trustees but instead it is payable direct to the beneficiary, in such cases the trustees are not assessable. In the case of *Williams v Singer* (1920) the trustees were resident in the UK; however, dividends from shares in a foreign corporation were paid, on the instructions of the trustees, direct to the beneficiary who was resident and domiciled outside the UK. It was held that the trustees were not liable to tax on the income.

| 14.2.4 | Residence of trustees |

Income tax is assessable on both persons resident in the UK and on income derived from a UK source. In the latter case it is usually taxable by deduction at source. Where trustees are resident, they are liable to tax in the usual way; similarly, where trustees are non-resident they will be taxable only on UK source income. What is the position where there are a number of trustees some of whom are resident in the UK and some of whom are not? In the case of *Dawson v IRC* (1989) it was held that where one only of three trustees was resident in the UK, he could not be made liable to tax. In that case he was neither in receipt of the income nor did he have any power to deal with the income when in the UK. As a consequence of this decision s 110 FA 1989 was introduced. This provides that where the trustees of a settlement include at least one person who is not resident in the UK and at least one person who is, then, if when the trust capital is settled the settlor is resident, ordinarily resident or domiciled in the UK, those trustees which are not resident shall be considered to be resident. Otherwise the trustees who are resident will be considered to be non-resident.

Section 686 ICTA 1988 provides for an additional tax charge on the trustees of certain trusts. For the year 1995–96, the additional rate is 10% on income charged at the basic rate and 15% on dividend income which would otherwise be chargeable at the lower rate. In effect the income of such trusts is charged at 35% in the hands of the trustees. The trusts in question are those to which the following four conditions apply:

- trusts where the income is to be accumulated, this may be at the discretion of the trustees or any other person or under s 31 TA 1925; and

- the income of which (before being distributed) is neither the income of any person other than the trustees nor treated for income tax purposes as the income of the settlor; and

- is not a trust established for either charitable purposes or for the purposes of providing certain pensions; and

- exceeds the income applied in paying trust expenses chargeable to income or which would be chargeable to income but for some provisions of the trusts deed.

The trusts to which s 686 ICTA 1988 applies are therefore those where the trustees have the power to accumulate income or have some say either over whether or not to distribute or to whom income is distributed. It should be noted that the last condition means that trust expenses are deductible for the purposes of the additional tax charge.

Because trustees comprise a body of persons, the actual identity of the trustees is irrelevant. Therefore, where the trustees carry on a trade, the replacement of all or any of the trustees will not result in the cessation of the trade. Similarly, where the trustees carry on a trade in partnership with another person, a change in the identity of the trustees will not result in the dissolution of the partnership and the creation of new one.

The trustees must pay any tax for which they are liable on the normal due date for the applicable schedule. However, the additional rate is not strictly charged under any schedule but is an amount charged by s 686 ICTA 1988; it is payable on 1 December in the tax year following the year of assessment.

There is no definition of income in s 686 ICTA 1988; therefore, the normal definition of income applies for trust purposes. Where the trustees receive a payment it is a question of trust law whether that payment is income or capital. Where, therefore, a company purchases its own shares the amount received by the trustees is a receipt of capital being a sum received for the disposal of an asset notwithstanding that the Taxes Act may treat the payment as income and taxable as such.

14.2.9   Section 687 ICTA 1988

Where income which has suffered tax at the additional rate under s 686 ICTA 1988 is distributed, the beneficiary is treated as receiving an amount grossed up at 35% (s 687 ICTA 1988). Thus, if the beneficiary receives £650 this is treated as £1,000. If the beneficiary has unused personal allowances, the tax paid by the trustees can be reclaimed by the beneficiary. However, once the income of the trust is accumulated any subsequent payment will be of capital and no credit will be given. This is notwithstanding the fact that some of the beneficiaries might have been able to reclaim the income tax had it been distributed as income.

14.3   Beneficiaries

The taxation of beneficiaries will depend upon the type of interest they have in the trust property. The beneficiary's interest can be described as:

* absolute;

* vested; or

* contingent.

It should be noted that a beneficiary may have one right in the income and a different right in the capital; for example, if the beneficiary has a life interest in a fund, the right to capital is vested but the right to the income may be absolute during the period in which the capital is vested. It is only the right to income with which we are concerned here.

14.3.1   Absolute interest

If a beneficiary has an absolute interest in the income, it belongs to the beneficiary as it arises. The trustees will be under an obligation to pay the income over to the beneficiary unless s 31 TA 1925 applies.

14.3.2   Vested interest

If a beneficiary has a vested interest, it means that the beneficiary has an interest for the time being but that the interest may be defeated on the happening of some event. For example capital may be settled on trust for X for life and then to Y absolutely. X's interest will terminate on X's death and the capital of any income it produces will then go to Y. In the meantime, however, the income produced by the capital belongs to the beneficiary.

If a beneficiary has a contingent interest, it means that there is no entitlement to income until such time as the contingency is satisfied. Once the contingency is satisfied, the interest may then be vested or absolute.

14.3.3   Contingent interest

A beneficiary who has a vested right to the income; ie a right to income as it arises or entitled to have it applied to his benefit, will be liable to tax on all the income arising regardless of whether it is paid to him (*Baker v Archer-Shee* (1927)). If, however, the beneficiary's right to the income is contingent or is vested but capable of being divested, it is not taxable as the beneficiary's income unless and until it is either paid to him or applied for his benefit.

14.4   Interest in possession trusts

Where the beneficiary is liable to income tax, the trust income will already have suffered tax at the basic rate in the hands of the trustees; it will also have had the trust expenses deducted from it. The beneficiary is therefore entitled to the residuary amount which is grossed up at the basic rate to take account of the tax that has been paid. Where the income includes dividend income, the beneficiary is entitled to a tax credit of 20%. Depending upon the beneficiary's personal circumstances, he may be able to recover some or all of the tax credit in respect of the tax paid by the trustees.

In the case of *Hamilton-Russels Executors v IRC* (1943) investments had been held on trust for the son of the settlor. The son became 21 on 17 October 1928 and at that point was entitled to end the trust and to have the investments assigned over to him. However, he did not do this until 18 January 1939. He was assessed to tax for the year 1938–39 on the whole of the income which had been accumulated. The Inland Revenue conceded that they could not assess any income which accumulated before 6 April 1938. It was held that the income on the investments was income of the taxpayer but that the taxpayer would receive a credit for tax already paid by the trustees.

Because the beneficiary is only entitled to a tax credit of 20% on dividend income, in determining what income of a trust is actually distributed, trust expenses are set against dividend income first.

14.5   Contingent interests

The converse of the rule that a beneficiary who has an absolute entitlement to income is taxable on it whether or not that income is received, is that a beneficiary who has a contingent right to income or has a right to income which is capable of being divested, is not liable to tax until such time as the income irrevocably belongs to the beneficiary.

The most common example of such a trust is the maintenance and accumulation settlement created by s 31 Trustee Act 1925. Section 31 TA 1925 has the effect of divesting an infant beneficiary of any vested right to income until the infant reaches 18. It should be noted that the section does not apply to divest an infant beneficiary where the infant has a vested right in the capital of the fund. The section can be specifically excluded by s 69(2) TA 1925. Many trusts do not exclude this provision and the consequence of it applying are as follows:

- where an infant beneficiary has an interest in trust property, it is converted into a maintenance and accumulation trust. This is so regardless of the interest that the infant has. Hence, an infant with an absolute interest in the income of the trust property will not be entitled to the income of the trust property but instead the trustees will be under a duty to accumulate so much of the income as they do not use to maintain, educate or apply to the benefit of the beneficiary;

- notwithstanding the terms of the trust, an infant on attaining the age of 18 will become entitled to a vested interest in the income of the trust property (which will included any income arising from income which has itself been accumulated); and

- any income which has been accumulated during the infancy of the beneficiary will either be payable to the beneficiary:

    (a) if the beneficiary becomes entitled to the property from which the income arose; or

    (b) if, but for the operation of the section the infant would have had a vested interest during his infancy; or,

    (c) if neither of those apply, the beneficiary will be entitled to any income arising from the accumulated income during his infancy. Any income which has been accumulated over that time is treated as an accretion to capital and will belong to whoever is entitled to the trust capital.

14.5.1   Contingent interests and income tax

For income tax purposes the consequences of the above are as follows:

- An infant beneficiary who has a vested and absolute interest in the trust income will be liable to higher rate tax on any income of the trust which is not distributed to him. Section 686 ICTA 1988 will not apply. If the infant were do die before reaching the age of 18, the trust property would still form part of his estate.

- An infant beneficiary who does not have an absolute interest in the income of the trust property is not liable to tax on the accumulated income because until he reaches the age of 18 it is not certain whether the accumulated income will pass to him. If such a beneficiary dies before reaching the age of 18 none of the trust property will form part of the estate. Instead, it will pass to whoever has an infant on the trust capital.

- An infant beneficiary who receives income from the trustees during his infancy and does not have a vested income in this capital will be liable to income tax on that income. Any such income will have suffered tax at 35% but s 687 ICTA 1988 will apply.

- Where the trust provides that a beneficiary is to be entitled to the trust property of attaining an age greater than 18. On attaining the age of 18 that person will be entitled to the income of the trust property and any income arising from any accretion to the trust property. He will therefore be liable on the trust income whether he receives it or not.

14.6   Capital or income?

Although trustees may pay amounts to a beneficiary out of trust capital, this does not mean to say that the amounts paid are capital in the hands of the beneficiary. In the case of *Brodies Trustees v IRC* (1933) the trustees of a deceased person were directed to make payments out of capital sufficient for the deceased's widow to receive £4,000 a year. It was held that although the payments were paid out of capital, the payments were annuities and assessable as income of the beneficiary with a consequent liability on the trustees to withhold basic rate tax on making the payments. Similarly, in *Cunnard's Trustees v IRC* (1946) certain discretionary payments made by the trustees of a will out of capital were held to be annual payments within Schedule D Case III. In the more recent case of *Stevenson v Wishart* (1987) the beneficiary under a discretionary trust suffered a heart attack in March 1978 and went into a nursing home. She died in January 1981. During this period between 1978 and 1981 the trustees made payments out of capital totalling £114,000 in order to pay the beneficiary's medical and nursing home expenses. Other beneficiaries of the trust included charities to whom the whole of the trust's income was distributed. The payments were, therefore, clearly payments out of the trust capital. The Inland Revenue assessed the trustees on the basis that the payments made to the beneficiary were income. The trustees appealed and the appeal was upheld in both the Chancery Division and the Court of Appeal. It was held that, notwithstanding that payments are made out of capital, they may still become income in the hands of the recipient; however, the fact that the payments were periodic and to pay for personal maintenance did not mean *per se* that they were income. There was nothing in the nature of those particular payments to indicate that they were income other than the fact that they were recurrent. The trustees were disposing of trust capital under a specific power given to them to appoint capital in the trust deed. The payments were therefore of a capital nature.

14.7	**The taxation of personal representatives, executors and beneficiaries under a will**	Personal representatives and executors are liable to income tax in the same way as trustees. However, they are not liable to the additional rate chargeable under s 686 ICTA 1988. Being individuals, they are not entitled to a personal allowance in their capacity as personal representatives or executors.
14.7.1	Legatees	A legatee under a will will be entitled to one of three types of interest:

- specific legacy;
- general legacy; or
- a legacy of residue.

14.7.2 Specific legacies

A specific legacy is a gift of specified items of property belonging to the deceased. Any income arising on a specific legacy is treated as being the interest of the legatee from the date of the deceased's death. Therefore, once the legacy has become vested in the specific legatee, any income which arose on that property during the course of the administration of the estate is related back to and taxed as the income of the beneficiary in the year that it arose. The will may, however, provide otherwise, for example, that the specific legacy is not to carry any interest. A specific legacy may take the form of an annuity. An annuity is payable from the date of the deceased's death and will be the income of the legatee from that date. Being an annuity, the personal representatives or executors are obliged to deduct tax under s 349 ICTA 1988; this is so notwithstanding that the annuity is paid out of capital.

14.7.3 General legacies

Any interest payable on a general legacy is treated as the income of the legatee and is chargeable under Schedule D Case III.

14.7.4 Residue

The taxation of a beneficiary with an interest in the residue will depend upon whether that interest is either an interest in the capital of the residue or an interest in the income only. It should be noted that an interest in the capital will carry with it an interest in the income derived from that capital.

Where the interest is in the capital of the residue any sum paid to the legate could represent capital or income derived from that capital. In order to differentiate between the two it is necessary to calculate the residue income of the estate. This is all the income of the estate minus expenses and any amounts paid on specific or general legacies. This is compared with any amounts paid to the beneficiary during the administration period. To the extent the amounts paid to the beneficiary during the administration period are equal to or less than the amount of the residue income, such amounts will be treated as income of the beneficiary. To the extent that any such amounts are greater than the residue income this is treated as a payment of capital from the residue estate. On the completion of the administration of the estate, if the beneficiary has not received the full entitlement to income, the amount by which the amount received is less than the entitlement is treated as being paid immediately before the end of the administration period.

The Finance Act 1995 introduced new provisions for the taxation of beneficiaries interested only in income of the residue estate. Sums which are paid out during the course of the administration of the estate are deemed to be the income of the beneficiary in the year in which they are paid. When the administration ends any amounts paid are treated as being the income of the beneficiary for the tax year in which the administration of the estate ended.

If the residue is held on discretionary trusts any amounts paid out to the discretionary beneficiaries will be treated as income of those beneficiaries up to the amount of the residual income. Any amounts over and above that will be treated as a distribution of capital.

14.8 Settlements – introduction

Historically, the provisions relating to settlements were very complex. In order to simplify matters, the Finance Act 1995 introduced new provisions relating to settlements and at the same time repealed all the old provisions. The new rules apply to all settlements from 1995–96 onwards regardless of when they were created. Under the new rules income is treated as that of the settlor unless some provision provides for it not to be; under the old rules the opposite was true: income was treated as belonging to the beneficiary unless, for some reason, it was treated as income of the settlor. There may, therefore, be instances where income has previously been treated as that of the beneficiary and is now treated as that of the settlor and *vice versa*.

14.9	**What is a settlement?**	In order for the rules to apply it is first necessary to identify a settlement. Section 660G ICTA 1988 provides that settlement includes 'any disposition, trust, covenant, agreement, arrangement or transfer of assets'. This is a very wide definition and includes, for example an outright gift. The definition is the same as under the previous legislation (s 681 ICTA 1988 now repealed) so it can be assumed that the case law on the old section will still apply in interpreting the new section. In the case of *Thomas v Marshall* (1953) it was held that an outright gift was a settlement so that when a father made gift to his infant children by paying amounts into the Post Office Savings Bank, the income derived from those investments could be assessed on the father. Although the case of *IRC v Plummer* (1980) was overturned in the case of *Moodie v IRC*, with regard to the application of 'the new approach' to certain annuity schemes, it is still regarded as good law in that it decided that a settlement requires an element of bounty ie, there has to be a gratuitous element to it or it is intended to benefit someone.
14.10	**Who is the settlor?**	Section 660G ICTA 1988 provides that the settlor of a settlement is any person by whom the settlement was made; this is further extended by sub-s (2) which provides that a person is deemed to have made a settlement if he has made or entered with the settlement either directly or indirectly and in particular if he has provided or undertaken to provide funds directly or indirectly for the purpose of the settlement or has entered into a reciprocal arrangement with another person to make or enter into a settlement.
14.11	**Section 660A ICTA 1988 – the charging section**	Section 660A ICTA 1988 is central to the whole regime. It provides that income arising under a settlement during the life of the settlor shall be treated for all purposes of the Income Tax Acts as the income of the settlor and not as the income of any other person unless the income arises from property in which the settlor has no interest. It is, therefore, irrelevant that the income has been paid out to a beneficiary the settlor is still liable to tax. Section 660A ICTA 1988 goes on to provide that the settlor shall be regarded as having an interest in property if that property or any property derived from it is, or will or may become, payable to or applicable for the benefit of the settlor or his spouse in my circumstances whatsoever. The words 'in any circumstances whatsoever' were considered, in the context of settlements, in the case of *Glyn v IRC* (1930). It was stated that the words had to restricted to mean any circumstances within the terms of the settlement. If this was not the case an outright gift to anybody would be a settlement because there would

always be a chance, however remote, that the donee might give the property back again.

Because the terms of s 660A ICTA 1988 are so wide, there are a number of exclusions. These are contained in sub-s (3)–(9) of 660A ICTA 1988.

14.12   Exclusions

Section 660A(3) ICTA 1988 provides that for the purposes of sub-s (2), ie income payable to the benefit of the settlor's spouse, spouse does *not* include:

14.12.1   Spouse

- a person to whom the settlor is not for the time being married but may later marry; or

- a spouse from whom the settlor is separated under a court order, or under a separation agreement or in such circumstances that the separation is likely to be permanent; or

- the widow or widower of the settlor.

An outright gift to the settlor's spouse is also excluded from the provisions by sub-s (6) unless:

- the gift does not carry a right to the whole of the income produced by the property gifted; or

- the property given is wholly or substantially a right to income.

A gift is not considered to be an outright gift if there are conditions attached; the legislation does not specify the type of condition necessary. Nor is a gift considered to be an outright gift if the property given or any property derived from it is or will or may become, in any circumstances whatsoever, payable to or applicable to the benefit of the donor.

Subsection (1) is also excluded where the settlement is made by one party to a marriage by way of provision for the other either:

- after the dissolution or annulment of the marriage; or

- while they are separated under a court order, or under a separation agreement or in such circumstances that the separation is likely to be permanent

where the income from the settlement is payable to or applicable for the benefit of that other party.

Section 660A(4) ICTA 1988 provides that the settlor is not to be regarded as having an interest in property or any property derived from it provided that it cannot become payable to the settlor except in certain specified circumstances. There are:

14.12.2   Specified exemptions

- the bankruptcy of some person who is or may become beneficially entitled to their property or any derived property; or

- in the case of marriage settlement, the death of both parties to the marriage and of all or any of the children of the marriage; or

- the death of a child of the settlor who has become beneficially entitled to the property or any derived property at an age not exceeding 25.

Section 660A(5) ICTA 1988 provides that the settlor is not to be regarded as having an interest in property provided that some person is alive under the age of 25 and the property cannot become payable to the settlor except by that person becoming bankrupt.

| 14.12.3 | Commercial and charitable exemptions | Section 660A(4) ICTA 1988 provides that income consisting of: |

- annual payments made by an individual for *bona fide* commercial reasons in connection with his trade profession or vocation; or

- covenanted payments to charity (under s 347A(7) ICTA 1988) is to be excluded from the charge imposed by s 660A(2) ICTA 1988.

14.13   Payments to unmarried minor children of the settlor

Section 660B ICTA 1988 provides that where a payment is not caught by s 660A ICTA 1988 but is made to an unmarried minor child of the settlor during the life of the settlor it is to be treated as the income of the settlor and not as the income of any other person.

14.14   The charge to tax

Income which is made income of the settlor by virtue of the settlement provisions is taxed under Schedule D Case VI (s 660C(1) ICTA 1988); however, in calculating the income chargeable the same deductions and reliefs are allowed to the settlor as would be allowed to him if the income actually belonged to him (s 660C(2) ICTA 1988). The income is treated as the highest point of the settlor's income (s 660A(3) ICTA 1988).

14.15   More than one settlor

Where the property in a settlement is derived from more than one settlor, it is necessary to identify the settlor of each item of property, the income derived from that property and to tax the settlor accordingly.

Income Tax –
Trusts and Settlements

Trustees are taxable as a separate entity; however, there are no specific provisions which impose a charge to tax on trustees. It is necessary to look at the appropriate charging provision to see whether the trustees are taxable. Normally, they are taxable in their capacity as a person 'entitled' to the income in that they are able to sue for it.

Trusts

Trustees are a body of persons and they are not individuals and therefore cannot claim personal allowances. A further consequence of being individuals is that the lower rate and higher rate of tax do not apply to them. They are therefore taxable at 25% unless the income received is dividend income in which case they are taxable at 20%.

Trust expenses are not deductible for tax purposes but are deductible for the purposes of calculating additional rate tax.

In order to be taxable on income, trustees have to receive it. Income paid directly to a beneficiary is therefore not the responsibility of the trustees.

Certain trusts are charged at a higher rate of tax. Such trusts must satisfy four conditions; these are that the income is to be accumulated, the income does not belong to any person other than trustees, the trust is not charitable and the income exceeds the amount applied in paying trust expenses.

The taxation of a beneficiary will depend upon the nature of the beneficiary's interest. Further, it is only the nature of the beneficiary's interest in the income which is relevant. A beneficiary who is entitled to the income as it arises will be taxable on it notwithstanding that the beneficiary never receives it. Conversely, a beneficiary who has a contingent right to income or has a right to income which is capable of being divested, is not liable to tax until such time as the income irrevocably belongs to the beneficiary. An example of such a trust is a maintenance and accumulation settlement created by s 31 Trustee Act 1925.

The nature of a payment to a beneficiary does not depend upon the nature of the payment by the trustees. Thus, if a beneficiary receives an annuity it will be taxable as income in the hands of the beneficiary notwithstanding the annuity is paid out of trust capital.

The taxation of legatees under a will depend upon the nature of the interest in the estate which they receive. A specific tax legacy carries interest from the date of the deceased's death unless the will provides otherwise. A beneficiary with an interest in the residue will be taxed according to whether that interest is in the capital or in income only.

Settlements

The Finance Act 1995 introduced new provisions relating to settlements. The new rules apply to all settlements from 1995–96 onwards regardless of when they were created. Under the new rules, income is treated as that of the settlor unless some provisions provides for it not to be.

The settlement includes a disposition, trust, covenant, agreement, arrangement or transfer of assets. However, in order to be a settlement there needs to be some element of bounty.

A person who provides funds directly or indirectly is the settlor of a settlement. Income arising under a settlement during the life of the settlor is treated for all purposes of the Income Tax Acts as the income of the settlor.

There are certain exclusions from the rule. Amongst them are:

- outright gifts to the settlor's spouse;
- settlements of a dissolution of a marriage;
- income which cannot become payable to the settlor except in certain specified circumstances;
- payments made for *bona fide* commercial reasons; and
- covenanted to payments of charity

Taxes chargsed under Schedule D Case VI where the settlor is given the same deductions and reliefs as would be allowed had the income actually belonged to the settlor.

Chapter 15

Income Tax – Special Cases

The rules applicable to the taxation of partnerships have been radically altered by the introduction of the current-year basis, which replaces the preceding-year basis for Schedule D Cases I and II. This chapter looks at the new rules as they apply to new businesses commencing on or after 6 April 1994. The new rules will also apply to existing businesses from 6 April 1997 and transitional rules will apply in the meantime. However, this chapter only deals with the new rules.

15.1 Partnership taxation – introduction

Partnerships have always had a strange place in English tax law. In England, partnerships are not separate legal entities (in Scotland they are) and yet many of the income tax rules did not fit easily with the notion of partnership. Indeed, there have never been many tax provisions specific to partnerships. In order to determine whether a partnership exists, it is first necessary to look at the general law; this is to be found in the Partnership Act 1890. Section 1 PA 1890 states that a partnership is '... the relation which subsists between persons carrying on business in common with the view to profit'. The distinguishing feature of a partnership is that the partners are jointly and severally liable for partnership debts. This was true for taxation also until the new rules were introduced. The effect of this was that each partner was ultimately liable for the other partners' tax liabilities in respect of partnership taxation.

15.2 Status of a partnership

Now, each individual partner will be assessed separately and the necessary tax collected from each individual partner in respect of that partner's own personal liability. Any joint liability for partnership tax will cease. The partnership profits are to be assessed as if the partnership were an individual. What this means is that a tax return will still be required from the actual partnership. However, each individual partner will be treated as carrying on a notional trade. The profits of the partnership are allocated to the partners according to their partnership share for the particular accounting period. The trade carried on by each individual partner begins when the partner joins the partnership and ceases when the partner leaves.

Under English partnership law when the constituent members of the partnership changes, one partnership is deemed to come to an end and a new partnership is deemed to commence. This used to cause substantial problems for the tax system because it meant that a partnership was deemed to come to an end and a new partnership commence each time a partner was either admitted or left. This meant that calculations for the closing-year rules, opening-year rules and transfers of assets between the old and new partnership had to be done notwithstanding that the majority of partners were common to the old and the new partnership. To prevent the inconvenience caused by this, it was possible to sign an election treating the old partnership and the new partnership as the same (a continuation election). However, the existence of such an election meant it was possible to manipulate partnership profits so as to achieve the best tax result and either deliberately cause a cessation without signing a continuation election or, where it was advantageous, sign a continuation election where there was a cessation. Under the new rules where each partner is treated as carrying on a separate notional trade, a leaving partner will simply be treated as ceasing her own notional trade, while the other partners will be treated as continuing their own individual notional trades which they were carrying on prior to the outgoing partner's departure. There is consequently no longer any need for a continuation election for tax purposes.

15.3 Special rules for determining income

Each partner will be allocated profits in accordance with the interest they have in the partnership during the accounting period which forms the basis for that particular year's assessment. Due to the nature of a partnership, there may be agreements between the partners as to the distribution of and the division of income and profits. It may be that one partner is given what is called a 'salary' by the partnership and, in effect, all the salary is in a first charge on profits given to a partner. So, if there are three partners and one is given a salary of £12,000 per annum, then particular partner will simply be allowed the first £12,000 profit before the rest of the profit is divided. In consequence, the £12,000 is still a division of the partnership profit and is not deductible when calculating that profit (see *Stekel v Ellice* (1973)). Similarly, any interest that is paid to a partner on the capital contributed is merely a first charge on profits in recognition of that fact. It might therefore be possible for a partnership having two partners to divide the profits equally but to allow interest at 10% of the capital contributed. If the capital contributed by partner A is £10,000 and that contributed by a partner B is £5,000, partner A will receive £500 more than partner B. This interest is again a division of the profit and is not allowable when computing the profits.

It may be that an individual partner owns property which is let to the partnership. Any rent paid by the partnership for this property will be deductible in computing profits, although the rent paid to the partner will be assessable on the partner as Schedule A income.

Section 628 ICTA 1988 provides that, where a person ceases to be a member of a partnership because of age, ill health or death, and where annual payments are made under:

15.4 Partnership retirement annuities

- the partnership agreement;

- an agreement replacing or supplementary to the partnership agreement; or

- an agreement entered into by an individual who has acquired the whole or part of the business carried on by the partnership,

then, where annual payments are made to that partner or a widow, widower or dependant of the former partner, those payments shall not be treated as investment income but instead will be treated as earned income up to a certain limit. The limit is 50% of the average of the best three years' profits of that partner in the last seven years that he was a partner. This amount is index linked.

This section takes a brief look at the international aspects of income tax. Where a person works in, or derives income from, two or more countries, the question arises as to which jurisdiction is able to tax the income. If all jurisdictions were entitled to tax the income it would be possible for a person to suffer tax greater than the income. If each jurisdiction left the others to tax the income, it would be possible for no tax to be payable. Most jurisdictions look at certain connecting factors in order to assume the right to tax a person's income. Where more than one jurisdiction claims the right to tax income, there may be a tax treaty between the various jurisdictions which states which jurisdiction has priority. In the UK, the Taxes Act contains provisions which allow relief against foreign tax suffered on income where there is no double tax treaty.

15.5 International aspects – introduction

The UK taxes individuals by reference to three connecting factors:

15.6 Connecting factors

- residence;

- ordinary residence; and

- domicile.

In general where an individual is resident or ordinarily resident in the UK, the UK taxes all of the individual's income regardless of where it comes from. Where an individual is neither resident nor ordinarily resident the UK will tax income which is derived from property in the UK, eg rent from UK properties and interest on UK bank deposits. Where a person is resident and not domiciled in the UK, income which is earned abroad whilst the individual is out of the country will only be taxed if it is brought into the UK.

<table>
<tr><td>15.6.1</td><td>Residence</td></tr>
</table>

There is no statutory definition of residence. The Inland Revenue have set out (IR 20) when they consider a person to be resident. This is based on case law but the cases relied upon are those which tend to favour the Inland Revenue. In practice, people tend to rely upon the Revenue guidelines.

A person is treated as resident in the UK if, in any year of assessment, the person spends more than six months in the UK. Six months is taken as 183 days regardless of whether the year in question is in leap year or not. The days on which a person arrives in the UK or leaves the UK are disregarded. A person is treated as in the UK if present at midnight. As workforces become more mobile interesting questions arise regarding people who, for example, live in France and work in the south of England.

Where a person leaves the UK to live abroad, that person will be treated as continuing to be resident in the UK if he or she makes visits to the UK which average 91 days or more in the year of assessment.

It used to be the case that where an individual had accommodation available in the UK, that person would be regarded as resident in the UK if they set foot in the UK regardless of whether they actually used the available accommodation. This test was abolished from 1993 in order to make the system more certain.

<table>
<tr><td>15.6.2</td><td>Ordinary residence</td></tr>
</table>

There is no statutory definition of ordinary residence. Again, the Inland Revenue have set down a list based on case law. Ordinary residence is habitual residence. A person can be resident in the UK without being ordinarily resident and *vice versa*. A person will be considered by the Inland Revenue to be ordinarily resident when they came to the UK with the intention of staying for more than three years. If a person comes to the UK with no intention of staying, that person will be treated as being ordinarily resident from the beginning of their third year.

Domicile is a concept of the general law and is not specific to tax. A person acquires a domicile at birth. A person can change their domicile in which case they acquire a domicile of choice. In general a person is domiciled in the place that they consider to be their real home this is not necessarily where they are resident. A person can be resident in a country for many years without ever becoming domiciled in that country.

15.6.3   Domicile

A partnership is resident in the country in which it is centrally managed and controlled. Therefore, it is possible for a partnership to be non-resident if the individual partners are resident in the UK and conversely a partnership may be resident in the UK even if individual partners are non-resident. Now that individual partners are taxed as if they carry on an individual trade, the residence of the partners will determine their liability to tax. Where the partnership source of income is the UK, members of the partnership will be taxed regardless of where a resident. If the source of income is abroad UK resident partners will be taxed whereas non UK partners will not.

15.7   Residence of partnerships

The UK now has two tests of residence. The first is where the company is incorporated in the United Kingdom; this test is applied since 15 March 1988. Second, a company is resident in the United Kingdom if it is managed and controlled in the United Kingdom. A company is managed in control in the United Kingdom if board meetings are held in the United Kingdom; however, where the board act in accordance with a shareholder's wishes a company may be resident where the shareholders reside. A company resident in the United Kingdom by virtue of its incorporation will not cease to be resident if it is managed and controlled abroad. However, a company which is not registered in the United Kingdom will still be resident here if it is managed and controlled in the United Kingdom.

15.8   Residence of companies

A trust is resident where the trustees are resident. This is given by ss 110–111 and 151 Finance Act 1989. Where the trustees of the settlement comprise a trustee and is UK resident, the trustees will be treated as being UK resident unless the settle of the trust was neither resident, ordinarily resident, or domiciled in the UK when either trust was set up or if later funds were provided to the trust.

15.9   Residence of trusts

The following paragraphs deal briefly with certain specific types of income and indicates how they are treated.

15.10   Specific types of income

15.10.1	Schedule D Cases I and II	A UK resident is taxed on all the profits of a trade, professional vocation which is carried in the UK where some part of the trade is carried on overseas, it is still treated as UK income. A non-resident is liable to tax on the profits of a business carried on in the UK. It is important to distinguish between a trade which is carried on within the UK and a trade which is carried on with the UK (see *Erichsen v Last* (1881)). A trade is carried on within the UK if the contracts are made in the UK. A contract is made in the UK if the offer is accepted in the UK. A person may trade with the UK if the contract is made outside the UK but with the person who is resident in the UK. Sections 78 and 83 TMA 1970 provide for an agent to be taxed if the agent receives income on behalf of a person who is not resident.
15.10.2	Schedule D Cases IV and V	Schedule D Case IV taxes income from non UK securities. For these purposes, securities does not include stocks and shares but does include debentures and debts. Schedule D Case V taxes income from possessions outside the UK. For these purposes, possessions include stocks and shares and rented property.
15.10.3	Schedule E	There are three cases of Schedule E. Case I was dealt with in Chapter 10 and taxes the earnings of people resident and ordinarily resident in the UK regardless of where those earnings are earned. Schedule E Case II applies to people who are not resident or not ordinarily resident and taxes their income for duties performed in the UK. Schedule E Case III taxes the income of people who are not domiciled in the UK and taxes their income on a remittance basis. A UK resident who is non-domiciled and is employed abroad by non-resident employer will, therefore, only be taxed on so much income as is remitted to the UK. It is not in common for non-domiciliaries to have two contracts of employment; one governing their UK employment and one governing any overseas employment.
15.11	**Taxation in marriages, separation and divorce – introduction**	This section examines the taxation of husband and wife and draws together certain aspects and matters discussed in other chapters in the book. The taxation of husband and wife has undergone a fundamental change in recent years. In his 1988 budget, the then Chancellor of the Exchequer Nigel Lawson, proposed an end to the system whereby the husband was responsible for his wife's tax affairs. The new system was introduced in 1990 with certain transitional provisions. Consequently, married women pay their own tax calculated on the basis of their own income and where necessary complete their own tax returns.

Each spouse is allowed a personal allowance for the tax year commencing 6 April 1995 of £3,525 (s 257(1) ICTA 1988). In addition, a married couple is entitled to the married couple's allowance which is £1,720. Up to and including the tax year 1993–94, the married couple's allowance could be set off against total income and, consequently, reduced tax at the highest rate; for example, if a husband was earning £50,000 the married couple's allowance would be set off against the highest slice of that income and so would save tax at 40%. From the tax year 1994–95 onwards the married couple's allowance has been restricted. This restriction is given effect by allowing a percentage of the married couple's allowance to be deducted from the final income tax bill; for example, for the tax year 1995–96 the married couple's allowance is given effect at 15%, which is achieved by multiplying £1,720 by 15% and deducting this amount from the total tax bill ie £258.

In order to qualify for the married couple's allowance a couple must be living together (s 257(1) ICTA 1988). The husband and wife are treated for income tax purposes as living together unless:

- they are separated under an order of a court of competent jurisdiction, or by deed of separation; or

- they are in fact separated in such circumstances that the separation is likely to be permanent (s 282 ICTA 1988).

In the case of *Holmes v Mitchell* (1991) the taxpayer had married in 1959. In 1982 he stated that he was going to seek a divorce which was granted in 1987. The taxpayer claimed the equivalent to the married couple's allowance for the years between 1982 and 1987. The Inspector of Taxes refused the claim and this decision was upheld by the General Commissioners who found that during these years, notwithstanding the fact that they were living together under the same roof, they had in fact lived as separate households and '... more or less ignored each other'.

It should be noted that for the purposes of the married couple's allowance a wife does not include a 'common law wife'. Thus in *Rignell v Andrews* (1990) the taxpayer's claim to the equivalent to the married couple's allowance was refused on the basis that the reference to 'wife' referred to a wife recognised by civil law.

Notwithstanding the more liberal attitude of the tax system in allowing a wife to deal with her own tax affairs, the married couple's allowance in the first place goes to the husband (s 257A ICTA 1988). However, a couple may elect to split the allowance between them in the most beneficial way (s

15.12   Income tax – allowances

257BA(2) ICTA 1988). If the wife unilaterally elects, she is automatically entitled to 50% of the married couple's allowance (s 257BA(1) ICTA 1988). The election must be made on a prescribed form and it will continue in force until it is revoked by making a subsequent election. Any election for a particular tax year must be made before the beginning of that tax year. Now that the benefit of the married couple's allowance is restricted to 15% of the amount of the allowance and does not depend upon the level of earnings of any particular taxpayer there is less scope for maximising a couple's income by making an election.

In the year of marriage the married couple's allowance is reduced by one-twelfth for every complete month prior to the date of marriage (s 257A(6) ICTA 1988). Thus, a couple getting married on 5 May will get the full married couple's allowance whereas one getting married on 6 May will have it reduced by one-twelfth which is £143.33 which at 15% is £21.49. Thus, by bringing the marriage forward by one day it may be possible to buy another couple of bottles of wine.

| 15.13 | **Income tax – mortgage interest relief** | A married couple are entitled to interest relief of £30,000. What this means is that interest on a loan of up to £30,000 can be reclaimed against the taxpayer's income. Like the married couple's allowance interest relief is given as a deduction in the amount of tax payable not against total income. However, as the vast majority of mortgage payments are within the MIRAS scheme, relief is given at source and as the rate of relief is unaffected by the level of the taxpayer's income, there is no need for it to enter the calculation at all. In the first instance the relief is split by reference to the ownership of the property. Therefore, if the property is in joint names the relief is split so that each spouse receives relief on £15,000. If the loan is in the name of only one spouse, he or she will be entitled to the full £30,000. If the couple do not wish these rules to apply, they can elect to split the relief in any way that they think fit (s 356B(1) ICTA 1988). |

| 15.14 | **Income tax – jointly held property** | As a wife is now entitled to run her own tax affairs, it has become necessary for the legislation to deal with the problem of jointly owned property. Previously, it was not necessary to consider this problem because all income was considered to be that of the husband. The problem is dealt with by stating that income from jointly held property is deemed to accrue in equal shares to the husband and wife. It is possible for a couple to elect that the income will accrue in different proportions; however, this can only be done only if at the same time they declare that the underlying asset is held in different |

proportions. Hence, it is not possible for the spouses to have a 40/60 split in income, a 60/40 split in the underlying assets. It should be noted that the 50/50 rule applies where no declaration has been made by the couple (ss 282A and 282B ICTA 1988). Therefore, even if the asset is held in unequal proportions, the 50/50 rule will apply unless the couple elect for the actual proportions to be used. It should be noted that the 50/50 rule only applies to assets which are beneficially held in joint names. It does not apply to partnership income where both spouses are partners in the same firm, nor does it apply when a couple separate.

Once a couple separate either by court order or in circumstances that are likely to be permanent for income tax purposes, they revert to being single people again. The married couple's allowance will continue to be given for the year in which the couple separate; this is because s 257A ICTA 1988 provides for a man to have the married couple's allowance if he proves that for the whole or *any part of the year* he is a married man whose wife is living with him. The additional personal allowance may also be claimed by a parent who maintains any children. Where a couple which have separated are reconciled in a later year of assessment, the couple receive the full married couple's allowance in that year. There is no reduction for time before the reconciliation (s 257A(6) ICTA 1988).	**15.15 Income tax – separation**
Notwithstanding the move to make the wife's tax position the same as that of her husband, in death not all things are treated equally. If the wife dies the husband is entitled to the full married couple's allowance for the tax year in which she dies. Following that, he will receive only his personal allowance. If the husband dies the wife is entitled to a personal allowance, to the widow's bereavement allowance for the year of death and the year following (assuming she does not remarry), possibly to the additional personal allowance if she has children living with her and also any unused amount of the married couple's allowance for the year of death.	**15.16 Income tax – death**
Although capital gains tax is not dealt with until Chapter 20 it is useful to illustrate its application in a matrimonial context now. Where a married man and his wife are living together any disposal between them is treated as having taken place at such consideration as neither a gain nor a loss will accrue (s 58 TCGA 1992). Consequently, the spouse acquiring the asset will acquire it at the same value as the spouse disposing of the asset did plus an allowance for indexation. However, for all	**15.17 Capital gains tax – general**

other purposes spouses are treated as separate individuals. They are each liable for their own gains and each is entitled to the annual exemption which for the year 1995–96 is £6,000. As a consequence of separate taxation losses incurred by one spouse cannot be offset against gains made by the other. Both spouses are entitled to retirement relief. Only one principal private residence exemption is available to a married couple. Jointly held property will be treated as being held 50/50 unless an election has been made to treat it otherwise. An election made for income tax purposes is effective for CGT.

15.18   Capital gains tax – separation

If a couple separate, the rules for married couples will not apply if the separation is in such circumstances that it is likely permanent; however, until such time as the couple is legally divorced they remain connected persons (s 286 TCGA 1992). The problem does arise in respect of the matrimonial home where one spouse leaves it as it will then cease to be that spouse's principal private residence. Under extra statutory concession D6, no charge will arise if, the partner who ceases to occupy the home subsequently, as part of a financial settlement, disposes of it to the other partner, provided that the partner that has left the matrimonial home had not elected for another property to be their principal private residence in the meantime, and the other spouse has continued to reside in it.

15.19   Inheritance tax

The parties to a marriage are treated as separate people for inheritance tax purposes. Each is entitled to all the various exemptions and reliefs. There is a specific exemption for transfers between spouses. However, unlike income tax and capital gains tax, it is irrelevant whether they are living together. Therefore, transfers between spouses will be exempt from IHT during their marriage; for these purposes the marriage will continue until any decree absolute.

Income Tax – Special Cases

Partnership taxation

The rules applicable to partnerships have been changed. The new rules will apply to new businesses commencing on or after 6 April 1994. Existing businesses will be taxed under the new rules from 6 April 1997 and, in the meantime, transitional rules apply.

A partnership is not a separate legal entity. To see whether a partnership exists, it is necessary to look to the general law which is found in the Partnership Act 1890. Under the general law, partners are jointly and severally liable for partnership debts. However, under the new tax provisions each individual partner will be assessed separately and the necessary tax is collected from each individual partner. Each individual partner is treated as carrying on a notional trade. The profits of the partnership are allocated to the partners according to their partnership shares. If a partner leaves the partnership, that partner is treated as ceasing her own notional trade. The other partners are treated as continuing.

A salary given to a partner is still a division of profit. It is treated as a first charge on the profits. Similarly, any interest paid to a partner is merely a first charge on profit.

Where a person ceases to be a member of a partnership because of age, ill health or death, then annual payments paid to the partner, widow or widower are not treated as investment income but as earned income.

International aspects

Where a person derives income from more than one jurisdiction, it is possible that that income is taxable twice. In order to prevent double taxation, most jurisdictions will look at certain connecting factors. In the UK these connecting factors are:

- residence;
- ordinary residence; and
- domicile.

The UK will tax all of a person's income if they are resident or ordinarily resident. If a person is domiciled in the UK, that person will only be taxed upon income which is remitted to the UK if it is owned abroad.

There is no definition of residence. A person is treated as resident in the United Kingdom if the person spends more than six years here. If a person leaves the UK in order to work abroad, the person will be treated as resident in the UK if they reside in the UK for more than 91 days in any one tax year.

There is no statutory definition of an ordinary residence. Ordinary residence means habitual residence. The Inland Revenue treat a person as being ordinarily resident if they come to the UK with the intention of staying for more than three years.

Domicile is a concept of the general law. The person is domiciled in the country which they believe to be their real home. A person acquires a domicile of origin at birth but this may be changed at a later date, provided they share the necessary intentions.

In general, a partnership is resident in the country in which it is centrally managed and controlled.

The UK has two tests of residence for companies. A company is resident in the UK if it is incorporated in the UK. Further, a company is resident in the UK if it is centrally managed and controlled in the UK.

A trust is resident where the majority of the trustees are resident.

Taxation, marriages, separation and divorce

It was not until the budget proposals of 1988 that women had complete control over their own tax affairs.

Each spouse is allowed a personal allowance for the tax year commencing 6 April 1995 of £3,525.00. Married couples are entitled to the married couple's allowance which is £1,720. Married couple's allowance is given effect by multiplying it by 15% and deducting the resulting figure from a tax liability. In order to qualify for the married couple's allowance a couple must be living together. In the first instance, the allowance goes to the husband. Or many like to split the allowance between them in the way most beneficial. The wife may unilaterally elect to have the benefit of the allowance and is entitled to 50%. In the year of marriage the married couple's allowance is reduced by one-twelfth for every complete month prior to the date of marriage.

Married couples are entitled to interest relief of £30,000. This means that interest on a loan of up to £30,000 can be reclaimed against the tax payers income. However, most mortgage payments are within the Miras scheme and relief is given at source. There is no need for the tax relief to enter the calculation at all.

Property held jointly is treated as belonging to each spouse equally. It is possible for a married couple to elect and have a separate split in which case the income will be apportioned in the elected proportions.

On separation, couples are treated as single people again. However, the married couple's allowance will continue to be given for the year in which the couple separate.

On death, the husband is entitled to full married couple's allowance for the year in which his wife dies. Following that he is only entitled to the personal allowance. On the death of the husband, the wife is entitled to a personal allowance, the widows bereavement allowance for the year of death and the year following and also any unused amount of the married couple's allowance on the year of death.

Married people are connected for the purposes of capital gains tax. It is liable for their own gains and entitled to the annual exemption in which the year 1995–96 is £6,000. Only one exemption for the principle private residence is available to a married couple.

On separation the laws for married couples cease to apply, however they continue to be connected persons until divorce.

For inheritance tax purposes, transfers between spouses are exempt and continue to be exempt until the date of divorce.

Chapter 16

Corporation Tax – The Charge to Tax

This chapter looks at corporation tax, its structure and how it is charged. The next three chapters look at specific aspect of corporation tax.

16.1   Introduction

The need for a separate corporation tax arises because of the distinction between those businesses where the proprietors have a direct interest in their management and those where they do not. Thus, partnerships and sole traders do not pay corporation tax; their proprietors are taxed on the full amount of the profits of the business. By contrast, a company has a separate legal personality which is distinct from its incorporators; very often the owners (ie the shareholders) are different from the management (ie the directors). A company can therefore retain its profits; whereas, a sole trader or partnership cannot. In effect, sole traders and partnerships are taxed as if all their profit is distributed each year. The problem with a company is that, if it is taxed only at the corporate level, each shareholder will in effect suffer the same rate of tax; ie the increase in the value of each shareholder's share will be equal and will be reduced by the tax borne by the company, the wealth of each shareholder will therefore be reduced by an equal amount. In a progressive system of taxation this is considered objectionable. However, if profit is only taxed when it is distributed, taxation could be postponed indefinitely. If, however, both the profit and any distributions are taxed, this would arguably lead to double taxation; and the profit having already been taxed means that any further tax on a distribution may be seen as a disincentive to companies to distribute their profits. The contrary view is that it is an encouragement to retain earnings and therefore investment. However, it can also be argued that efficient investment is achieved by shareholders choosing how to invest the profits not by forcing a company to invest as a result of a desire to minimise taxation.

16.2   Theories of corporation tax

There are three basic systems of corporation tax, each gives rise to its own difficulties. The three systems are generally known as:

16.3   The three systems of taxation

- the classical system;
- the imputation system; and
- the split rate system.

| 16.3.1 | The classical system |

Under the classical system profits are taxed both at the company level and then again when distributed to shareholders. As stated above, the classical system is criticised because it is said to lead to double taxation. However, the system arises out of the desire of governments to tax retained earnings and to provide a progressive system of taxation; as has already been stated, if only profits were taxed, all shareholders would suffer the same rate of tax; if only distributions were taxed, tax could be postponed indefinitely.

The second criticism levelled at the classical system is the disincentive for companies to distribute income. The greater the distribution the higher the rate of tax suffered by the shareholder.

Notwithstanding these criticisms, some major economies do operate the classical system, most notably the USA.

| 16.3.2 | Imputation system |

Under an imputation system some of the tax paid by the company is imputed to the shareholder. Because of this, the rates of corporation tax in an imputation system are often higher than those under a classical system; however, in recent years the UK has moved towards relatively low rates of corporation tax notwithstanding the fact that it has an imputation system.

An imputation system works by allowing the shareholder a credit against income tax for tax which has been paid by the company. Thus, if a company has £100 of profit on which it pays tax at 40%, it will have a net £60. If it then distributes half of this, the shareholder will received £30. Assuming that a quarter of the tax paid by the company is imputed to the shareholder, the shareholder will be treated as having received £40 (£30 + £10 tax credit). Further, assuming that the shareholder's rate of tax is £25%, the shareholder will be liable to £10 tax on the £40. This will be satisfied by the tax credit. The shareholder will have nothing more to pay. The £10 of tax paid by the company is used to satisfy the tax liability of the shareholder.

Where all the tax paid by the company is imputed to the shareholder, double taxation is eliminated completely. In the UK only part of the tax is imputed. Note, however, that the system currently operated in the UK is a partial imputation system not because higher rate taxpayers are liable to tax over and above the imputed amount, but because the tax credit allowed to a shareholder is only a proportion of the tax paid by the company. A partial imputation system can still eliminate double taxation where the credit eliminates tax on the shareholders' dividend.

Further, notwithstanding that the imputation system is intended to eliminate the bias away from distributing profits, a full imputation system can still produce such a bias if the personal rate of tax is higher than the amount of the fully imputed tax credit resulting in further tax being payable on the receipt of a dividend.

Under a split rate system retained profits and distributions are taxed at two different rates. In theory this gives an incentive to the company to distribute. However, the split rate system can be looked at as a partial imputation system with the difference between the rate of tax on retained profits and the rate of distributed profits being the tax credit. The disincentive brought about by dividends being taxed at higher rates is therefore, still present.

16.3.3   Split rate systems

Corporation tax dates back to 1965 when it was introduced to replace income tax and profits tax on companies' profits. The tax introduced in 1965 was a classical system. In 1973 an imputation system was introduced. The rate of tax remained unchanged at 52% until 1984 when it was gradually reduced. It now stands at 33%.

16.4   United Kingdom corporation tax

Corporation tax is charged by reference to financial years. A financial year runs from 1 April to 31 March and is referred to by reference to the year in which it starts. Hence, the financial year 1996 runs from 1 April 1996 to 31 March 1997.

16.4.1   Financial years

A consequence of the imputation system operated in the UK is that profits should only be taxed once whilst in the corporate sector. Thus, the company making the profits is taxed, if it then distributes these profits to a shareholder which is a company, that shareholder will not be taxed on that receipt. In fact, whilst ever those profits are distributed to a company which is within the charge to corporation tax no more tax will be due. A company in receipt of dividends can therefore use that receipt to pay a dividend without incurring a tax liability in respect of it.

Corporation tax is charged on companies by s 6 ICTA 1988. A company is defined by s 832 ICTA 1988 as any body corporate or unincorporated association, but does not include a partnership, a local authority or a local authority association. Company therefore includes trade unions and sports clubs. Section 9 ICTA 1988 provides that notwithstanding that companies are liable to corporation tax, the amount of income liable to corporation tax is to be calculated in accordance with income tax principles unless otherwise provided. Thus, a

16.5   Charge to corporation tax

company's income is calculated in accordance with the rules applying to the various schedules and then charged to corporation tax.

A company is chargeable to corporation tax if it is resident in the UK which means either it is incorporated in the UK or managed and controlled in the UK. By s 11 ICTA 1988 if a company which is not resident in the UK trades in the UK through a branch or agency it is chargeable to corporation tax on its chargeable profits wherever arising. At first sight this would appear to make a non-resident company liable to corporation tax on its worldwide profits by virtue only of trading through a branch or agency in the UK. However, the liability is restricted by the definition of chargeable profits in s 11(2) ICTA 1988 which limits chargeable profits to any trading income arising directly or indirectly through or from the branch or agency, income from property or rights held by the branch or agency, and any chargeable gains accruing on the disposal of any assets situated in the UK and used in the branch or agency. Consequently, there needs to be a connection between the profits and the branch or agency.

Having made companies liable to corporation tax, s 6(2) ICTA 1988 exempts from income tax:

- companies resident in the UK; and

- income of non-resident companies which satisfies the definition of chargeable profits described above.

However, this does not mean that all other non-UK resident companies are exempt from UK tax. A non-UK resident company which derives income from the UK, for example from letting property, will be liable to income tax not corporation tax. This is for two reasons, first, letting properties is not a trade (*Fry v Salisbury House Estates*, see Chapter 5) and secondly, it is doubtful whether a let building is a branch or agency of a non-resident company.

A company is charged to corporation tax by reference to the profits of an accounting period (s 12 ICTA 1988). The concept of the accounting period is central to UK corporate taxation. In no circumstances can an accounting period exceed 12 months (s 12(3)(a) ICTA 1988). An accounting period will also end on the date to which a company makes up its accounts. Most companies make up their accounts on an annual basis; the period of their accounts will therefore be coincident with the accounting period for tax purposes.

An accounting period can also end on the happening of any one of the following events:

- the company begins or ceases to trade;

- the company begins or ceases to be resident in the UK;

- the company ceases to be within the charge to corporation tax (eg it ceases to have a source of income); or

- the company is wound up, on the commencement of the winding up.

An accounting period will commence on the happening of one of the following events:

- the company comes within the charge to corporation tax; or

- an accounting period of the company comes to an end.

The fact that an accounting period cannot exceed 12 months means that if a company alters its accounting date by, for example, making up accounts for an 18 month period, the 18 month period will be split into two accounting periods; the first of 12 months and the second of six months.

Because tax is charged by reference to financial years and calculated by reference to the profits of a company's accounting period where, as is often the case, a company's accounting period straddles more than one financial year, an apportionment may need to be made where the rate of tax in the two financial years is different.

Example

Company I Ltd makes its accounts up to 30 September each year. Its profits for the year ending 30 September 1994 were £100,000. The rate of tax for the financial year 1983 was 50% and for 1984 was 45%. The £100,000 is there apportioned as to £50,000 for 1983 and £50,000 for 1984. The 50,000 for 1983 will be aggregated with the other profits (as apportioned) for 1983 and be taxed at 50%. The £50,000 for 1984 will be aggregated with the other profits for 1984 and taxed at 45%.

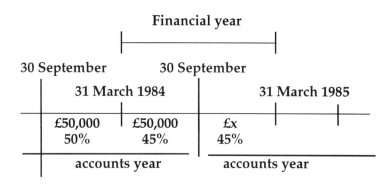

16.6	Small companies' rate

As many companies make up their accounts to 31 December an apportionment is often necessary.

When the imputation system was first introduced in 1973 so, also, was a reduced rate of tax for small companies. In fact, small company is a misnomer. The reduced rate of tax applies to companies with profits below a certain level. A major UK company which had a bad year and made only a small profit would be a 'small company' for these purposes. The reason for the reduced rate is twofold; first, small companies are dependent to a greater extent on retained earnings, therefore to impose a high rate of tax on the company in the expectation that a part of it would be imputed to the shareholders would penalise small companies where the profits were not distributed. Secondly, small companies are often the result of a sole trader or partnership deciding to incorporate. The small companies' rate therefore helps effect a transition between one business medium and another.

When the small companies' rate was introduced the rate equated to the basic rate of income tax. Therefore, if the company only distributed income to the shareholders up to the basic rate band the whole of the companies tax was imputed to the shareholder; there was therefore no element of double taxation. This state of affairs continued until quite recently when the rate of tax on dividends was reduced to 20% and the imputed tax likewise, the small companies' rate remained at 25%.

For the financial year 1995, the small companies' rate applies to companies whose profits are below £300,000.

For companies whose profits are above £300,000 but below £1,500,000 tapering relief applies. The way this relief applies is often misunderstood. Once the lower limit is exceeded the profits of the company are taxed at the full rate and then relief is given against this full rate. In effect in order to arrive at the full 33% tax charge at the upper limit, the profits between the lower and upper limit must be taxed at a higher average rate than the rate of corporation tax.

A company's profits, are its income profits plus its chargeable gains plus its franked investment income ('FII'). FII is dividends received from other companies grossed up to take into account the imputation tax. It should be noted that although FII is not charged to tax in the hands of the company it is taken into account when calculating the company's profits for the purposes of the small companies' rate.

The FII is grossed up by applying the fraction:

$$\frac{100}{100-L}$$

where L is the lower rate of tax.

Tapering relief works by applying a statutory fraction to the figure given by the following formula:

$$(M–P) \times \frac{I}{P}$$

where   M is the upper relevant amount (£1,500,000)

I is the company's income (profits minus FII)

P is the company's profits

(where a company has no FII $^1/_P = 1$ and can be ignored).

The statutory fraction for 1995–96 (financial year 1995) is $^1/_{50}$.

This fraction can be calculated in the following way. The difference between the full rate of corporation tax and the small companies' rate is 8%. The full benefit of this 8% reduction is received when profits are £300,000. The benefit reduces to zero at £1,500,000. The tapering fraction is therefore:

$$8\% \quad \times \frac{300,000}{1,500,000–300,000} = {}^1/_{50}$$

A number of points need to be noted.

The small companies' rate does not operate as a relief on the first £300,000 of all companies' profits; if it did, all companies would benefit and not just those with small profits.

Between £300,000 and £1,500,000 the marginal rate of tax is higher than the corporation tax rate.

The marginal rate can be calculated as follows:

£300,000 at 25%   = £75,000

£1,500,000 at 33%   = £495,000

Therefore, in order for the tax rate on £1,500,000 to be 33%, £420,000 of tax needs to be raised on the £1,200,000 between the lower and upper rates.

The % rate of tax on this £1,200,000 will therefore be:

$$\frac{£420,000}{1,200,000} \times 100 = 35\%$$

The effect of this is that there may be disincentive for companies to increase their profits above £300,000. The marginal rate of tax is higher than the basic rate of income tax; therefore, if the extra £1 above £300,000 can be taken out of the company in a way which attracts basic rate tax it will be more tax efficient. One way this can be done is if the directors pay basic rate tax. An extra £1 of remuneration will reduce the profit by £1. This £1 will be taxed in the hands of the director at 25%. A tax saving of 7 pence.

Without any special provisions shareholders could reduce their tax by splitting a trade which, for example, made £1,500,000 of profit, into five separate companies each making £300,000 and thus being eligible for the small companies' rate. Section 13 ICTA 1988 provides that where a company has associated companies, the upper and lower limits are divided by one plus the number of associated companies. In the above example the upper limit would be reduced for each company to:

$$\frac{£1,500,000}{1+4} = £300,000$$

Thus none of them would be eligible.

A company is associated with another if at any given time one of the two has control of the other or both are under the control of the same person or persons (control for these purposes is defined in s 416 ICTA 1988, see Chapter 18).

The small companies' rate only applies to UK resident companies. Therefore a branch or agency of a non-resident company trading in the UK would still be taxed at 33% regardless of the level of profit.

The small companies' rate does not apply to close investment holding companies. These are dealt with in Chapter 18.

16.7 Calculating a company's profit

When calculating the income of a company, the same principles are applied as when calculating the income of an individual. Thus, the amount of income and the time when it arises are calculated as if an accounting period of the company were a year of assessment. The income tax law to be applied for an accounting period is that in force for the year of assessment in which the accounting period ends. A trading company will therefore calculate its trading income in accordance with the rules for Schedule D Case I and deduct expenses in accordance with s 74 ICTA 1988.

A sample proforma for calculating profits and the corporation tax due is given below.

	[Notes]	£	£
Schedule D Case I	16.7.1	X	
Schedule A		X	
Schedule D Case III		X	
Schedule D Case V	16.7.2	X	
Other Income	16.7.3	X	
Add Chargeable Gains	16.7.4	X	
			X
Less Charges	16.7.5		(X)
Profits Chargeable to Corporation Tax			X
Corporation Tax on profits @ 33%	16.7.6		X
Less: Double Taxation Relief	16.7.7		(X)
Less: ACT set-off			(X)
Less: Income Tax on UFII	16.7.8		(X)
Tax Credit on BSI			(X)
Mainstream Corporation Tax Liability			X

16.7.1 Schedule D Case I

The computation of Schedule D Case I income is the same as for income tax except that annual interest, annual payments and annuities cannot be deducted as a trading expense; instead, they must be deducted as a charge on income. However, an exception to this is annual interest, which can be deducted as a trading expense provided that it is payable to a bank carrying a *bona fide* banking business in the UK.

In certain circumstances the Inland Revenue can substitute a different value than that which is entered in the company's books. Section 770 ICTA 1988 is aimed at transfer pricing.

Without s 770 ICTA 1988 a company could charge reduced prices to another company in the group which was not resident in the United Kingdom. This would depress the UK company's profits and inflate those of the buyer. It may be the case that the foreign company is exempt from tax or suffers tax at a lower rate than the UK company. The group's profits overall would, therefore, be increased. The UK company may also realise a loss as a result of undercharging. The Inland Revenue can therefore substitute market value if the vendor and the purchaser are 'associated'; which means either one has control over the other or both are controlled by some third party. The provisions do not apply where the purchaser is resident in the UK because, of course, any under value in the vendor's books will result in a profit chargeable to UK tax in the purchaser's books. Section 770 applies not only to sales of goods but also to lettings and hirings of property, grants and transfers of rights, interests and licences and the giving of business facilities of any kind. The Inland Revenue consider that these latter words include transactions such as interest free loans.

Capital allowances are deducted as a trading expense of the trade carried on by the company and if there is a balancing charge this is treated as a trading receipt (s 144(2) CAA 1990).

16.7.2   Schedule D Case V

A company which wishes to trade abroad can do it in one of two ways; first, it can set up a foreign subsidiary and, second, it can trade through a foreign branch or agency. If it trades through a subsidiary, the subsidiary's profits will be transferred to the UK by way of dividend; this will be chargeable to tax under Schedule D Case V as income from a foreign possession. The income from a foreign branch, however, will be included in the company's Schedule D Case I profits. In both cases, the foreign profits may have already suffered tax in the foreign territory and, consequently, the company may be entitled to relief in calculating the UK tax in respect of the foreign tax.

16.7.3   Other income

A company may receive other income eg building society interest or debenture interest. Where these are received under deduction of tax, the amount is 'grossed up' and included in the company's profits. Relief is given at a later stage in the computation for tax deducted at source.

16.7.4   Capital gains

Corporation tax is charged on a company's profits which includes both income and chargeable gains. A company's chargeable gains (and losses) are computed in the same way as for an individual; however, many of the reliefs available to an individual are not available to a company. Further, notwithstanding that a company's income and chargeable gains are aggregated for the purpose of determining profits a distinction must still be drawn between the two for the purpose of dealing with losses. A trading loss can only be carried forward and used against profits of the same trade in future accounting periods. A capital loss can only be set against capital gains, it cannot be set against other income. Nor can a capital loss be surrendered to other group companies.

Charges on income include:

- annual interest, eg debenture interest but not annual interest paid to a bank and which has been deducted in calculating the company's Schedule D Case I profits;

- other interest, eg short interest (note short interest on a bank loan, ie overdraft interest, is usually deducted as a trading expense);

- annual payments AND covenanted payments to charities;

- qualifying donations, ie those made under s 339 ICTA 1988; and

- patent royalties.

Section 338 ICTA 1988 specifically excludes as a charge on income any dividend or other distribution.

A charge on income is deductible in the accounting period in which it is paid not in that in which it is payable. Therefore, if a charge on income has been accrued in the company's books as an expense without being paid, it will be disallowed. Further, a company should ensure if at all possible that charges on income are paid towards the end of its accounting period so as to obtain tax relief for the payment as early as possible, ie as soon after the payment as possible. Note that short interest (ie interest other than annual interest) paid to a bank and which is deductible as a charge on income may be deducted if it has been debited in the books of the person to whom it is owed although it has not been paid (s 388(2) ICTA 1988).

Certain other conditions need to be satisfied in order for the charge to be deductible:

- the payment must be made out of the company's profits brought into charge to corporation tax (s 338(1) ICTA 1988);

- the payment must be charged to (ie paid out of) income unless it is interest in which case it can be charged to capital account (*Chancery Lane Safe Deposit and Offices Co Ltd v IRC* (1966); s 338(5) ICTA 1988);

16.7.5   Charges on income

- the payment must be borne by the company; therefore, if the company is reimbursed the expense it will not be borne by the company;

- the payment must be made under a liability incurred for valuable and sufficient consideration (*Ball v National and Grindley's Bank Ltd* (1971)).

The above rules apply for all charges. Where the payment is of interest, certain other conditions also need to be satisfied. The payment must be:

- paid by a trading company; or

- wholly and exclusively for the purposes of company's trade;

- paid by an investment company; or

- eligible for relief under s 338A ICTA 1988 (to interest for loans to buy land).

Further, conditions are imposed when the charge is paid to a non-resident. These are:

- the payment must be made under deduction of tax and the amount deducted accounted for to the Inland Revenue (s 338(4)(a) ICTA 1988); or

- the payment is made out of Case IV and V income (s 338(4)(d) ICTA 1988); or

- it is interest payable out of foreign trading income (ss 338(4)(c) and 340 ICTA 1988).

Where a company makes a covenanted donation to charity, the amount paid can be deducted as a charge. In order to be a covenanted donation, the following conditions need to be satisfied:

- it must be made to a body of persons or trust established for charitable purposes only; and

- the period for which the payments are to be made must be *capable of* exceeding three years; and

- the obligation to make the payments must be terminable only with the consent of the charity entitled to the payments; and

- must be made otherwise than for consideration in money or money's worth.

A covenanted donation to a charity cannot be a distribution (s 339(6) ICTA 1988) therefore, it can vary with a company's profits. Because of this, a charity which wishes to carry on a commercial venture will set up a company which covenants to pay its profits to the charity. The amount paid therefore becomes a deduction from the profits and thus reduces the profits of the company to nil and thereby eliminates the charge to tax. Profits upon which the charity would otherwise be chargeable are taken out of the charge to tax.

A *covenanted donation* to a charity must be distinguished from a *qualifying donation* to a charity (s 339 ICTA 1988). A company can make a qualifying donation if it is UK resident and deducts tax on making the gift and if it also provides the charity with a certificate showing the tax deducted. A payment cannot be a qualifying donation if it is a covenanted payment or it is otherwise deductible as a trading expense. A qualifying donation to a charity is treated as charge on income.

The amount at this point of the calculation is aggregated with the company's franked investment income to ascertain whether the small companies' rate applies. Franked investment income from another group company is ignored for these purposes. Franked investment income is treated as coming from another group company if it could be made the subject of a group income election. Group income elections are dealt with under s 247 ICTA 1988 (see Chapter 19) and apply generally if one company is a 51% subsidiary of another.	16.7.6 Small companies' rate

It should be remembered that if a company's profits exceed £300,000 corporation tax is charged at 33% but relief is given on the tapering scale.

For the financial year 1995 the small companies' rate is 25%.

Where a company earns profits abroad, these profits may have already been taxed. For the UK to tax them again would result in double taxation and would probably act as a disincentive to companies to trade abroad. There are, therefore, a number of ways in which the UK tax system mitigates the harshness of double taxation. The first is treaty relief. The UK has entered into double taxation treaties with many countries which state, in the event of double taxation arising, which country shall have priority to tax the company and how credit shall be given by the other country for the tax levied. The second is by way of unilateral relief. Unilateral relief applies either because there is no treaty with the country concerned or, if there is a treaty, it does not deal with the particular tax in question. Where there is a treaty it will apply in preference to unilateral relief. The amount of unilateral relief available is for the amount of foreign tax paid on those profits.	16.7.7 Double taxation relief

| 16.7.8 | ACT set-off | Once the corporation tax charge of the company has been determined, the company can set off advance corporation tax paid when distributing profits during the year. The amount of ACT which can be set off is restricted to the amount of ACT which would have been payable if the company had distributed an amount which together with the ACT payable on it would equal the profits for that period. |

As a consequence of setting double taxation relief off before ACT, the company may have an amount of surplus ACT which cannot be set-off. In recent years this has been a major problem for UK companies. Surplus ACT which can never be set off because of a company's profit earning structure, in effect, means that a company is being subjected to a higher rate of tax than the stated 33%.

| 16.7.9 | Income tax credit | Where income is received which has had income tax deducted, for example building society interest, to the extent that the tax credit has not been used in making payments without having to account for tax, it can then be set against the tax bill for that year. |

16.8   Trading losses

Where a company makes a trading loss, it can be utilised by the company or, if the company is a member of a group it may be surrendered to another member of the group. Group losses are dealt with in Chapter 19, the following paragraphs deal with the use of losses by the company making the loss.

| 16.8.1 | Carry forward – s 393 ICTA 1988 | Where a company incurs a trading loss under Schedule D Case I, the loss can be carried forward and set against the income of the same trade for succeeding accounting periods provided that the company continues to carry on that trade in those succeeding accounting periods (s 393 ICTA 1988). |

This is the general rule. No election need be made. If the profits of the subsequent accounting period is insufficient, s 393(8) ICTA 1988 allows the losses to be set against interest or dividends on investments which would be taken into account as trading receipts but for the fact that they have already been subject to tax.

Section 393(1) ICTA 1988 applies to trading losses under Schedule D Case V as well as those under Schedule D Case I.

Where there is an excess of charges on income over and above the profits chargeable to corporation tax and those charges on income were made wholly and exclusively for the purposes of the trade then the company can treat as a loss an amount up to the amount of the excess or the amount of the charges, whichever is the loss.

In para 16.8.1 above, it was stated that the losses will be carried forward if the company takes no action, under s 393 ICTA 1988 a company can elect to set a Schedule D Case I trading loss incurred in an accounting period against profits of whatever description of the same accounting period; this includes both non-trading income and capital gains. For any remaining loss, the company can elect to set it against the profits of the three years immediately preceding the accounting period in which the loss was occurred provided the company had been carrying on the trade in those previous three years. If one of the earlier accounting periods straddles the three year date then the profits of that period must be apportioned and the losses set against that part falling within the year period.

A further condition is that the trade must have been carried on under some statutory authority or it must be shown that the trade was carried on with a view to commercial gain either in the trade itself or of some larger concern of which the trade forms a part.

Unlike s 393 ICTA 1988, s 393A ICTA 1988 does not apply to Schedule D Case V losses.

16.8.2 Current year and previous year

If the company incurs a loss under Schedule D Case VI, there is only provision for the loss to be set off against other Case VI profits either of the same year or succeeding years (s 396 ICTA 1988).

16.8.3 Other losses

Although companies are chargeable to corporation tax, the rules relating to capital gains are the same as those for individuals. Therefore, if a company makes a capital loss on the disposal of a chargeable asset, that loss may be set against either, chargeable gains for that year of assessment or, carried forward and set against gains of a succeeding accounting period. In the ordinary course, there is no provision for setting capital losses against trading income.

16.8.4 Capital losses

A new system for paying corporation tax came into force on 1 October 1993. It affects any company with an accounting period ending on or after that date. The new system is referred to as 'pay and file'. The reason for this is that if a company is not to incur a liability for interest it must pay its corporation tax nine months after the end of the accounting period; this is regardless of whether an assessment has been issued. Three months later (ie 12 months after the end of its accounting period) the company must file a return, unless the company receives a notice from its inspector in which case the return must be filed within three months of the notice. The return will contain such details and be accompanied by such documents

16.9 Paying corporation tax

as are necessary to assess the company's liability to corporation tax. The assessment may be more or less than the amount paid; if more, then interest is payable on the extra from the nine month date; if less, a repayment with interest is due from the Inland Revenue. However, the interest rates are different and when making the decision to pay at the nine months date, the company will have to decide whether to err on the side of caution and pay more than may be necessary or risk a higher interest bill if it underestimates the payment.

Corporation Tax – The Charge to Tax

There are three systems of corporation tax: the classical system, the imputation system and the specific rate system. The United Kingdom operates an imputation system of corporation tax. Under the imputation system, some of the tax paid by a company is imputed to the shareholders.

Corporation tax is charged by reference to financial years. A financial year runs from 1 April to the following 31 March. It is identified by the year in which it starts. Corporation tax is charged on companies. Corporation tax is calculated by reference to the information arising under the various schedules. The tax is calculated by reference to accounting periods. Because tax is charged by reference to financial years and yet calculated by reference to accounting periods, it may be necessary to make an apportionment for tax purposes. For small companies, that is companies earning under £300,000 in profit, a special rate is applied and called the small companies' rate. Companies whose profits are below £300,000 are taxed 25%, those above £1,500,000 are taxed at the full rate of 33%. Between £300,000 and £1,500,000 a sliding scale operates. The affect of the sliding scale is to tax the profits between these two amounts at a rate higher than the normal rate of corporation tax. Consequently, the combined total of the lower rate plus the tax of the sliding scale means that the tax paid by the company gradually increases and all the profits are taxed at the full rate of corporation tax, when profits reach £1,500,000.

A company's profit is calculated in the same way as for income tax. The total amount is then aggregated and charged to corporation tax. However, there are certain specific rules which apply to corporation tax only. For example, capital allowances are deducted as a trading expense.

A company's chargeable gains are computed just the same way for an individual; however, many of the reliefs available to an individual are not available to a company.

Certain amounts are deductible as charges on income. These include annual interest, annual payments, covenanted payments to charges and patent royalties. Once the amount chargeable to tax has been calculated, the correct rate of corporation tax is then applied. ACT is then deducted. The amount of ACT deductible is such an amount as would have been payable if the company had distributed an amount which together with the ACT thereon equalled the profits chargeable to tax.

Chapter 17

Corporation Tax – Tax Distributions, ACT and Schedule F

When a company makes a distribution of its profits to shareholders, it must make a payment of advance corporation tax ('ACT'). The ACT has two uses. First, it can be set against the company's corporation tax bill at the end of the year; second, it satisfies the shareholder's liability to tax at the lower rate on the dividend.

In this way the part of the tax paid by the company, ie the ACT, also serves to satisfy part of the liability of the shareholder; it is imputed to them. It is often thought that ACT is an essential part of an imputation system, as will as explained in para 17.4 this is not so; however, ACT greatly helps the administration of the system.

17.1   General overview

Because a distribution is made out of after tax profits, it cannot be deducted in computing profits. For this reason the definition of distribution, which is to be found in s 209 ICTA 1988 is very wide in order to catch payments which are really distributions but which have been disguised in such a way so as to look like a deductible expense.

Individuals are charged to income tax on distributions under Schedule F. Companies are not taxable on the receipt of a distribution because the distribution represents profits which have already been subject to corporation tax in the hands of the payer, instead they receive franked investment income ('FII'). The uses to which FII can be put are discussed in para 17.5.2. The most common types of distribution are described in the following paragraphs.

17.2   Distributions – general

This is the most common type of distribution, a cash dividend paid to shareholders. A capital dividend is one paid out of profits which are subject to corporation tax on capital gains although it is rarely referred to as a capital dividend.

17.2.1   Dividends – s 209(2)(a) ICTA 1988

The distribution must be out of assets of the company; this can be in cash or otherwise. It must also be to a shareholder in his capacity as a shareholder. A return of capital is not a distribution. If the shareholder gives new consideration, there is no distribution to the extent of that new consideration.

17.2.2   Distribution out of assets of the company – s 209(2)(b) ICTA 1988

| 17.2.3 | The issue of bonus redeemable shares and securities – s 209(2)(c) ICTA 1988 | To the extent that bonus redeemable shares are issued for new consideration they are not treated as a distribution; to the extent that the issue is made out of a share premium account which was created on the subscription for shares at a premium, this is treated as new consideration for these purposes (s 254(5) ICTA 1988). |

| 17.2.4 | Securities which carry on excessive rate of interest – s 209(2)(d) ICTA 1988 | Interest is deductible expense of a company in arriving at its profit for tax purposes; by charging an excessive rate of interest a company would receive a deduction for what was, in effect, the paying out of profit. |

To the extent that the payment represents a repayment of the principal amount of the debt or some part of it, that part of the payment is not a distribution; neither is any part which represents that element of the interest which is at a commercial rate.

The distribution does *not* need to be made to a shareholder.

It should be noted that where s 209(2)(d) ICTA 1988 applies, if the company which is in receipt of the distribution is within the charge to UK tax then the s 209(2)(d) ICTA 1988 is disapplied by s 212 ICTA 1988. This is because there will be no loss of tax to the UK revenue, because although the payer will receive a deduction the payee will be chargeable to tax on the excessive interest.

| 17.2.5 | Transfers of assets or liabilities – s 209(2)(f) and (4) ICTA 1988 | It is only the excess of the market value over the amount of any consideration received which is treated as a distribution. |

| **17.3** | **The distinction between qualifying and non-qualifying distributions** | Section 14 ICTA 1988 provides that where a company makes a qualifying distribution it shall be liable to pay an amount of corporation tax (advance corporation tax). It is therefore necessary to determine what amounts to a qualifying as opposed to a non-qualifying distribution. The answer is to be found in s 14(2) ICTA 1988 which makes all distributions qualifying distributions except: |

- the issue of any redeemable share capital with s 209(2)(c) ICTA 1988 (para 17.2.3 above); or

- a distribution by a company of any share capital which has been received by that company which with regard to the company issuing it is redeemable.

Why, then, is redeemable share capital not treated as a qualifying distribution? The answer lies in an analysis of the balance sheet of the issuing company. When a company makes a distribution falling within any subsection of s 209 ICTA 1988 other than s 209(2)(c) ICTA 1988 (ie a qualifying distribution) value is transferred from the company to the shareholder or other person receiving the distribution; consequently, the assets of the company are reduced. Where, however, a company issues redeemable shares there is no immediate reduction in the company's assets. There will only be a reduction in the company's assets when the shares are ultimately redeemed. Similarly, where a company has received redeemable securities from another company and then distributes them nothing is at that time leaving the corporate sector.

When the shares are subsequently redeemed, money will pass out of the company and into the hands of the shareholder. Without more, this would be considered a repayment of share capital. However, s 211 ICTA 1988 provides that where a company issues bonus shares (which will include bonus redeemable shares) other than for the receipt of new consideration, the amount of any distribution in respect of them shall not be considered a repayment of share capital. The amount paid on redemption will fall in s 209(2)(b) ICTA 1988 and will therefore at the time of redemption be a qualifying distribution.

The shareholder is treated as receiving a distribution on both occasions; however, there are provisions preventing double taxation (see para 17.7).

When a company makes a qualifying distribution, it must pay an amount of corporation tax ('ACT'). The amount of ACT payable is expressed as a fraction of the distribution. This fraction is calculated using the formula:

17.3.1   Qualifying distributions – company

$$\frac{I}{100 - I}$$

where I is the percentage at which income tax at the lower rate is charged.

The company must account to the Inland Revenue for the ACT 14 days after the end of the quarter in which the distribution is made. For these purposes a final distribution is paid where it becomes due and payable (s 834(3) ICTA 1988) an interim dividend is paid when it is actually paid. The quarters are 31 March, 30 June, 30 September and 31 December. Where the company's accounting period ends on a date other than one of the quarter dates the company must account for ACT 14 days from the end of the accounting period for any distribution made between the end of a quarter and the end of the accounting period.

A qualifying distribution plus the associated ACT is called a franked payment. Consequently, if a company pays a dividend of £800 the ACT on the distribution will be £200 and the franked payment will be £1,000.

The ACT which the company pays can be set-off against the company's mainstream corporation tax.

The amount of ACT which can be set-off is, however, restricted to the amount of ACT which would be payable had the company made a distribution at the end of the accounting period of an amount which, together with the ACT thereon equals the company's profits charged to corporation tax in that period.

The excess is referred to as surplus ACT. Section 239(3) ICTA 1988 provides that where a company has an amount of surplus ACT it can elect, within two years after the end of the accounting period in which the surplus ACT arose, to carry the surplus back and treat it as ACT paid in an accounting period beginning in the six years preceding that accounting period.

The ACT used in this way must be set against later years before earlier years.

To the extent that surplus ACT cannot be carried back, it can be carried forward indefinitely.

To generate the maximum cash flow dividends should be paid as late in the accounting period as possible but as early in the quarter.

17.4   ACT theory

At first sight it may be surprising that a company can generate surplus ACT or that there should be some restriction on the amount of ACT that a company can set against its mainstream corporation tax.

Surplus ACT can arise for a number of reasons. In recent years it has arisen because of companies earning overseas profits with a foreign tax credit which is set against profits before ACT. This means that a company might be left with a higher distributable profit than taxable profit.

Previously surplus ACT arose because of the discrepancy between accounting profit and tax profit. The UK's system of capital allowances and other deductions meant that the accounting profit could be higher than the tax profit.

ACT is a system which is designed to alleviate the problem of the government not having the cash when it needs to repay the credit. ACT is paid when the distribution is made so the government has the cash to cover the tax credit. Because MCT is paid nine months after the end of the accounting period, a distribution made within the accounting period would otherwise result in a tax credit which would not be financed until much later.

Secondly, the amount of ACT capable of set-off is restricted to the amount that would have been payable had the taxable profit been distributed. Thus, the ACT set-off can never reduce the mainstream corporation tax payment to below zero; if it did, there would be an argument that the ACT should be repaid, however, the amount required to be repaid may also be required to repay a shareholder who pays no tax. The ACT system is therefore an administrative system designed to ensure that the tax credit of the shareholder is financed at the time the distribution is made. The restriction imposed on a company for the set-off of ACT may result in surplus ACT. Surplus ACT may also arise if in year one a company does not distribute its profit but in year two it distributes years one and two's profit. The company can carry the surplus ACT from year two to year one and reclaim the MCT paid the effect is as if the distribution had been made in year one.

It should be noted that ACT is *not* therefore an essential feature of an imputation system. It is an administrative device which ensures that the tax imputed to the shareholder is paid when the shareholder receives the profit. In countries where taxable profit effectively equates to tax profit, there is no ACT. Where the tax credit may exceed tax revenue there is often a special tax imposed to cover the difference, an example of such a system is France where the additional tax is called the *précompte*. Nor is ACT a withholding tax. It is, as its name suggests, an advance payment of corporation tax which tax is imputed to the shareholder.

The treatment of a qualifying distribution in the hands of the recipient will depend upon whether the recipient is an individual or a company.

17.5 Qualifying distributions – shareholders

Where an individual receives a qualifying distribution, the amount received is treated as the amount of the distribution 'grossed up' to take account of the associated ACT. It is, in reality, the amount of the franked payment discussed in para 17.3.1. If the amount of the franked payment is not known, the distribution is grossed up using the formula:

17.5.1   Individuals

$$\frac{100}{100 - I}$$

where I is the lower rate of tax.

The taxation of the distribution in the shareholder's hands is discussed in para 17.6.

17.5.2   Companies

As was stated in para 17.2 once profits have been subjected to corporation tax they will not be taxed again whilst in the corporate sector. A company receiving a qualifying distribution will receive a tax credit. Income in the hands of a company resident in the UK to which a tax credit attaches is called franked investment income (s 238 ICTA 1988). The amount of the FII is the distribution plus the tax credit.

A company can use franked investment income to frank its own distributions to shareholders. Section 241 ICTA 1988 provides that a company making qualifying distribution need only pay ACT to the extent that its franked payments exceed its franked investment income.

A UK company which is exempt from corporation tax, eg a charity, can reclaim the tax credit. In general other companies can use it to frank their own distributions. If the company making the distribution is a member of a group then it can elect to pay the distribution without ACT (see Chapter 19).

The advantages of a company receiving franked investment income is to defer the payment of corporation tax. The company can make a distribution without accounting for ACT. The company's MCT is increased but the tax bill remains the same.

17.5.3   Uses for surplus
franked investment
income

A company receiving franked investment income may not pay dividends or may pay insufficient dividends so as to leave the company with a surplus.

Section 241(3) ICTA 1988 provides that where a company has surplus franked investment income it may be carried forward to the next following accounting period and treated as surplus franked investment income arising in that period. Because it is treated as surplus franked investment income arising in the next following accounting period it can again be carried forward under s 241(3) ICTA 1988 if there is surplus in that period.

Surplus franked investment income cannot be carried back to previous accounting periods, it can only be carried forwards. However, s 242 ICTA 1988 provides an alternative use to which it can be put. The tax credit in the surplus franked investment income can be released. The system is quite complex and gives the company a temporary cash flow advantage. The company is allowed to set the following against the FII:

• trading losses;

- charges on income;

- management expenses; and

- certain capital allowances.

However, for these purposes surplus franked investment income does not include surplus franked investment income carried forward from previous years (s 242(9) ICTA 1988).

In effect the company is treated as having received profits equal to the franked investment income which has borne tax at 20%. By setting the losses against this profit the tax is repaid.

However, this repayment is reversed in the future if the company makes franked payments. The reason for this is that although a s 242 ICTA 1988 claim is advantageous in the short term, releasing funds to the company, in the long term the company would lose out. To take losses as an example, losses which could, if carried forward result in a tax saving of 33% have been used to reclaim tax at 20%; the reduction in the amount of FII would result in more ACT being paid in the future.

When the company is next able to make a distribution it must pay ACT in the normal way (it no longer has the surplus franked investment income); the amount of the loss which was used to release the ACT is re-instated. However, the amount of ACT reclaimed under s 242 ICTA 1988 is carried forward and that amount of ACT paid on subsequent distributions is unavailable for set off against MCT (s 244(2) ICTA 1988). Thus, the loss is reinstated and the ACT repaid is clawed back.

The reduction in the amount of ACT payable on a distribution of 25% to 20% was intended to alleviate the ACT problem. However, the reduction did not solve the problem and further measures were called for. Section 138 Finance Act 1994 introduced the foreign income dividend or FID. In essence, the new legislation allows a company which receives foreign income to pay a dividend out of that foreign income. The company pays ACT on the FID but it may then recover it subject to complex rules. In order to pay a FID, the company must make an election no later than the date on which the dividend is paid. Once the dividend has been paid the election cannot be withdrawn in respect of that particular dividend. The dividend must be paid in cash. As far as the shareholder is concerned a FID does not carry a tax credit. An individual shareholder is treated as receiving an amount grossed up at the lower rate, as if there were a tax credit. However, no repayment claim can be made. To the extent that a company has shareholders within each class of taxpayer ie nil rate, lower rate and higher rate, the payment of the FID will be

17.5.4   Foreign income dividends ('FIDs')

disadvantageous to the nil rate taxpayer. A company cannot elect to pay a FID on certain shares and not on others. As far as a company is concerned it will not be treated as receiving franked investment income, however, if a company has received a FID and pays a FID it will only have to account for ACT on the excess of FIDs paid over FIDs received. To the extent that it receives more FIDs than it pays in an accounting period, the excess can be carried forward to frank FIDs paid by it in a future accounting period.

17.6   Schedule F

An individual shareholder is charged to tax on distributions from UK companies under Schedule F (s 20 ICTA 1988). The system of taxing dividends has recently become more complex as a result of the government's desire to reduce the surplus ACT problem.

The taxation of individuals can be expressed by a number of simple rules:

- the amount of the distribution carries a tax credit which for 1995 is equal to one-quarter of the amount of the distribution;

- the aggregate of the distribution and the tax credit enters the calculation as the taxpayer's income;

- distributions received by a shareholder are treated as the top slice of the individuals income; thus, one can imagine the different types of income being stacked up with Schedule F income at the top;

- to the extent that the distribution income does not exceed the higher rate threshold it is to be charged at the lower rate not the basic rate. It is now possible for a person's income tax rates to be as follows:

1st slice	nil	–	personal allowance
2nd slice	20%	–	lower rate
3rd slice	25%	–	basic rate
4th slice	20%	–	lower rate Schedule F
5th slice	40%	–	higher rate Schedule F

- If the taxpayer is not liable to income tax because, for example, the income is covered by the personal allowances, the taxpayer can claim to have the credit repaid.

17.6.1   Overseas shareholders

Unless there is relief under a double tax treaty, an overseas shareholder is not entitled to a tax credit. However, s 233(1) ICTA 1988 provides that where a person is not entitled to a tax credit, no assessment shall be made on them at the lower rate, and to the extent that a person is liable at the higher rate the amount of that assessment shall be reduced by as sum equal to tax at the lower rate.

Note that a tax credit is only available to UK residents; therefore the amount of the distribution upon which a non-resident is chargeable is the amount of the actual distribution disregarding the credit.

When a company makes a non-qualifying distribution it does not have to pay ACT and the individual recipient does not receive a tax credit. The individual is not liable to basic rate tax on the distribution but *is* liable to higher rate tax (s 233 ICTA 1988). Note that the amount upon which the individual is liable to higher rate tax is the amount of the non-qualifying distribution.

17.7 Non-qualifying distributions – individuals

Note that the reduction of liability by an amount equal to the lower rate is not a tax credit in the way that ACT is a tax credit, it is not that someone else has paid the tax it is that the individual is not liable to tax on that income.

If the shares which were the subject of the non-qualifying distribution are later redeemed, this redemption will amount to a qualifying distribution (s 209(2)(b) ICTA 1988). The recipient will receive a distribution together with a tax credit for the ACT paid at that time. However, if the shareholder has to pay higher rate tax on the income he will receive a credit for the higher rate tax paid when the shares were first issued.

The idea behind the credit being given for the higher rate tax is to prevent double taxation in respect of both the issue and redemption of the shares. Where the shares are held at redemption by the person to whom they were issued, this is achieved. Where, in the meantime, the shares have been sold, there is an element of double taxation because the person holding the shares at redemption will not have paid higher rate tax on the non-qualifying distribution.

When a company receives a non-qualifying distribution it does not receive franked investment income as no ACT was paid in respect of it. If the shares are later redeemed, they will then be a qualifying distribution and the company will be in receipt of franked investment income. A company can, of course, distribute shares which it has itself received as a non-qualifying distribution, such a distribution will itself be a non-qualifying distribution but there will be no question of the company having to pay ACT in respect of those shares as any redemption will be by the issuing company and the person receiving the qualifying distribution will be the ultimate holder of the shares.

17.7.1 Non-qualifying distributions – companies

| 17.7.2 | Non-qualifying distributions – the company | When a company makes a non-qualifying distribution there is no liability to ACT. If the securities issued are later redeemed this will be a qualifying distribution and ACT will then be due. |
| 17.7.3 | Small companies' rate and ACT | Prior to the introduction of the lower rate of tax ACT was payable at 25% and franked the basic rate liability to tax. Where the company paying a dividend was a company which qualified for the small companies' rate of corporation tax, the ACT paid by the company equalled its mainstream corporation tax liability ie 25%. For companies, therefore, the UK tax system was a total imputation system as the whole of the companies' tax liability was imputed to the shareholder and satisfied by the tax credit. With the introduction of the lower rate, this symmetry has been lost. |

Corporation Tax – Tax Distributions, ACT and Schedule F

It is a feature of the UK corporation tax system that it is necessary to identify when profit is being extracted from a company.

Because a distribution is a payment made out of profits, it cannot be deducted in computing profits. The definition of distribution is therefore very wide in order to prevent a company getting a deduction for what is, in effect, a distribution of profits. Distributions include: dividends paid by the company; distributions out of assets of the company (whether in cash or otherwise); issues of bonus redeemable shares; any interest on securities where the interest is excessive; and transfers of assets where the value of the asset is greater than the consideration received.

Where distribution is made, the company is liable to pay advanced corporation tax. The advanced corporation tax is payable 14 days after the end of the quarter in which the distribution is made. For the company, ACT can be set against the mainstream corporation tax liability. Obviously, the payment of ACT gives a cash flow disadvantage in that it accelerates the date for payment of tax.

A tax payer who receives a distribution is chargeable to tax under Schedule F if the recipient is an individual. Otherwise, if the recipient is a company, no further tax is charged. An individual is entitled to a tax credit on the distribution equal to the amount of ACT which has been paid in respect of it. If the tax payer is a nil rate tax payer, the repayment is due.

A company receiving a dividend will also have a tax credit. The dividend income is called a company's franked investment income and it can be used to pay dividends without having to account for ACT.

Where a company receives a dividend out of foreign income, it can pay a Foreign Income Dividend ('FID'). Although the company pays ACT on the FID it can recover this amount subject to certain complex rules. A FID must be paid in cash and a company cannot elect to pay the FID to certain shareholders but not to others. The FID does not carry a tax credit; however, an individual shareholder is treated as receiving an amount grossed up at the lower rate as if there were a tax credit. A nil rate tax payer is therefore at a disadvantage because there is no repayment for this notion on tax credit.

A company subject to the small company's rate of corporation tax, also had to account for ACT when paying dividends. Because of the amount of the tax credit and the small companies rate, this is almost a total imputation system.

Chapter 18

Corporation Tax – Close Companies

This chapter looks at a special class of companies called close companies: close companies which in general terms are companies that are not at arm's length with their shareholders, are the subject of special rules. The first part of the chapter looks at how to identify a close company; the second part looks at the rules applicable to them. The final part of the chapter looks at close investment-holding companies; a sub-species of the close company.

When corporation tax was introduced in 1973 it was recognised that certain business could be carried on as either a partnership or as a company. If the members chose to adopt the partnership, they would be taxed on the profits earned each year. If, however, they chose to operate through a company, they would be taxed only if the profits were distributed. Consequently, two identical businesses could be operated in two different ways but the rates of tax suffered would be different. The decision as to how to carry on the business would therefore be affected by tax factors rather than commercial factors. At that time income tax rates were far higher than corporation tax rates. A company could therefore be used as a means of avoiding or deferring tax. The close company rules were meant to prevent the use of companies as 'incorporated piggy banks'. The main thrust of the legislation was to tax the shareholders as if the company's profits had actually been distributed.

Gradually the rates of income tax and corporation tax were reduced and the rates of capital gains tax have were assimilated with those of income tax. There was, therefore, no need for the distinction between close companies and others. Consequently, in 1989 the complex rules by which the income of the company was apportioned to its shareholders were abolished. However, some of the other provisions were retained to prevent other perceived abuses of the tax system. Further, a new type of company, the close investment-holding company was introduced, these are subject to the full rate of corporation tax notwithstanding that they would otherwise qualify for the small companies' rate of tax.

18.1 Introduction

18.2 Why distinguish close companies?

18.3	**Close company – definition**	A close company is defined in s 414(1) ICTA 1988 as one which is:

'under the control of five or fewer participators, or of participators who are directors ...'

There are therefore two criteria either:

- the company is under the control of five or fewer participators; or

- it is under the control of its directors who are participators however many that may be.

Certain companies which might otherwise satisfy this definition are stated not to be close, these are:

- a non-UK resident company (s 414(1)(a) ICTA 1988);

- a registered industrial and provident society (s 414(1)(b) ICTA 1988);

- a company controlled on behalf of the Crown (s 414(1)(c) ICTA 1988);

- a company which is controlled by a company which is not a close company (generally, this prevents a wholly owned subsidiary of a non-close company being close); however, a subsidiary of a foreign company which, if it was resident in the UK, would be a close company, will be a close company (ss 414(1)(d), 414(5) and 415 ICTA 1988); and

- a company in which 35% of the shares are beneficially held by the public and the shares of which have within the preceding 12 months been dealt in and quoted on a recognised stock exchange (s 415 ICTA 1988).

18.4	**Close company – further definitions**	In order to ascertain whether or not a company is close from the definition given above it is necessary to define the following terms:

- control;

- participator; and

- director.

At first sight identifying a close company would appear to be quite straightforward. Each of the terms used has an extended definition.

18.4.1	Control	Control is defined in s 416(2) ICTA 1988. A person is taken to have control of a company if he exercises, or is entitled to exercise, or is entitled to acquire, direct or indirect control over the company's affairs and in particular if he possesses or is entitled to acquire:

- the greater part of the share capital or issued share capital of the company or the voting power in the company; or

- such part of the issued share capital of the company as would entitle him to receive the greater part of the income of the company if the whole of it were distributed; or

- such rights as would, in the even that the company was would up entitle him to receive the greater part of the assets of the company.

The definition of control is therefore very wide, encompassing not only actual holdings but also rights to acquire such holdings in the future. A person who holds options over shares may, therefore, have control.

A 'participator' is a person who has a share or interest in the capital or income of the company and includes: **18.4.2   Participator**

- a person who possesses or is entitled to acquire share capital or voting rights in the company (s 417(1)(a) ICTA 1988);

- a loan creditor of the company (s 417(1)(b) ICTA 1988) (but not a bank lending on normal commercial terms (s 417(9) ICTA 1988));

- any person who possesses or is entitled to acquire the right to participate in distributions of the company (s 414(1)(c) ICTA 1988); or

- any person who is entitled to secure that income or assets (whether present or future) of the company will be applied directly or indirectly for his benefit (s 414(1)(d) ICTA 1988).

'Loan creditor' is defined by s 417(7) ICTA 1988 as a creditor in respect of any debt incurred by the company:

- for any money borrowed or capital assets acquired by the company; or

- for any right to receive income created by the company; or

- for consideration the value of which to the company was (at the time the debt was incurred) substantially less than the amount of the debt; or

- a creditor in respect of any redeemable loan capital of the company.

Without more, a bank could become a loan creditor of a company, s 417(9) ICTA 1988 therefore provides that a person carrying on the business of banking will not be considered to be a loan creditor in respect of any loan capital or debt issued or incurred by the company for money lent by the bank to the company in the ordinary course of that banking business.

In determining whether a participator has control it is necessary to look not only at the rights of the participator but also at the rights of the participator's nominees and associates. A nominee is a person who holds assets for another, often referred to as a bare nominee, one who holds assets in name only.

18.4.3   Associate

An associate of a participator is:

- any business partner or relative of the participator (which means any spouse, parent or remoter forebear, child or remoter issue or brother or sister) (s 417(3)(a) ICTA 1988); and

- any trustee or trustees of a settlement of which the participator is or any relative of his was the settlor (regardless of whether the relative is still living (s 417(3)(b) ICTA 1988)).

It should be noted that in taking into account the rights of an associate they are to be attributed to the participator but excluding any attributions which have been made to the associate; however there is nothing in the legislation to prevent an associate being counted as a participator after being included as an associate of another participator or to prevent that other participator from being included as an associate (s 416(6) ICTA 1988).

18.4.4   Director

A director is any person who occupies the position of director or any person in accordance with whose directions or instructions the directors are accustomed to act. Often this type of person is referred to as a shadow director. The term director also includes a manager of the business who, either on his own or with one or more associates, is able to control 20% or more of the ordinary share capital of the company (s 417(5) ICTA 1988).

18.5   The consequences of a company being close

One of the major consequences of a company being close, namely the apportionment of its income to its participators, was abolished by the Finance Act 1989. Nigel Lawson, the then Chancellor of the Exchequer, said that 'the rules for the so called apportionment of close companies' income are notoriously complex, taking up some 20 pages of impenetrable legislation'. However, two other consequences remain:

- an extended meaning of distribution; and

- the special rules applying to loans to participators.

In addition to the normal type of distribution in s 209 ICTA 1988, s 418(2) ICTA 1988 provides that where a close company incurs expense in or in connection with the provision for any participator of living or other accommodation, of entertainment, of domestic or other services, or of any other benefits or facilities of whatever nature, the company shall be treated as making a distribution to the participator of an amount equal to so much of that expense as is not made good to the company by the participator. Where the participator is a director or a person earning more than £8,500 a year such amounts would be benefits in kind and consequently liable to income tax in the hands of the recipient under ss 154–165 ICTA 1988 and s 145 ICTA 1988. Section 418(3) ICTA 1988 therefore provides an exemption from the extended meaning of distribution if the benefits charged under those provisions. Similarly, expense incurred in the provision of any pension or similar payment paid to the spouse, children or dependents of a participator is excluded from the extended distribution charge. The amount of the expense treated as a distribution is the same as the cash equivalent calculated under the benefit in kind rules. Those caught are typically shareholders who are neither directors nor employees earning more than £8,500 a year.

An extended distribution is treated in the same way as other qualifying distributions. The company will have to account for ACT and the shareholder will receive a tax credit equal to the lower rate of tax.

Because of the nature of close companies, it would be easy for them to make loans to shareholders for indefinite periods creating what would, in effect, be a distribution of profit without the adverse tax consequences usually associated with a distribution. Section 419 ICTA 1988 therefore provides that where a close company makes a loan or advances money to a participator or to an associate of a participator there shall be due from the company an amount equal to the amount of ACT that would have been due if the loan had been a distribution. The amount is due as if it were an amount of corporation tax and consequently non-payment will result in interest and penalties. Although the amount is equal to the amount of ACT that would be payable, it is not ACT and it cannot therefore be set against the company's mainstream corporation tax liability. It is more akin to a forced loan to the Inland Revenue.

A company is treated as making a loan to a participator if the participator incurs a debt to the company.

18.5.1   Distributions

18.5.2   Loans to participators

A loan is also treated as having been made where a debt, which is due to a third party from a participator, is assigned to the company.

The amount due to the Inland Revenue is payable 14 days after the end of the accounting period in which the loan is made. In default of payment interest runs from that date. Interest will be due notwithstanding that the loan has, in the meantime, been repaid. Two further points should be noted; first, where the loan is at a low rate of interest the loan may be a benefit in kind for the purposes of s 160 ICTA 1988 and chargeable accordingly; second, the Companies Act 1985 prohibits certain loans to directors, however, the amount is still payable notwithstanding that it is illegal under the Companies Act 1985.

The provisions do not apply in these circumstances; first, where the loan is made in the ordinary course of the company's business carried on by it which includes the lending of money; second, where a debt is incurred for the supply by the close company of goods or services in the ordinary course of its trade or business unless the credit given exceeds six months or is longer than the period normally given to its customers; and third, where the borrower is either a director or an employee and works full time for the close company or an associated company and does not have a material interest (ie more than 5% of the shares) in the close company or an associated company then the company is permitted to make loans which in aggregate do not exceed £15,000. Where such a person subsequently acquires a material interest in the company he is treated as having made a loan of the amount then outstanding on the day that he acquires a material interest. A company is associated with another if at that time or any time within the previous 12 months one company had control of the other or both are under the control of the same person or persons.

Where a sum of money is misappropriated by a participator this does not amount of a loan because the necessary consensus for a loan is not present (*Stephens v T Pittas Ltd*).

Where the loan is repaid to the close company by the participator the company is entitled to reclaim the amount paid to the Inland Revenue when the loan was originally made. Any repayment supplement due is calculated from the later of the date the loan is repaid or the date the amount equal to the ACT is paid. The repayment is equal to the amount of ACT which would have been payable on the amount repaid at the rate prevailing when the loan was originally made.

Where, instead of the loan being repaid, the debt is released or written off, the participator is treated as receiving a distribution equal to the amount released or written off. The sum paid by the company to the Inland Revenue at the time the loan was made becomes irrecoverable; however, it is not treated as ACT and hence it cannot be set against the company's mainstream corporation tax liability. Notwithstanding that the amount paid to the Inland Revenue was calculated on the rate of ACT prevailing at the time the loan was made, the release is grossed up at the rate of ACT prevailing when the debt is released. However, although the participator does not have any lower rate liability on the distribution, if he is a nil rate taxpayer he is not entitled to a repayment of the tax credit.

In the case of *Collins v Addies* (1992) a loan which had been made by a close company was novated to a third party. The participator was assessed to tax on the basis that there had been a release. The participator argued that as another person had been substituted as debtor, the company had received good consideration and therefore there had been no release. It was held that 'release' was no restricted to gratutitious release. It was also stated, during the course of argument, that such an interpretation led to an anomaly on the basis that the person to whom the loan was novated would have to account for a further sum equivalent to the ACT.

The Inland Revenue would, therefore, have received two such sums with a liability to repay only one when the loan was ultimately repaid. It was stated in the Court of Appeal that this may be an anomaly in the drafting.

The close investment-holding company ('CIC') was introduced in order to prevent an individual's investment gains being taxed at a lower rate than would be the case if held by the individual. An individual who was taxed at 40% could place his investments in a company which would be taxed at the small companies' rate of 25%. The income could be reinvested and a higher rate of return received by virtue of the lower rate of tax.

18.6   Close investment-holding companies

A CIC is defined by way of exclusion. A close company is a CIC if throughout the accounting period in question it is not:

- a 'trading company' (ie one that exists wholly or mainly for the carrying on of a trade on a commercial basis) (s 13A(2)(a) ICTA 1988);

- a 'property investment company' (ie one that exists wholly or mainly for the purpose of commercial property investment) (s 13A(2)(b) ICTA 1988);

- a 'passive holding company' (ie one which exists wholly or mainly for the purpose of holding shares in trading companies and/or property investment companies) (s 13A(2)(c) ICTA 1988);

- an 'active administration company' (ie one that co-ordinates the administration of trading companies and/or property investment companies) (s 13A(2)(d) ICTA 1988); or

- a 'service company' (ie one that exists wholly or mainly for the purpose of a trade or trades or property investment carried on by other members of the group)(s 13A(2)(e), (f) ICTA 1988).

18.6.1   Consequences of being a CIC

There are two consequences of being a CIC. First, a CIC does not qualify for the small companies' rate of corporation tax. A CIC will, therefore, always pay tax at 33%. It should be noted that if a CIC does other things eg carries on a trade, these profits will also be taxed at 33%. In such circumstances it would be better to move the trade to a new company which existed wholly or mainly for the purposes of carrying out that trade. Secondly, in certain circumstances the repayment of the tax credits on distributions may be restricted; this will usually happen where there exists a special class of share held by lower rate taxpayers (ie children) and the distribution is targeted at these shareholders.

Corporation Tax – Close Companies

Close companies are subject to special rules. These rules recognise that in general a close company is not at arm's length with its shareholders.

A close company is one which is under the control of five of fewer participators, or of participators who are directors. Therefore, if a company is under the control of its directors, it does not matter how many directors there are for the company to be close. Certain companies which might otherwise be close are specifically excluded: non-UK resident companies; a company which is controlled by a company which is not a close company; and a company which 35% of the shares are beneficially held by the public and which have been dealt with on a recognised stock exchange.

A person has control of a company if he exercises, or is entitled to exercise, or is entitled to acquire, direct or indirect control over the company's affairs. It is necessary to look at the rights of the participator in determining whether the participator has control but also the rights of any associate. Associates include relatives and trustees of settlement created by a participator.

A director is a person who either occupies the position of director or a person in accordance with whose directions or instructions the real directors are accustomed to act.

The consequences of being a close company are that there is an extended meaning of distribution and that special rules apply to loans to participators.

Where a close company incurs an expense in or in connection with the provision for any participator who is living or other accommodation, of entertainment, of domestic or other services, or of any other benefits of facilities of whatever nature, the company is treated as having a distribution to the participator.

Where a close company makes a loan to a participator, the company is required to pay an amount equal to the ACT that would have been payable had the loan been a distribution. The purpose of these provisions is to prevent a close company making an indefinite loan to a participator which is tantamount to a distribution which would otherwise avoid liability to pay ACT. Once the loan to the participator is repaid, the amount paid to government is also repaid. If the loan to the participator is written off or released, the amount paid to the government is treated as an amount of ACT payable on a distribution.

There is a special type of close company called a close investment-holiday company. Such companies are not entitled to the small companies rate of corporation tax. They are intended to prevent individuals putting their investments into companies and thus being taxed at a lower rate than if they had been held as an individual.

Chapter 19

Corporation Tax – Groups of Companies and Transactions

Although company law treats a company as a separate legal entity (see *Salomon v A Salomon & Co Ltd*), the tax legislation occasionally treats a group of companies as a commercial entity and allows transfers of reliefs between them and certain payments to be made without being subject to tax.

However, there may be a conflict between tax law and company law. Although the tax legislation may treat the group as a commercial entity, the directors of each company must still act in the company's best interests and not the group's best interests. Often the two will not conflict, but in practice it is necessary for the directors to consider the point.

19.1 Scope of the chapter

Depending upon which type of relief or payment is being considered different definitions of 'group' will apply. Thus, two companies may be in a group for one type of relief but not in a group for another. In order to ascertain the group, it is necessary to understand the parent/subsidiary relationship.

There are basically four types of relationship:

- 51% of subsidiary
- 75% of subsidiary;
- consortia; and
- 90% subsidiary.

A company is a 51% subsidiary of another company if it is UK resident and the holding company is also UK resident, and beneficially owns directly or indirectly more than 50% of the ordinary share capital (s 838(1) ICTA 1988). A company is a 75% subsidiary if the above conditions apply but the holding company beneficially owns 75% of more of the ordinary share capital. Companies form a consortium if they together own more than 75% of the ordinary share capital of a company and each owns more than 5%. A 90% subsidiary must be held directly.

19.2 Defining the group

Group relief and consortium relief allows a company with profits (the 'claimant company') to set the unrelieved losses of another company (the 'surrendering company') against its profits thus reducing the tax that it would otherwise pay.

19.3 Group relief and consortium relief

In order for the relief to apply the two companies must be in the same 75% group or in a consortium. A 75% group is one in which one company holds directly or indirectly not less than 75% of the issued ordinary share capital of the other, or a third company owns directly or indirectly not less than 75% of the issued ordinary share capital of the surrendering and claimant company.

In the event that one member owns 75% of the issued ordinary share capital, it will be entitled to group relief which means it will be entitled to all losses. Not only can losses be surrendered but also charges on income and mangement expenses.

If the claimant company pays for the losses, the receipt by the surrendering company will not be taxable (but neither will the amount be deductible by the claimant company) provided the amount paid does not exceed the amount of the loss. Note that it is the amount of the loss, not the amount of the tax saved. A group can therefore use the provisions to move money around the group. However, directors would have to consider whether it would be right to do so.

Where the claim is made by a 75% subsidiary, the claim can be for the whole amount of the loss. Where the claim is by a consortium company, the amount of the loss that can be claimed is such proportion as the claimant company's shareholding bears to its share in the consortium.

Where a company claims group relief, the losses so claimed must be used in the year of surrender. The losses cannot be carried back and they must be deducted from the total profits of the claimant company. The claimant company need not claim the full amount of the loss, nor need it claim so much as is neccessary to eliminate its profits although, in practice, companies do.

19.4   Making a claim

A claim must be made within two years from the end of the surrendering company's accounting period. A claim must be in writing and show the following:

- the name of the claimant company;

- the accounting period of the claimant company for which relief is claimed;

- the identify of the surrendering company or companies where more than one;

- the relevant accounting period for each of the surrendering companies;

- the amounts claimed;

- the amount of profit to be covered by the group relief.

A claim will normally be signed by the company secretary of the claimant company, being the proper officer; however, the Inland Revenue will accept claims by any person authorised by the company. A consent to surrender must still be signed by the company secretary.

If may be that the accounting periods of the claimant company and the surrendering company do not coincide; where this happens, the group relief is restricted to those parts that are common to both.

19.5   Corresponding accounting periods

Dividends can be paid from a 51% subsidiary to its parent without having to account for ACT. Dividends so paid are called 'group income'. Note this provision only applies to dividends not to distributions; therefore, where assets are given to a shareholder as a distribution in specie the company will still have to account for ACT.

19.6   Group income

For dividends to be paid as group income a joint election must be made setting out the facts necessary to show that the companies are entitled to make the election. Once it has been submitted, the Inspector of Taxes has three months in which to satisfy himself that the election is validly made. A dividend paid within three months of making the election will not be paid under the election unless the Inspector has signified that he is satisfied.

Once an election is made it remains in force until one of the companies withdraws the election or the group relationship is broken because of a change in shareholdings.

A dividend may be paid outside the election whilst it is still in force by notifying the Inspector. In practice, therefore, the election is made for all qualifying companies and notification is made when a payment to be made outside it.

The recipient of group income will not be entitled to a tax credit and it will not therefore be franked investment income.

The effect of a group income election is to improve the payer's cash flow.

Charges paid between members of a 51% group can be paid without deduction of income tax. Charges paid in this way can be between parent and subsidiary, subsidiary and parent or between two subsidiaries. Consortium members can also pay charges without deduction of tax but only from the consortium company to the consortium members and not *vice versa*.

A joint election must be made. There is a separate election from the group income election. However, unlike the group income election, all payments made when the election is in force must be paid under it; if it is required to pay a charge outside the election the election must be withdrawn, the charge paid and a new election submitted.

19.7   Surrender of ACT

Where a company has paid ACT in respect of a dividend or dividends in an accounting period it may surrender the benefit of that ACT to any company which is a 51% subsidiary.

The subsidiary must have been a subsidiary throughout the accounting period. In order to determine when the benefit of the ACT arose the subsidiary is treated as having paid a dividend on the same day as the dividend on which the parent company paid the dividend.

ACT surrendered to a subsidiary cannot be treated as surplus ACT of the subsidiary capable of being carried back six years. However, in determining how much surplus ACT a subsidiary has, the subsidiary can set off surrendered ACT before ACT paid on distributions made by it. In this way the subsidiary can generate ACT to be carried back.

A claim to surrender ACT must be made within six years after the end of the accounting period in which it arose and the claim requires the consent of the subsidiary or subsidiaries concerned.

No payment made for the surrender of ACT is to be taken into account to the extent that does not exceed the amount of ACT surrendered; nor is the payment deductible.

19.8   Capital gains

Although a company can surrender trading losses to another company in the group by way of group relief, it cannot surrender capital losses. Without more, a situation could arise whereby one member of a group has capital gains on which it would be taxable while at the same time another company has unrelieved capital losses. A company which operated through divisions (ie all trades in one company) would be at an advantage to a group. This problem is alleviated by the legislation providing that transfers of capital assets with a group take place at such a value that the disposing company realises neither a gain nor a loss (s 171 TCGA 1992).

The effect of this is that no tax liability arises until the asset leaves the group.

Most groups, therefore, make all capital asset disposals through one company so that all gains and losses are matched. However, the system would be open to abuse because an asset could be sold to a company which itself was then sold. A third party could therefore acquire the company and with it the asset without any charge to CGT arising. To prevent this s 179 TCGA 1992 provides that where an asset is sold intra-group and within six years the company to which it was sold leaves the group, there will be a deemed disposal and reacquisition which will thus crystallise the gain. A group for capital gains purposes comprises the parent company (called the principal company) and all its 75% subsidiaries. When a company is not a 75% subsidiary if it has 75% subsidiaries then it may be a principal company and thus a group may contain a number of capital gains tax groups.

Corporation Tax – Groups of Companies and Transactions

Although a company is a separate legal entity, the tax legislation occasionally treats a group of companies as a commercial entity and allows transfers of reliefs between them and certain payments to be made without being subject to tax. Losses can be transferred by either group relief or consortium relief. For group relief, one company must be a 75% subsidiary of another or two companies must be 75% subsidiaries of a third company. Losses can be surrendered between any member of the group. A consortium exists if 75% of the issued ordinary share capital belongs to companies in aggregate, each of the companies owning not less than 5% nor more than 75%. A consortium company can surrender losses to members of the consortium and *vice versa*. The amount of the losses which can be surrendered depends upon the proportion of shares owned by each consortium member.

Dividends can be paid from a company which is a 51% subsidiary of another company without having to account for ACT. Such dividends are called group income. These provisions do not apply to distributions but only to dividends. Charges on income can also be paid between such members without having to deduct basic rate tax.

Where a company has paid ACT in respect of a dividend or dividends in an accounting period, it may surrender the benefit of that ACT to any company which is a 51% subsidiary. ACT surrendered cannot be treated as surplus ACT.

Transfers of assets within a 75% group take place at such value that neither nor a loss will arise to the transfer or company. A transferee company acquires the asset at the transferor's base cost adjusted for inflation. There is therefore no tax on the disposal until the asset leaves the group.

Capital gains tax is charged at the marginal rate of income tax for individuals or at the corporation tax rate for companies. For a charge to tax to arise, there has to be a disposal of an asset by a person within the charge to tax. Assets includes all forms of property. Case law shows that a right can be an asset if it can be taken into account notwithstanding that a transfer of an asset is impossible. A disposal of an asset can result in the acquisition of a further asset, namely the right to further consideration.

Certain assets are not chargeable, eg passenger vehicles, sterling and national savings certificates.

A person is chargeable to capital gains tax if they are resident and ordinarily resident in the United Kingdom during the year of assessment. A person carrying on business through a branch or agency in the UK is chargeable to tax but a disposal of any assets used by the branch or agency.

Disposal is not defined by the Act. However, it carries its ordinary meaning and a disposal therefore occurs when a person divests themselves title to the assets. Certain events are treated as disposals for the purposes of the Act eg where a capital sum is received by way of compensation for damage or injury to an asset, or a capital sum is received under an insurance policy, where a capital sum is received in return for the forfeiture or surrender of rights or refraining from exercising rights, and the capital sum is received in consideration for the exploitation of an asset. Where an asset becomes negligible value, a claim can be made to treat the asset as having been disposed of and immediately required, thus realising any loss. A subsequent disposal at a gain would of course be chargeable to tax. An asset subject to a mortgage is treated as being disposed of by the mortgagor not by the mortgagee and hence mortgagee takes the proceeds free of any tax liability being the responsibility of the mortgagor.

A disposal will also be treated as taking place where people act together to exercise votes such that value passes out of shares belonging to one person and passes into shares belonging to another.

The disposal takes place where there is an unconditional contract on the date of the contract is made. Where there is a conditional contract, it is the date on which the condition is satisfied.

Chapter 20

Capital Gains Tax – The Charge to Tax

Capital gains tax ('CGT') was first introduced in 1965. Prior to this tax had been charged on short term capital gains under Schedule D Case VIII. With the introduction of CGT, the Schedule D Case VIII charge was abolished. CGT has always been relatively expensive to administer when compared with other taxes. However, its introduction was prompted more by a desire to be fair than by a desire to raise revenue.

20.1 Introduction

For many years CGT was charged at a flat rate of 30%. This meant that there was an incentive to convert income into capital especially when income was chargeable at rates of up to 98%. In 1988 the rate of tax was assimilated with income tax. CGT is now charged at the taxpayer's marginal rate of tax, and so can be charged at 20%, 25% and 40% depending upon the level of the taxpayer's income in the tax year in which this gain is realised. Like income tax, the tax year runs from 6 April to 5 April.

20.2 Rate of tax

Section 1(1) TCGA 1992 provides that tax shall be charged in accordance with the TCGA in respect of capital gains that is to say chargeable gains computed in accordance with the TCGA and accruing to a person on the disposal of assets.

20.3 The charging provision

There are therefore three components required:

- an asset;

- which is disposed of;

- by a person within the charge to tax.

In order for a charge to CGT to arise there must be a disposal of an asset.

20.4 Assets

Section 21(1) TCGA 1992 provides that for CGT purposes, all forms of property are assets, whether they are situated in the UK or otherwise and assets includes all options, debts, incorporeal property, currency other than sterling and property which either has been created the person who is disposing of it or which is owned but which has not been acquired by the person disposing of it; for example, goodwill.

Although it is clear that all forms of property are assets, does this mean that in order to be an asset the thing must be property? In other words, which is wider the word asset or the word property?

20.4.1   *O'Brien v Benson's Hosiery (Holdings) Ltd*

The answer is to be found in the case of *O'Brien v Benson's Hosiery (Holdings) Ltd* (1979) in which the taxpayer company had entered into a seven year service contract with one of its directors. The director wished to be released from the contract prematurely and the company agreed to the release in exchange for a payment of £50,000. The company was assessed to tax on the £50,000. The Inland Revenue argued that the rights under the service contract were assets from which the company had derived a capital sum. The taxpayer argued that the in order to be an asset, it needed to have a market value, which meant that it had to be transferable. The rights under the service contract could not be assigned; therefore, there was no market value.

The argument of the taxpayer succeeded in the Court of Appeal but failed in House of Lords where it was held that the fact that the company could exact a sum from the employee for the employee's release from the contract meant that the rights released were an asset of the company which could be and were turned to account. The fact that the ways in which the asset could be turned to account were restricted, because of the nature of the asset, was irrelevant. Therefore, although the rights were not property they still amounted to an asset for CGT purposes.

20.4.2   *Davis v Powell –* compensation

Notwithstanding the very wide interpretation of the word asset in the *O'Brien* case, there have been a few cases where the courts have held that capital sum has not come from an asset but some other source. In *Davis v Powell* (1977) the taxpayer received £591 compensation for disturbance under the Agricultural Holdings Act 1948 because he had been served with notice to quit by his landlord. It was held that the compensation was not derived from the lease but instead was a statutory payment for loss incurred by the taxpayer. It was held that as the sum was paid to compensate for a loss, it could not give rise to a chargeable gain. This is not necessarily true see *Zim Properties Ltd v Procter* (1985) below.

20.4.3   *Davenport v Chilver –* compensation

The case of *Davis v Powell* can be compared with the case of *Davenport v Chilver* (1983) in which the taxpayer received compensation under the Foreign Compensation (Union of Soviet Socialist Republics) Order 1969 in respect of her mother's land which had been appropriated by a foreign government. It was held that the compensation had been derived from an asset and was liable to CGT.

If, instead of focusing on the compensation, the courts had focused on the asset, it would have been seen that to the extent that the compensation reimbursed part of the cost of the asset there would have been no gain. Only if the compensation exceeded the acquisition cost would a profit, and hence a CGT charge, have arisen. If the assets in question had been sold on the open market, there would have been no question that tax would have been payable if a gain had arisen. The fact that there was a forced disposal and compensation was payable ought not make any difference. In *O'Brien v Benson's Hosiery Holdings Ltd* there was no acquisition cost and so the whole amount received was taxable.

It would be tempting to argue that following *Davenport v Chilver*, *Davis v Powell* is no longer good law; in *Davis v Powell* the Crown did not argue that the statutory right itself might be an asset. However, *Davis v Powell* was reaffirmed as good law in the case of *Drummond v Austin-Brown* (1984). Again, however, the Crown did not argue that a statutory right itself was an asset. In *Drummond* the taxpayer was entitled to compensation under the Landlord and Tenant Act 1954; it was held that the right to compensation was conferred by Parliament; if Parliament took that right away, the lease which had been surrendered would not have conferred such a right therefore the right did not derive from the lease. It has been suggested that the distinction in these cases is that in *Davis v Powell* and *Drummond v Austin-Brown* the sum paid was to compensate for a loss; whereas in *Davenport v Chilver* there was no loss because the asset compensation was in respect of the taxpayer's mother's land and therefore the loss had been suffered by the mother. However, in each case there was a disposal of an asset and a sum was received. The fact that the disposal was not voluntary is irrelevant.

20.4.4   *Drummond v Austin-Brown*

In *Marren v Ingles* (1980) it was again necessary to identify what was the relevant asset. The taxpayers sold shares in a company for £750 each; however, there was to be a further payment if the shares were later listed on the stock exchange and any further amount was to be calculated by reference to the price of those shares when listed. The taxpayers became entitled to a further £2,825 per share. The question arose: how was this later consideration to be charged? Section 48 TCGA 1992 provides that where further consideration is due after the time of disposal, that extra consideration is to be brought into account at the time of disposal and, if the extra payment does not materialise, a repayment is made. Where, as in the *Marren*

20.4.5   *Marren v Ingles*

v Ingles case, the further amount cannot be ascertained how can it be charged? The answer, according to the Court of Appeal was that when the taxpayers disposed of their shares, the consideration they received comprised two elements. First, they received the cash sum; and secondly, they received a right to further consideration. This right could itself be valued and sold in the market, the value of this right was further consideration which was chargeable on the date of disposal. When the further sum was received, there was a second disposal; this time of the right to the deferred consideration. The acquisition cost of the right was its market value when acquired and hence, there was no element of double taxation.

20.4.6   *Zim Properties Ltd v Procter*

The definition of asset probably reached its zenith in the case of *Zim Properties Ltd v Procter* (1984). The taxpayers wished to sell a property; however, they were unable to show good title and the sale fell through. When they finally came to sell the property they received £69,000 less than they would have received in the original sale. The taxpayers sued their solicitors for the £69,000 and the action was settled. It was held that the £69,000 was derived from the right to sue which was itself an asset for capital gains purposes; accordingly, it was taxable.

However, if in a case like *Drummond v Austin-Brown*, the landlord refuses to pay the statutory compensation and the tenant sues, is the sum received taxable as arising out of a right of action? or not taxable because if it had been paid without suing it would not have been derived from an asset? The *Zim* decision was not favourably received and in consequence the Inland Revenue issued Extra Statutory Concession D33 which provides that where there is an underlying asset the sum received can be treated as deriving from the underlying asset. Where there is no underlying asset then any capital sum received will not be chargeable. In the *Drummond* case therefore, the right will derive from the statute not the lease and as such will not be chargeable. However, the fact that a concession is required shows that there is an underlying conceptual flaw.

The problem with ESC D33 is that in *Zim* Warner J was faced with the choice between either the sum being derived from the asset or the sum being derived from the right of action; he chose the latter. The Inland Revenue having argued for this course have now issued an ESC which allows the taxpayer to opt for the former. Thus, the taxpayer is now taxed at the discretion of the Revenue not by the law. It would be possible to amend the legislation to provide for the gain to be taxed only if there is an underlying asset; however, this course has not been adopted.

The conclusion to be drawn from the cases discussed above is, perhaps, that where a capital sum is received by a taxpayer, in nearly all circumstances, it will be derived from the disposal of some asset. Only in very few circumstances ie *Davis v Powell* and *Drummond v Austin-Brown*, will the sum be treated as being derived from something else.

Certain assets are stated by the legislation not to be chargeable assets and accordingly, no chargeable gain accrues on their disposal. Taxpayers cannot claim an allowable loss if one is incurred. The three most common type of assets which are not chargeable are:

- Passenger vehicles (s 263 TCGA 1992); vehicles within this exemption must be 'constructed or adapted for the carriage of passengers, except for a vehicle of the type not commonly used as a private vehicle'. Thus, in the case of *Bourne v Auto School of Motoring (Norwich) Ltd* a driving instructor's car fitted with dual controls was held not to be the type commonly used as a private vehicle. Most cars will, in any event, fall into other exemptions eg as a wasting asset or as tangible movable. However, the exemption may still be important for classic cars, which are often sold at very high prices. In this regard care must be taken because many old cars were single seaters and as such they are not 'constructed or adapted for the carriage of passengers'. Note also that most cars, being depreciating assets, usually give rise to a loss on disposal. Section 263 TCGA 1992 far from being generous to the taxpayer, prevents numerous loss claims reducing the take of the Revenue.

- Sterling (s 21 TCGA 1992). The measure by which a gain is charged is in sterling. Sterling is therefore exempted as it is impossible for it to appreciate against itself.

- National Savings Certificates and Premium Bonds (s 121 TCGA 1992). Certain government securities are exempted.

It should be noted that sometimes the legislation provides that a gain shall not be a chargeable gain; for example, the gain made on the disposal of an individual's main residence. The difference between something being a non chargeable asset and something being a non-chargeable gain is that in the former case there are no circumstances in which the asset *per se* is chargeable; in the latter case the asset is chargeable, ie a house, but if the conditions are satisfied, ie it is the taxpayer's only or main residence, the gain is not.

20.5   Chargeable persons

A person is chargeable to capital gains tax if they are resident or ordinarily resident in the United Kingdom during the year of assessment. A person is chargeable notwithstanding, that they are only resident in the United Kingdom for part of a year. A person who is chargeable is chargeable on all their assets wherever they are situated. However, under Extra Statutory Concession D2, where a person ceases to be resident in the United Kingdom during a year of assessment, the Inland Revenue will not seek to charge tax on gains made by that person once they have ceased to be resident. In the case of *R v IRC, ex p Fulford-Dobson* (1987), the taxpayer's wife had inherited certain property which she considered selling. The taxpayer was unemployed and accepted work in Germany. The taxpayer's wife, therefore, transferred the property to him by deed of gift and he then left the country in order to take up residence in Germany. Eleven days after ceasing to be resident in the UK, he sold the property. He sought to rely on Extra Statutory Concession D2 on the basis that having ceased to be resident part way through the year, the Inland Revenue should not tax him on gains made following his departure. It was held that where an extra statutory concession is used for the purpose of tax avoidance, its application can be denied and hence the taxpayer was chargeable to tax. It should be noted that had he delayed the sale of the property and sold it in the following tax year the concession would have had no application and the gains would have been exempt. As it was, he sold it on 17 September and the gain became chargeable.

Where a person carries on business through a branch or agency in the UK, that person is chargeable to capital gains tax on any gains accruing on the disposal of assets used by the branch or agency which are situated in the United Kingdom. It would be a simple matter to avoid such a charge by either taking the asset outside the UK and then disposing of them (in the case of movable property) or, alternatively, ceasing to trade prior to the disposal. Section 25 TCGA 1992 provides that where an asset is moved outside the UK, the owner is deemed to have made a disposal of the asset immediately before the time it became situated outside the UK; and where a business ceases to trade, it is deemed on so ceasing to have disposed on the asset and to have immediately reacquired it at market value. Thus, a charge to tax is triggered by the deemed disposal.

Where a non resident company operates in the UK through a branch or agency and transfers the assets from that branch to a UK registered company, there would be a charge to tax under the above provisions on the branch ceasing to trade. However, s 172 TCGA 1992 excludes the operation of s 25

TCGA 1992 and provides that the assets so acquired by the UK resident company are treated as being acquired as such a value that neither a gain nor loss will accrue on the disposal to the branch or agency. The gain is in effect held over until such time as the UK registered company disposes of the asset.

The capital gains tax legislation contains no definition of disposal. However, in its ordinary sense a disposal occurs where a person divests themselves of title to an asset. However, a disposal does not necessarily have to involve an acquisition by someone else; if a person destroys an asset, there has obviously been a disposal yet no one else has made an acquisition. The capital gains tax legislation, therefore, although not providing a general definition of disposal, provides that certain specific transactions do amount to a disposal.

20.6   Disposals

In its ordinary sense, a person disposes of an asset when the asset is transferred to another person, eg by way of sale or gift. The interest with which the CCT legislation is concerned is the beneficial on equitable interest.

20.6.1   Actual disposals from one person to another

Section 22 TCGA 1992 provides that where a capital sum is derived from an asset, the asset is treated as having been disposed of notwithstanding the fact that no asset is acquired by the person paying the capital sum. This section sets out four particular examples:

20.6.2   Capital sums derived from an asset

- A capital sum is received by way of compensation for damage or injury to an asset, or for the loss, destruction or dissipation of an asset, or for any depreciation or risk of depreciation of an asset (s 22(1)(a) TCGA 1992). If the sum received is of an income nature, it will be chargeable to income tax not capital gains tax; for example, where a trader receives a sum for loss of trading profits that sum will be brought into the trading account and thus chargeable to income tax (see *London and Thames Haven Oil Wharves Ltd v Attwooll*).

- A capital sum received under an insurance policy for damage or injury to, or the loss or depreciation of assets.

- A capital sum is received in return for the forfeiture or surrender of rights or for refraining from exercising rights. Thus, the sum received in *O'Brien v Benson's Hosiery (Holdings) Ltd* would be such a payment. However, it should be noted that the right must be a legally enforceable right and thus, in the case of *Kirby v Thorn EMI plc* (1988) it was held that a capital sum paid to restrict a company from trading was not chargeable to CGT because the right to trade was not legally enforceable; similarly, a capital sum received for restriction on the right to work or the right to get married would not be chargeable. However, in the *Kirby* case it was held that the restriction on trading activities amounted to a disposal of goodwill which was itself an asset and hence the capital sum was chargeable.

• A capital sum received is consideration for the use or exploitation of assets; for example, a lump sum received to allow a person to use a copyright.

Where a capital sum is received in the circumstances set out above, it would be unfortunate if the taxpayer wished to replace the asset and yet had been taxed on the insurance proceeds which therefore meant that he could not afford a replacement asset. Similarly, where a replacement is obtained or an asset is repaired, it may be that not all of the proceeds are used by the taxpayer. Section 23 TCGA 1992 provides that in these circumstances a charge for tax will not arise providing certain conditions have been satisfied. Where the asset is not lost or destroyed these conditions are:

• that the capital sum is wholly applied in restoring the asset; or

• the capital sum is applied in restoring the asset and to the extent that it is not the amount that is not used is small; or the amount of the capital sum which is received is small, as compared with the value of the asset. For these purposes the Inland Revenue consider that 5% is small.

Where these conditions are satisfied the amount is deducted from the allowable expenditure on the asset. Consequently, the taxpayer is placed in the same position as would have been the case had the asset not been damaged.

Where the asset is lost or destroyed, the condition is:

• that the capital sum received by way of compensation is within one year of the loss or destruction, or such longer period as the inspector may allow, applied in replacing the asset which was lost or destroyed.

Where this condition is satisfied, the asset which was lost or destroyed is treated as it were disposed of at a value that neither a gain or a loss would arise; and the acquisition cost of the new asset is reduced by so much of the compensation as exceeds the value so taken and any scrap value of the original asset.

In both the situations discussed above the taxpayer must make a claim in order for the relief to apply.

Where an asset is lost, destroyed, or becomes of negligible value, it is treated as a disposal regardless of whether any sum is received by way of compensation or otherwise (s 24(1) TCGA 1992). Hence, this may give rise to an allowable loss.

20.6.3   Total loss or destruction of an asset

Where an asset becomes negligible value, the owner can make a claim the effect of which is to treat the asset as being disposed of and immediately reacquired. The effect of this is to crystallise the loss and to give the taxpayer a new but lower acquisition cost (s 24(2) TCGA 1992).

For the purposes of the above two rules buildings and land are treated as two separate assets. However, where the building is destroyed in order to calculate the gain both assets are treated as having been disposed of and reacquired at the then market value. It is the corresponding gain or loss which is taken into account.

As stated in para 20.6.2 above, where the asset is lost or destroyed and a sum of money is received in compensation, provided the money is used to acquire a replacement asset within a year of receipt to acquire a new asset, the gain will be treated as being rolled into the new asset.

The granting of a mortgage over a property does not give rise to a disposal (s 26 TCGA 1992). If the mortgagee has been forced to realise the security and in consequence sells the asset to pay off the mortgage debt, it is not treated as a disposal by the mortgagor to the mortgagee and a further disposal by the mortgagee. Instead, the mortgagee is treated as disposing of the asset on behalf of the mortgagor. Any gain is therefore that of the mortgagor.

20.6.5   Mortgages

Where an asset which is subject to a mortgage is disposed of, the assumption of the liability to pay the mortgage by the person acquiring the asset is further consideration for the asset. This is so even if the disposal purports to be by way of gift.

In three circumstances a person may be treated as making a disposal notwithstanding the fact that no asset is disposed of and it is not lost or destroyed. These three circumstances are:

20.6.6   Value shifting

- where a person having control of a company exercises control so that value passes out of shares in the company owned by him or a person with whom he is connected and passes into other shares of the company. In such a case the person who exercises control is treated as disposing of the shares out of which the value has passed.

Suppose X owns the majority of ordinary shares in a company. His daughter owns the preference shares. X exercises his majority vote to alter the articles of the company so as to increase the dividend rights of the preference shares. The preference shares will, as a result, increase in value. There will be a disposal for the purposes of s 29 TCGA 1992;

- where, following a transaction in which the owner of land or other type of property becomes a lessee of the property, there is an adjustment of the rights and liabilities under the lease which is favourable to the lessor, it is treated as if the lessee had made a disposal of an interest in the property;

- where there is some sort of restriction or right over an asset, the extinction or abrogation of the whole or part of that right or restriction by the person entitled to enforce it is treated as a disposal by that person of that right or restriction.

Section 30 TCGA 1992 provides that where there has been a disposal of an asset or before the disposal a scheme has been effected or arrangements have been made (before or after the disposal) whereby:

- the value of the asset has been materially reduced; and

- a tax free benefit has been or will be conferred on either:
  - the person making the disposal or a person connected with that person; or
  - any other person

then the allowable loss or chargeable gain arising on the disposal of the asset shall be calculated as if the consideration for the disposal were increased by so much as the Inspector considers to be just and reasonable having regard to the scheme and the tax free benefit.

| 20.6.7 | Part disposals |

Section 21 TCGA 1992 provides that the reference to a disposal of any asset includes a reference to a part disposal. A part disposal is defined in s 21(2)(b) TCGA 1992 as occurring when an interest or right in or over an asset is created by the disposal, as well as where it subsists before the disposal, and generally, there is a part disposal of an asset where, on a person making a disposal, any description of property derived from that asset remains undisposed of. Thus, the creation of a lease is a part disposal. However, s 144 TCGA 1992 provides that the grant of an option is a disposal not a part disposal.

Where a person disposes of their whole interest in property that is a full disposal notwithstanding that the interest which the person had was only a part interest in the property. The question whether there is a disposal or part disposal therefore does not depend on the type of interest which a person has but the amount of the interest which is disposed of.

In the normal case it will be relatively easy to identify the time at which the disposal takes place. Generally, it will be when property passes in the asset. However, in a number of circumstances the question is more difficult.

20.7 When does the disposal occur?

Section 28 TCGA 1992 provides that where an asset is disposed of and acquired under a contract the time in which the disposal and acquisition is made is the time of the contract and not, if different, the time at which the asset is conveyed or transferred. Therefore, where a person sells a house, the disposal will take place on the exchange of contracts and not upon completion. However, if completion does not take place, has there been a disposal at the date of contract? It is considered that the answer to this is no. Section 28 TCGA 1992 provides that where an asset is acquired and disposed of, the date of disposal is the date of contract. Where completion does not take place here has been no acquisition and disposal. Therefore s 28 TCGA 1992 is not applicable. Where completion does take place, the date of disposal is related back to the date of contract which was the date when beneficial ownership is deemed to have passed. A problem arises where these is a long period between exchange and completion. In this situation, once completion has happened it is obvious that the charge to tax arose on the date of exchange. If the period between exchange and completion is longer than, say, two years, the date for payment of tax may have passed and a liability to interest and penalties for non payment may arise. However, until completion it will not be certain that a disposal has occurred. The alternative to this is that the taxpayer ought to pay tax on the due date as if completion is going to take place and then receive a repayment in the event that it does not. The problem with this is that under s 28 TCGA 1992 a disposal takes place at exchange only where there is an acquisition and disposal. Until completion this has not happened; arguably, there is therefore, no charge to tax.

20.7.1 Acquisition under a contract

Section 28(2) TCGA 1992 provides that if the contract is conditional, the time when the disposal and acquisition is made is the time when the condition is satisfied. The type of condition which is being talked about is a condition precedent. That is, a condition the occurrence of which brings the contract into operation not a condition upon which performance of the other party is dependent (*Eastham v Lee London and Provincial Properties Ltd* (1971)).

20.7.2 Conditional contracts

20.7.3	Capital sums derived from assets

Where a capital sum is derived from an asset which is chargeable to tax under s 22 TCGA 1992, the date of the disposal is the date upon which the capital sum is received.

Where a claim is made that an asset has become of negligible value, a disposal takes place on the date that the Inland Revenue accepts the claim. This may not be the year in which the asset became of negligible value but some later date when the claim is allowed. In the case of *Williams v Bullivant* (1983), the taxpayer made a claim in 1978 that certain shares become of a negligible value in 1974. The resulting loss would offset a gain made in the tax year 1973/74. The claim was rejected on the basis that the disposal and reacquisition is deemed to occur when the claim is made not when the shares actually became of negligible value. However, under Extra Statutory Concession D28 the Revenue will allow a claim for a disposal to have been made on a particular date provided the claim is not made later than 24 months after the end of the tax year in which that date fell, provided that the asset is of negligible value both when the claim is made and at the earlier date.

Capital Gains Tax – The Charge to Tax

Capital gains tax is charged at the taxpayer's marginal rate of income tax. It is charged on disposals of chargeable assets.

Assets include all forms of property. It also includes rights, choses in action and other intangibles. Compensation payments are derived from an asset if the payment does not reimburse a loss.

Certain assets are not chargeable assets and no charge will arise on their disposals, these include sterling, National Savings Certificates and Premium Bonds.

A person is chargeable to CGT if they are UK resident. A non-resident who carries on business in the UK through a branch or agency is also chargeable in respect of assets used in the branch or agency.

A disposal is not defined. A disposal will occur when a person loses the beneficial title to an asset whether it be by sale, gift or the assets destruction.

Where only a part of an asset is disposed of, the proportion of the acquisition cost attributable to the part disposed of is ascertained using the formula:

$$\frac{A}{A + B}$$

A disposal occurs at the time of contract or, if the contract is conditional, when the condition is satisfied.

Chapter 21

Capital Gains Tax – Computation

This chapter looks at the method of calculating the capital gains tax charge or any allowable loss. Some of the rules are complex and beyond the scope of this book. However, it is necessary to have an understanding of the mechanics and the conceptual basis on which the tax is based.

21.1 Scope of chapter

Capital gains tax is charged by s 1 TCGA 1992 on chargeable gains computed in accordance with the act. The scheme of the act is to charge tax according to the following calculation. The calculation is applied to each asset and therefore a loss is calculated in the same way as a gain (s 16(1) TCGA 1992).

21.2 The basic computation

The basic computation for capital gains tax can be described as follows:

	£	£
Disposal proceeds		X
Minus: Acquisition cost	X	
Incidental costs of acquisition	X	
		(X)
Minus: Incidental costs of disposal		(X)
Indexation		(X)
Net gain		X
Minus annual exemption (if not previously allowed)		(X)
		X
(Minus brought forward losses)		(X)
Chargeable gains (or loss)		X

The acquisition cost is usually referred to as the base cost. The various aspects of the computation are dealt with in the paragraphs following.

It is trite to say that the disposal proceeds are the consideration received by the person making the disposal; however, if that was all there was to it, capital gains tax would be a much more simple than it is. Although the starting point is the amount received, the legislation substitutes a different amount in certain circumstances.

21.3 Disposal proceeds

21.3.1	Arm's length disposals	Another amount will not be substituted where the disposal is at arm's length. An arm's length disposal is not defined. However, examples of various disposals which are not arm's length disposals are given by the legislation and these include a gift, a transfer into a settlement, or a distribution (s 17 TCGA 1992). In normal circumstances, an ordinary commercial transaction is an arm's length disposal. Where an arm's length disposal is made the disposal proceeds is the amount received by the vendor; this is not necessarily the market value. Where the vendor makes a bad bargain or sells at a low figure for a quick sale in order to realise cash the fact that a higher price could be achieved is irrelevant.
21.3.2	Non-arm's length disposals	Where a transaction is not at arm's length, market value must be substituted in place of the actual consideration (if any) (s 17(1)(a) TCGA 1992).

The market value of an asset is also substituted where the consideration received by the person disposing of the asset cannot be valued or the consideration given for the disposal is the performance of services (s 17(1)(b) TCGA 1992).

Section 17 TCGA 1992 also provides for market value to be substituted where the consideration:

- is given for loss of office; or

- is given for services given in any office or employment.

However, market value is not substituted in two situations these are:

- where there is no corresponding disposal of the asset (s 17(2)(a) TCGA 1992); and

- there is no consideration in money or money's worth or the consideration is of an amount or value lower than the market value of the asset (s 17(2)(b) TCGA 1992).

The purpose of s 17(2) TCGA 1992 is to counter what are known as reverse Nairn Williamson schemes (following the case of *Harrison v Nairn Williamson* (1976). Such schemes allowed people to receive assets with very high base costs where no consideration has been given.

A transaction between two connected persons is deemed to be a transaction not at arm's length (s 18 TCGA 1992). Market value will be substituted. (Spouses are treated differently, see below.) There are four categories of connected persons (s 286 TCGA 1992):

- **Family**

  A person is connected with an individual if that person is the individual's:

  (a) spouse;

  (b) brother, sister, parent, grandparent, children or grandchildren;

  (c) the spouse of anyone in (b) above;

  (d) a relative of the individual's spouse.

- **Settlements**

  A person who is the trustee of a settlement is connected in that capacity to:

  (a) the settlor;

  (b) any person connected with the settlor;

  (c) and any company connected with the settlement in s 681 ICTA 1988.

- **Partnerships**

  A person is connected with any partner and the spouse or relative of any partner.

- **Companies**

  A company is connected with another company if:

  (a) the same person controls both companies; or

  (b) a person has control of one and another person connected with that person has control of the other;

  (c) of a group of two or more persons has control of each company and the groups either consist of the same persons or could be regarded as doing so if one or more of these persons was treated as replaced by a person connected with them.

A further restriction affecting transactions between connected persons is that where such a transaction gives rise to a loss that loss can only be used against a gain made between the same connected persons.

The connected persons rules do not apply to disposals between spouses. Section 58 TCGA 1992 provides that where an asset is disposed of between spouses, the transaction is treated as taking place at such consideration that neither a gain nor a loss will accrue.

As no loss can arise on a disposal between spouses no question of restricting the loss arises.

21.3.3 Exchanges of assets	Where one party to a transaction disposes of an asset in consideration for another asset, the consideration for each disposal is not the market value of the other asset, instead the consideration is any agreed value which the parties have put on the assets. In the case of *Stanton v Drayton Commercial Investment Co Ltd* (1982) Drayton agreed to acquire investments from an insurance company. The consideration was expressed to be £3,937,632 to be satisfied by 2,461,226 shares in Drayton at their issue price of 160p per share. The sale was conditional upon Drayton's shares being listed on the Stock Exchange. The shares were issued on 11 October. On 12 October they were quoted at 125p per share. Later Drayton sold some of the investments and was assessed to tax on the basis that the shares in Drayton should be valued at 125p when the investments were acquired. Drayton appealed. It was held by the House of Lords that as there had been an honest arm's length valuation of the shares at 160p there was no reason to go behind this. Market value could only be substituted where there was no agreed value. If the parties were to put an unrealistic value on assets it is probable that market value would be substituted.
21.3.4 No gain/no loss disposals	In certain circumstances the legislation provides that notwithstanding the actual consideration given, or the market value of the asset, the disposal is treated as taking place at such value that neither a gain nor a loss will accrue to the person making the disposal. One example of 'holdover' relief has already been given; namely, transfers between spouses. Another example is a transfer of business property which is not at arm's length, ie a gift.
	Section 165 TCGA 1992 provides that where an individual disposes of business assets which includes an interest in an asset used for the purposes of a trade profession or vocation which is carried on by the individual or the individual's personal company. Then the transferor and transferee can elect for the transferee to be treated as acquiring the asset of such value that neither a gain or loss accrues.
21.4 Acquisition cost – general	Section 38(1)(a) TCGA 1992 allows the deduction from the disposal proceeds of the amount or value of the consideration, in money or money's worth, given by the person disposing of the asset wholly and exclusively for the acquisition of the asset.
	It also allows, the incidental costs of the acquisition. When capital gains tax was first introduced, the computation of the gain was based solely upon the difference between the disposal cost and the acquisition cost. This meant that CGT

was a tax on inflationary gains as well as real gains. Consequently, the disposal of an asset which in real terms had devalued could still give rise to a chargeable gain. A number of changes were introduced in the 1980s so as to ensure that only real gains were taxed; however, in the November 1993 budget the tax took a step backwards. Although an examination of the history often helps in understanding the present, in this area of tax the history is so convoluted that it could easily cause confusion and it has therefore been left out. In the paragraphs that follow the law is stated for a disposal taking place after November 1993.

In simple terms, the acquisition cost of an asset is the amount in money or money's worth which was paid for it. However, it must be remembered that one person's disposal cost is another person's acquisition cost; therefore, where the legislation substitutes market value for a disposal, that value will also apply for the corresponding acquisition. If A gives an asset to B, this is not a bargain at arm's length and market value will be substituted. A will be taxed on any gain thus arising. B's acquisition cost will also be market value; the Inland Revenue cannot have it both ways.

Because of the introduction of an allowance to take account of inflationary gains, it was necessary to restate the acquisition cost of many assets; consequently, the date of acquisition is important.

Where an asset was acquired after 31 March 1982 it is not necessary to adjust the acquisition cost. Where, however, an asset was acquired before that date, it is possible to 'rebase' the acquisition cost; to do this the asset is treated as being disposed of and reacquired at market value on 31 March 1982. The market value on that date then becomes the acquisition cost for the purposes of the computation. However, this may prejudice the taxpayer if the asset had a lower value on 31 March 1982 than when it was acquired. The legislation therefore provides for a series of tests. Generally, the result which applies is that which is most beneficial to the taxpayer, although there are exceptions. Often the use of a simple graph helps.

The rules can be stated as follows:

• An asset which the taxpayer owned on 31 March 1982 is deemed to have been disposed of by the taxpayer on that date and immediately reacquired by the taxpayer at the market value (s 35 TCGA 1992). The deemed disposal is not liable to tax; thus, the base cost is raised to market value as at 31 March 1982.

21.4.1   Acquisition cost

21.4.2   Rebasing

- Where the use of the actual acquisition cost (instead of 31 March 1982 value) would result in a smaller gain or a smaller loss the taxpayer must use the actual gain or loss based on the original acquisition cost.

- Where rebasing would substitute a loss for a gain or a gain for a loss, the taxpayer will be deemed to have made neither a loss nor a gain.

- Where using the actual acquisition cost would result in a no gain/no loss disposal or if the legislation provides for the disposal to be at such a value that no gain or loss will accrue, the taxpayer will not be entitled to rebase.

Because of the problems of doing the calculations and the need to keep detailed records each time the taxpayer makes a disposal, the taxpayer can elect for all disposals to be rebased. Thus, a loss can be converted into a gain. The taxpayer must make the election within two years of the end of the year of assessment in which the first such disposal takes place. Once made, the election is irrevocable and applies to all disposals, even those made before the election was made. There are two points to note regarding the election; first, although at first sight it may seem beneficial, it requires all assets to be valued as at 31 March 1982 this can be both time consuming and expensive; second, a taxpayer who knows that the making of the election will be beneficial is not precluded from making the election.

| 21.4.3 | Acquisition costs – wasting assets |

A wasting asset is one which has a predictable useful life of less than 50 years (s 38 TCGA 1992). The time at which the decision is taken as to whether an asset is a wasting asset or not is when the acquisition is made. Wine is therefore a wasting asset notwithstanding that some wines can be very old.

Plant and machinery are always wasting assets. As wasting assets will, by definition, nearly always generate a loss because they will be disposed of for less than they were acquired; s 46 TCGA 1992 requires that the acquisition cost of the asset be written off at a uniform rate over the predictable life of the asset. Although, this will increase the amount of the chargeable gain, in the majority of cases it will reduce the amount of the allowable loss. In the case of a lease of less than 50 years, Sch 8 TCGA 1992 provides for the acquisition cost of the lease be reduced, not on a straight line basis, but on a basis whereby the amount written off increases towards the end of the asset's life. It should be noted that because one looks to the date of acquisition, a lease of 70 years which as assigned when there is 35 years left will become a wasting asset on the assignment.

Section 38(2) TCGA 1992 provides for the base cost to be increased by the incidental costs of acquisition. These consist of expenditure wholly and exclusively incurred for the acquisition of the asset; being fees, commission or remuneration paid for professional services of any surveyor or valuer, or auctioneer, or accountant, or agent or legal adviser and the costs of transfer or conveyance (including stamp duty). Where the asset disposed of is a wasting asset, the incidental costs of acquisition are written off from the date that the expenditure was incurred to the date of disposal on a straight line basis. Where the asset was made by the person disposing of it, eg a painting, the costs are any expenditure wholly and exclusively incurred by him in providing the asset.

21.5   Incidental costs of acquisition

Allowable expenditure includes any expenditure which was incurred wholly and exclusively by the person making the disposal in establishing, preserving or defending title to the asset or to a right over the asset is allowable; thus, for example, legal costs incurred in a boundary dispute would be allowable.

21.5.1   Costs of defending title or enhancing value of an asset

Any expenditure incurred wholly and exclusively for the purpose of enhancing the value of the asset, being expenditure which is reflected in the state or nature of the asset at the time of disposal is also allowable. Expenditure which is not reflected in the state of the asset, eg architect's fees for plans which were not carried through, are not allowable.

The incidental costs of disposal are defined in identical terms to those of acquisition. In addition there is included the costs of advertising to find a buyer and also any costs reasonably incurred in making any valuation or apportionment required by the Act in order to compute the gain including any expenses reasonably incurred in ascertaining the market value of the asset.

21.6   Incidental costs of disposal

Of the three costs above, the acquisition cost and the incidental costs of acquisition are to be further adjusted by the indexation. The idea behind this is to increase the expenditure so as to take into account the effect of inflation. The disposal proceeds are not indexed, presumably this is because the draftsman thought that such costs would be incurred at the time of disposal. However, it is possible that advertising costs are incurred some time before the disposal takes place, in such a case no indexation will be allowed.

21.7   Indexation

Indexation increases an allowable deduction by the increase in the Retail Prices Index between the date on which the cost was incurred and the date of disposal. However, following the Finance Act 1994 indexation cannot create a loss nor can it increase a loss. There are transitional provisions for individuals and trustees.

21.7.1 Computation of the indexation allowance

The indexation allowance is calculated by using the formula:

$$\frac{RD - RI}{RI}$$

where RD is the retail prices index figure for the date of disposal and RI is the retail prices index figure for the date of acquisition. The figure is expressed as a decimal to the nearest three decimal places. Thus, a figure of 0.3015 would become 0.302 and would mean that between the date of acquisition and the date of disposal there had been a 30.2% rise in the retail prices index. Each item of expenditure is indexed separately. There is no indexation for costs of disposal even if these costs were incurred some time before the actual disposal takes place.

Indexation only applies from 1 April 1982; therefore, if the expenditure was incurred before that date, the allowable expenditure is only adjusted by the increase in the Retail Price Index since 1982.

If the asset disposed of was acquired before 1 April 1982 the indexation allowance can be calculated on the basis of the market value of the asset at 31 March 1982 if this is more favourable. Note that if the market value is used, the incidental costs of acquisition are not taken into account. If an election has been made for all assets to be rebased, the 1982 value has to be used.

21.7.2 Transitional relief

The Finance Act 1994 abolished the rule that indexation could create a loss or increase a gain. There was much discontent with this and it was generally seen as a way of raising revenue rather than measure designed to counter tax avoidance. Following complaints, the government introduced a measure of relief for individuals and trustees.

In order for the relief to apply, the disposal must be made on or after 30 November 1993 but before 6 April 1995.

A disposal made on or after 30 November 1993 but before 6 April 1995 which, but for the restriction would have given rise to an indexation loss, will still do so and can be used to reduce chargeable gains to the amount of the annual exemption (£6,000). Any loss incurred which results from indexation can be carried forward to the following year. An indexation loss in the year 1994–95 can be used to reduce any chargeable gains in that year; however, any incurred indexation losses cannot be carried forward to the next year. The maximum aggregate amount of indexation loss allowed to be used in this way is £10,000.

Certain disposals are deemed to take place at such value that neither a gain nor a loss will accrue to the person disposing of the asset. When this happens, the cost of disposal is the base cost as increased by inflation.

21.7.3   No gain/no loss disposals

Capital gains tax was introduced with effect from 6 April 1965. In accordance with the principle that tax should not be imposed retrospectively, only those gains accruing since that date are liable to tax (s 35(9) TCGA 1992). The method by which this is achieved is to assume that the value of the asset has increased at a uniform rate over the ownership of the asset and to time apportion the gain. The taxpayer can elect for market value on 6 April 1965 if this is more favourable.

21.8   Assets held before 6 April 1965

In the case of *Smith v Schofield* (1993) the House of Lords held that indexation is to applied *before* time apportionment. Generally, this gives a result more favourable to the revenue. The House of Lords expressed regret at their conclusion on the basis that as indexation was intended to apply to gains accruing after 1982 it could not have been the intention of Parliament for it to apply to gains arising prior to 1965.

Where a person disposes of only part of an asset, it is necessary to ascertain the relevant part of the acquisition cost which is attributable to each part of the asset. This is done by applying the formula:

21.9   Part disposals

$$\frac{A}{A+B}$$

where A is the value of the part disposed of and B is the value of that remaining (s 42 TCGA 1992).

Once the computation has been done the gains and/or losses on all the disposals made in the year of assessment are aggregated. If there is a net loss this can be carried forward to the following year.

21.10   Net gain or loss

If, however, the gains exceed the losses (ie there is a net gain) the annual exempt amount then is deducted.

The annual exempt amount for 1995–96 is:

- individuals £6,000;

- trustees £3,000;

- personal representatives £6,000 (in the year of death and the two following tax years.)

Note: Companies do not have an annual exemption.

The annual exemption is dealt with in more detail in the next chapter. Once the exemption has been deducted any remaining gain can be reduced by the amount of any brought forward losses. In theory, the losses are deducted first, but the amount to be deducted is restricted to such an amount as would leave a gain equal to the annual exempt amount.

If the annual exemption exceeds the net gains the excess *cannot* be carried forward to be used in the following tax year and is therefore lost. Losses and gains for a year are aggregated before using the annual exemption and it is therefore lost, but losses carried forward are used after applying the annual exemption.

Capital Gains Tax – Computation

Although the consideration for the disposal will normally be the amount received, in certain circumstances the legislation substitutes a different amount. Where the disposal is a non-arm's length disposal, market value will be substituted. Market value will also be substituted where the consideration is either given for the loss of office or is given for services given in any office or employment. Market value will not be substituted where there is no corresponding disposal of the asset and there is no consideration in money or money's worth or the consideration is of an amount or value of lower than the market value of the asset. Transactions between connected persons are treated as being non-arm's length. People are connected if they are members of the same family or connected through a settlement or in partnership.

Where assets are exchanged, a consideration attributed to those assets provided there is evidence to show that the values attributed are reasonable.

In certain circumstances transfers are treated as taking place at no gain or loss. The principle example of this is transfers between spouses.

The acquisition cost of the asset is the amount paid in money or money's worth. Where, however, the asset was acquired on a non-arm's length disposal and market value was substituted, then the market value will be taken as the acquisition cost.

Where the asset was acquired before 1982 the acquisition cost will be rebased to market value in 1982 provided this does not make the taxpayer worse off.

Where the asset is a wasting asset, the acquisition cost will be written off over the life of the asset.

The incidental cost of acquisition and incidental costs of disposal are also deductible. The acquisition cost is adjusted to take into account the increase in inflation since acquisition.

Where only part of an asset is disposed of, it is necessary to ascertain the relevant part of the acquisition cost which is attributable to part of the asset disposed of.

This is done by applying the formula:

$$\frac{A}{A+B}$$

where A is the value of the part disposed of and B is the value of that remaining.

Chapter 22

Capital Gains Tax – Reliefs and Exemptions

Capital gains tax has a number of exemptions and reliefs. The exemptions are often designed to prevent an allowable loss occurring rather than specifically to exempt gains from tax. Major exception to this rule is the exemption from tax on the disposal of an individual's residence. A number of exemptions, for example the exemption from tax where the disposal consideration is less than £6,000, are included primarily to prevent administrative hassles for transactions which will yield very little tax.

22.1 Introduction

The exemptions and reliefs dealt with in this chapter are:

- annual exemption;

- residence exemption;

- replacement of business assets;

- retirement relief;

- relief for re-investment in shares;

- small disposals; and

- miscellaneous exemptions.

Section 3 TCGA 1992 provides for the first £6,000 of chargeable gains to be excluded from charge. The figure is reduced to £3,000 for trustees. The figure should be increased by inflation automatically (s 3(3) TCGA 1992); however, it is open to parliament to prescribe a different figure.

22.2 Annual exemption

The annual exemption is applied after deducting losses on assets disposed of in the year but before deducting losses which are carried forward from previous years.

Although often called the 'principal private residence relief', these words appear nowhere in the legislation. Section 222 TCGA 1992 defines dwelling house for the purpose of s 223 TCGA 1992 which provides that no part of the gain on the disposal of a dwelling house shall be a chargeable gain if the dwelling house or part of the dwelling house has been the individual's only or main residence throughout the period of ownership, or throughout the period of ownership except for all or any part of the last 36 months of that period. For these

22.3 Principal private residence relief

purposes, land of up to 0.5 of a hectare included in the sale is also exempt; however, if the house has more land than this, it may also be exempted if the Commissioners are satisfied that, with regard to the size and character of the dwelling house in question, the extra land is required for the reasonable enjoyment of it as a residence.

Where the dwelling house has not been the individual's main residence throughout the period of ownership, the gain is apportioned. The fraction of the gain which is not chargeable is the length of the period of ownership during which it was the individual's main residence together with the last 36 months in any event divided by the length of the period of ownership. For these purposes, certain periods of non-residence are treated as residence. These are:

- a period of absence not exceeding three years (or periods of absence which together do not exceed three years);

- any period of absence throughout which the individual was employed outside the United Kingdom and of which all the duties were performed outside the United Kingdom; and

- any period of absence not exceeding four years, in which the individual was prevented from residing in the dwelling house, either as a consequence of working away from the house or as a consequence of the conditions imposed by his employer requiring him to live elsewhere provided that the condition was reasonable.

In order for these three conditions to apply the individual must reside in the house both before and after the periods of absence.

Much of the case law in this area has focused on the question of to what extent separate buildings can form part of a main residence. In the case of *Batey v Wakefield* it was held that more than one building can qualify. Most of the cases depend upon the finding of fact in front of the Commissioners. Thus, in the case of *Williams v Merrylees*, a house together with a lodge, which was sold at a different time from the house, both qualified as part of the main residence. In contrast, in the case of *Markey v Sanders* relief for other buildings was denied. In the most recent case to look at this point, *Lewis v Lady Rook*, it was held that it is necessary to find the 'entity' which is the residence and provided that the separate buildings form part of this entity the whole would qualify for relief.

22.4   Relief – the replacement of business assets

Sections 152–58 TCGA 1992 provides relief where a business replaces chargeable assets. If no relief were given, each time a business disposed of its assets and suffered a tax charge, it would have less cash as a result to replace the assets; consequently, businesses would be penalised and would not seek to reinvest.

Where a trader sells a qualifying business asset, ie land, buildings, plant and machinery, aircraft, ships, and goodwill, and replaces it with a new qualifying asset, the gain on the old asset is rolled over into the new asset. The way this is done is that the consideration given for the new asset is treated as being reduced by the gain on the old asset; thus, when the new asset is disposed of the gain will be correspondingly higher. When the new asset is disposed of, it may itself qualify for the relief if the proceeds of sale are used to buy another qualifying asset. Therefore, provided the proceeds of sale and always invested in a new qualifying asset, no chargeable gain will ever arise.

In order to qualify for relief, the new qualifying asset must be purchased either one year before or three years after the disposal of the old asset. It is therefore not right to say that it has to be the proceeds of sale of the old asset which are reinvested as it would be impossible to do this where the new asset is acquired one year before the disposal of the old asset. It may be that due to economic conditions, a new asset is purchased, but it is impossible to sell the old asset within the one year time limit. In these circumstances, the Inland Revenue have discretion to allow roll-over relief but it will be necessary to show that active steps were taken to sell the asset.

The asset must be taken into use immediately upon acquisition.

Where the asset is disposed of by a company, any gain made by that company can be rolled into an asset acquired by another company, provided that it is a member of the first company's capital gains tax group.

22.5   Retirement relief

Where a person retires from business, they are entitled to an exemption from capital gains tax on a disposal of assets which were used in the business. To a certain extent, the retirement relief is seen as a reward for having built up the business throughout the taxpayer's life. Although the relief is called retirement relief, it is available if an individual reaches the age of 55 or has to retire earlier due to ill health. The gains which are eligible for relief are those made on a disposal of either assets of a family business, or shares in a personal company. A company is a person's personal company if they can exercise 5% or more of the voting rights in it. In order to qualify, the disposal must be of assets which were used in a trade or shares in a personal company which was a trading company or the holding company of a trading group. In order to qualify for the relief, the business must have been run, or the shares must have been held for at least one year. Maximum relief is given if the business has been run for, or the shares held for, 10 years. Thus, if shares which have been held for five years are disposed of, 50% relief will be available. The gains which are exempt are those up to £250,000. Between £250,000 – £1,000,000, the gains are exempt.

22.6   Re-investment relief

This new relief was introduced in 1993 and applies to a material disposal of a qualifying investment after 16 March 1993. It allows an individual who has disposed of assets which would otherwise qualify for retirement relief to re-invest in at least 5% of the ordinary shares of an unquoted trading company and to claim roll-over relief. Retirement relief is given in priority to re-investment relief. Therefore, to the extent that a taxpayer's gains are not covered by retirement relief they can be reinvested and roll-over relief obtained.

22.7   Disposals for less than £6,000

Under s 262 TCGA 1992 where the consideration for the disposal of tangible movable property is less than £6,000 the gains are exempt. Where the consideration is over £6,000 five-thirds of the gain on the excess is chargeable to tax. In other words, the excess is subject to a higher rate of tax than otherwise would be the case. In effect, this is a claw-back on the amount under £6,000 and this amount will continue to be charged until the whole consideration is chargeable at the normal rate of CGT.

22.8   Miscellaneous reliefs

Certain assets are exempt from charge. Amongst these are:

- private motor cars and vehicles (s 263 TCGA 1992);

- declarations for gallantry, if disposed of by the person who was awarded them (s 268 TCGA 1992);

- gains arising from the disposal of foreign currency which has been used for private purposes on holiday (s 269 TCGA 1992);

- the disposal of a debt where the person disposing of it is the original creditor, ie if the debt has been purchased and sold the gain will be chargeable (assuming it has not been bought or sold in the course of dealing in debts); if the debt is between the original parties, no gain or loss will arise from its disposal;

- gambling winnings are exempt. This is not so much to prevent winnings from being chargeable as to prevent losses from being allowable (s 51(1) TCGA 1992).

Capital Gains Tax –
Reliefs and Exemptions

The first £6,000 of chargeable gains are excluded from charge. For trustees the figure is £3,000.

The disposal of a person's principal private residence is exempt from tax. So is land of up to 0.5 of a hectare. More land than this may be exempt if the Commissioners are satisfied that with regard to the size and character of the dwelling house in question, the extra land is required for the reasonable enjoyment of it as a residence. The last 36 months of ownership are ignored. Certain periods of absence during the period of residence are also ignored provided that the person was resident both before and after the period of absence. A separate building can form part of the main residence provided that it forms part of the entity.

Relief is available from capital gains tax where a business replaces its assets. If no relief were available, a business will be disadvantaged because the proceeds of sale of any asset will always be reduced by tax and therefore could not be reinvested. The trader must sell a qualifying asset, eg land or buildings and the relief is given by reducing the acquisition cost of the new asset by the amount of the gain on the old asset. When the new asset is sold relief can be claimed again.

When a person retires from business they are entitled to an exemption from capital gains tax. Relief is given on a sliding scale. The assets must be held for at least one year and maximum relief is given when they have been held for 10 years. The maximum relief is £250,000 of gains being exempt, between £250,000 and £1,000,000 half of the gains are exempt.

Where an individual disposes of an asset which would otherwise qualify for retirement relief, reinvestment relief is available provided that the individual reinvests in at least 5% of the ordinary share capital of an unquoted trading company.

Where the consideration for the disposal of tangible movable property is less than £6,000 the gains are exempt. Above £6,000 five-thirds of the gain is taxable until the whole consideration is taxable at the normal rate.

There are certain miscellaneous reliefs, eg private cars and motor vehicles, decorations for gallantry, disposal of foreign currency, disposals of debts by the original creditor and gambling winnings.

Chapter 23

Capital Gains Tax –
Settled Property and Death

This chapter examines the treatment of settled property for the purposes of capital gains tax and also looks at the treatment of the person's assets on death.

23.1   **Introduction**

For the purposes of capital gains tax, settled property is defined in s 60 TCGA 1992 as any property held in trust other than property which is held as a nominee or trustee for infants or disabled persons absolutely entitled to the property. Trustees are regarded as a single and continuing body of persons and consequently, where the trustees change, there is no disposal (s 69 TCGA 1992). Where property is transferred into a trust, this will constitute a disposal by the person making the transfer. The disposal will not be at arm's length and therefore, market value will be substituted (s 70 TCGA 1992). Similarly, where property is disposed of from a trust either by passing to a beneficiary or on a sale, there will also be a disposal by the trustees. Where an asset is transferred to a beneficiary, the disposal will be deemed to take place at market value. Where a beneficiary disposes of an interest in a trust, no charge to CGT will arise unless the interest in the trust was acquired for money or money's worth, in which case normal CGT principles will apply. Where a beneficiary disposes of a life interest by reason of the terms of the trust, eg the beneficiary attains a certain age, there will be no disposal of trust assets.

23.2   **Settlements**

Where the settlor of the trust retains an interest in the trust assets, any gains made by the trustees are deemed to be those of the settlor.

The assets owned by an individual on death are treated as passing to the individual's personal representatives at market value. Therefore, there is no charge to tax on the death of an individual. Any disposal by the personal representatives will only attract tax if the assets have increased in value since the date of the death. It should be noted that personal representatives are entitled to the deceased's annual exemption for the two years following death. Where assets are transferred under a will, the legatee receives the assets at the market value which was acquired by the personal representatives.

23.3   **Death**

Capital Gains Tax –
Settled Property and Death

Where assets are transferred into a settlement, there is a disposal by the settlor. The trustee is regarded as a single and continuing body of persons, and consequently, a change of trustees does not create a disposal. No disposal arises when a life interest comes to an end. Where trustees dispose of assets in the trust, that will constitute a disposal. Where the settlor of a trust retains interest in the trust asset, any gains made by the trustee are deemed to be those of the settlor.

Assets owned by an individual on death are treated as being acquired by the personal representatives without a disposal having been made by the deceased. There is, therefore, what is called a step up on death and no chargeable gain arises.

Index